Marshall McLuhan
The Man and His Message

Marshall McLuhan
The Man and His Message

Introduction by John Cage

George Sanderson and Frank Macdonald
Editors

Fulcrum, Inc.

Book Design by
Bryan Dahlberg

Cover Photograph Courtesy of
Corinne McLuhan

Library of Congress Cataloging-in-Publication Data

Marshall McLuhan: The Man and His Message
    1. McLuhan, Marshall, 1911–1980.
    2. Mass media specialists—Canada—Biography.
    I. Sanderson, George. II. Macdonald, Frank.

P92.5.M3M345   1989   001.51'092'4 [B]   89-1608
ISBN 1-55591-035-1

Printed in the United States of America
1   2   3   4   5   6   7   8   9   0

Fulcrum, Inc.
Golden, Colorado

Contents

Acknowledgments   vii

Credits   ix

Introduction   *John Cage*   xi

A McLuhan Mosaic   *Marshall McLuhan*   1

Herbert Marshall McLuhan   *Claude T. Bissell*   5

Technology and the Human   *Marshall McLuhan with*
    Dimension   *Louis Forsdale*   12

McLuhan as Teacher:
    The Saint Louis Years   *Walter J. Ong*   25

McLuhan Probes   *Marshall McLuhan*   32

The Role of New Media
    in Social Change   *Marshall McLuhan*   34

The Unknown McLuhan   *T.W. Cooper*   41

Media and the Inflation CROWD   *Marshall McLuhan*   56

The McLuhan Festival:
    On the Road to San Francisco   *Gerald M. Feigen*   65

At the moment of Sputnik the
    planet becomes a global theater
    in which there are no spectators
    but only actors   *Marshall McLuhan*   70

Marshalling McLuhan   *Matie Armstrong Molinaro*   81

McLuhan Probes   *Marshall McLuhan*   89

Violence of the Media   *Marshall McLuhan*   91

Marshall's New York Adventure:
    Reflections on McLuhan's
    Year at Fordham University   *John Culkin*   99

A McLuhan Symposium   111

Making a Movie with McLuhan   *Jane Jacobs*   121

Why the TV Child Cannot See Ahead:
    The Unconscious Bias of the
    Visual Mode: A Note on the
    Meaning of Mosaic   *Marshall McLuhan*   124

Monday Night Sessions   *Fred Thompson*   131

McLuhan Probes   *Marshall McLuhan*   138

Inside on the Outside, or the
    Spaced-Out American   *Marshall McLuhan*   140

Via Media with Marshall
    McLuhan   *Barrington Nevitt*   149

Electric Consciousness   *Marshall McLuhan with*
    and the Church   *Hubert Hoskins*   159

Marshall McLuhan and the
    Rules of the Game   *Louis Forsdale*   169

The Brain and the Media:
    The Western Hemisphere   *Marshall McLuhan*   179

Watch the Background,
    Not the Figure   *Wilson Bryan Key*   186

A Last Look at the Tube   *Marshall McLuhan*   196

The Genesis of
    Laws of the Media   *Eric McLuhan*   201

Laws of the Media   *Marshall McLuhan*   205

The Man in the Coach House   *George Sanderson*   210

McLuhan Probes   *Marshall McLuhan*   218

Notes   221

Contributors   228

Acknowledgments

The process that culminated in this book began in 1983 with the receipt of a grant to *The Antigonish Review* from the Canadian Studies Program of the Secretary of State (then the Honorable Gerald Regan). The application also benefited from the good offices of the Honorable Alan J. McEachen, then Minister of Finance. Anne Scotton, the program officer, helped us negotiate bureaucratic hurdles. Additional funding was received from a number of Canadian firms: Spar Aerospace, Teleglobe Canada, Maritime Tel. and Tel and Dartmouth Cablevision. Luc Jutras, of the Canada Council, was a continuous source of encouragement and support.

Saint Francis Xavier University was especially generous in every way, contributing office space, secretarial assistance and funds. The support of the university president, Reverend Greg MacKinnon, was of key importance.

Corinne McLuhan's gracious encouragement and assistance were invaluable in maintaining our energy in what turned out to be a long process. Matie Molinaro, Marshall McLuhan's agent since 1968, and following his death in 1980, Corinne McLuhan's representative, extended a cordial expertise and friendship. Her advice, her constant availability and her knowledge were crucial in all areas dealing with our attempt to re-present McLuhan's work. George Thompson, McLuhan's executive assistant, worked tirelessly to assist in the procurement of articles and the compilation of addresses of potential contributors. Furthermore, he communicated, through anecdote and remembered incidents, an invaluable portrait of the human side of McLuhan. During this period Marge Stewart, McLuhan's long-time secretary, though ill, proffered valuable advice and encouragement. Eric McLuhan, Marshall's son, was also very generous with his time and comments as was Teri McLuhan, Marshall's daughter.

In 1984 I met Frank Macdonald, a long-time McLuhan admirer, with a background in marketing design, who became a friend and coeditor of this book.

Many people responded positively to our request for articles and submissions. Some contributors maintained contact and offered suggestions and encouragement through the years. Dr. Gerry Feigen of San Francisco must be mentioned among this number, along with Professor Bill Kuhns of Ottawa, and Barrington Nevitt, Bruce W. Powe and Professor Derrick de Kerckhove, all of whom reside in Toronto.

Dawn Currie, who was my secretary during the initial organization of the book, was always helpful and cheerful. My wife Gertrude, an editor of *The Antigonish Review,* participated fully in every phase of the long process, reading and commenting on the clarity and contents of the contributions, as well as making valuable suggestions for the organization of the book. My sons Eric and Brendan were always supportive and interested.

Finally I must acknowledge that my own interest in McLuhan was elicited in 1968 by R.J. MacSween—one of the great teachers at Saint Francis Xavier University, whose love of knowledge and whose curiosity about history, culture and contemporary events are of the same nature and scope as that of McLuhan.

George Sanderson
Antigonish, Nova Scotia
January 1989

Credits

We wish to thank Corinne McLuhan (McLuhan Associates Ltd.) for permission to publish the articles by her late husband and for permission to use various statements by Marshall McLuhan that appear in the "McLuhan Mosaic" section and in pages entitled "Probes." Matie Molinaro, Corinne McLuhan's business agent, was present throughout the negotiations and oversaw the organization and wording of the documents. The "Probes" are culled from the more than six hundred articles written by McLuhan, although the majority are taken from articles written in the late sixties and seventies.

We also wish to thank the following persons and publishers who made material on McLuhan available to us, and for the publishers listed who gave permission, or from whom permission was requested, to use citations in the "Mosaic" and "Symposium" sections. The following list is not exhaustive and we apologize to anyone inadvertently omitted.

Sources for the "McLuhan Mosaic"

Australian Broadcast Company TV, "Monday Conference" (229), Monday, June 27, 1977, p. 9; interview with Eric Norden, *Playboy*, Vol. 16, no. 3 (March 1969); *McLuhan: Hot and Cool*, edited by Gerald E. Stearn (Dial Press 1967), p. 285; *Maclean's*, March 7, 1977; Barry Day, interview, 1968.

Sources for the "McLuhan Symposium"

From letters sent to the editors in response to a request for remarks on McLuhan:
  Robert Hittell, Edward T. Hall, Margaret Stewart, Walker Percy, John Cage
Excerpts from other materials submitted to the editors:
  William Kuhns, John Wain, Bruce Powers, Gerald O'Grady
From Stephanie McLuhan's TV Program "The Man and His Message":
  Norman Mailer, Corinne McLuhan, Arthur Schlesinger, Jr.
From Derrick de Kerckhove's interviews:
  Martin Esslin, Pierre Trudeau, Patrick Watson, Tom Wolfe
Other sources:
  Barry Day, an envoi to Marshall published in the trade magazine *Campaign*, 1981
  Hugh Kenner, "McLuhan Redux," *Harper's* (November 1984)
  Harold Rosenberg, *McLuhan: Hot and Cool*, edited by Gerald E. Stearn (Dial Press, 1967)
  Pierre Emmanuel, *Le Devoir* (May 16, 1967)
  George Steiner, *Language and Silence* (Atheneum, 1967)
  George Thompson, Nancy Cole interview (1986)
  Charles Weingartner, book review in *Et Cetera* (June 1977)
  Bruce W. Powe, *The Antigonish Review*, no. 50 (Summer 1982)

John Cage

Introduction

At one of our meetings in the sixties Marshall McLuhan suggested that I write some music using the ten thunderclaps of *Finnegans Wake*. They were a history, he said, of technology and they were the subject of a book by his son. I received a typescript of the book from Eric McLuhan and fully intended to make *Atlas Borealis* with *The Ten Thunderclaps*. It would have been for orchestra and chorus transformed electronically so that the singing would fill the envelopes of actual thunderclaps, and the playing of the strings those of actual raindrops, falling first on earth, successively on different materials down through history, and finally remaining in the air. Going to the concert would have been like going to a storm. I never started it. At the University of Illinois, where I was invited to work with a computer facility, the composition *HPSCHD* took two years rather than one.

It was through Mildred Constantine of the Museum of Modern Art in New York City (known in Rockland County, where I was living, as Connie Bettleheim) that I first heard of Marshall McLuhan. She was enthusiastic, and after reading *The Agenbite of Outwit*, Location 1:1 (1963) and, more recently (1985), *Tyuonyi 1*, so was I ("Money is obsolete . . . work is obsolete," etc.). In my thoughts about world improvement I put McLuhan together with Buckminster Fuller ("No need for politicians, they may be sent off to the moon."). And for the source material of my current Norton lectures at Harvard I link them. They were often together at conferences in the sixties, once with Margaret Mead in Greece (1964) for a Doxiades Symposium held on a yacht in the Aegean Sea.

I remain stimulated and convinced, full of belief in Fuller and MuLuhan. If as world people we ever come to our senses, their separate works will help us initiate intelligent action.

This book alternates articles by McLuhan himself with articles about him by people who knew him. I had been saddened in the late sixties to hear of his illness—described in the article by John Culkin. Matie Molinaro's article, which describes the lingering illness and silence from the time of his stroke in 1977 until his death in 1980, brought tears to my eyes. What a great loss it was for all those who are living that he died. I had lunch with him once in Toronto, and he asked me a question about pattern recognition that I couldn't answer. My mind doesn't work his way. I don't always understand McLuhan, nor do I understand anything else that I actually need and can use. Of my own work, that interests me most which I have not yet made, and I think that was McLuhan's attitude toward his own ideas. In his writings I like the way he leaps from one paragraph to the next without transition. This also happens in the *Journal* of Henry David Thoreau ("The best form of government is no government at all."). Each one leaves space in his work in which a reader, stimulated, can do his or her own thinking.

Marshall McLuhan

A McLuhan Mosaic

Today, in the electronic age of instantaneous communication, I believe that our survival, and at the very least our comfort and happiness, is predicated on understanding the nature of our new environment, because unlike previous environmental changes, the electric media constitute a total and near-instantaneous transformation of culture, values and attitudes. This upheaval generates great pain and identity loss, which can be ameliorated only through a conscious awareness of its dynamics. If we understand the revolutionary transformations caused by new media, we can anticipate and control them; but if we continue in our self-induced subliminal trance, we will be their slaves.

The point to remember here is that whenever we use or perceive any technological extension of ourselves, we necessarily embrace it. Whenever we watch a TV screen or read a book, we are absorbing these extensions of ourselves into our individual system and experiencing an automatic "closure" or displacement of perception; we can't escape this perpetual embrace of our daily technology unless we escape the technology itself and flee to a hermit's cave. By consistently embracing all these technologies, we inevitably relate ourselves to them as servomechanisms.

How do we become aware of the effects of alphabet or print or telegraph in shaping our behavior? It is absurd and ignoble to be shaped by such means. Knowledge does not extend but restricts the areas of determinism. And the influence of unexamined assumptions derived from technology leads quite unnecessarily to maximal determination in human life. Emancipation from that trap is the goal of all education.

One of the peculiarities of electric speed is that it pushes all the unconscious factors up into consciousness. This began with Freud and Einstein back in 1900, but the hidden aspects of the media are the things that should be taught because they have an irresistible force when invisible. When these factors remain ignored and invisible they have an absolute power over the user. The sooner the population—young or old—can be taught the effects of these forms the sooner we can have some sort of reasonable ecology among the media themselves.

For many years until I wrote my first book, *The Mechanical Bride,* I adopted an extremely moralistic approach to all environmental technology. I loathed machinery. I abominated cities, I equated the Industrial Revolution with original sin and mass media with the Fall. In short, I rejected almost every element of modern life in favor of a Rousseauvian utopianism. But gradually I perceived how sterile and useless this attitude was, and I began to realize that the greatest artists of the twentieth century—Yeats, Pound, Joyce, Eliot—had discovered a totally different approach, based on the identity of the processes of cognition and creation. I realized that artistic creation is the playback of ordinary experience—from trash to treasures. I ceased being a moralist and became a student.

Values, in so far as they register a preference for a particular kind of effect or quality, are a highly contentious and debatable area in every field of discourse. Nobody, in the twentieth century, has ever come up with any meaningful definition or discussion of "value." It doesn't work any longer in economics, let alone humanistic affairs. It is rather fatuous to insist upon values if you are not prepared to understand how they got there and by what they are now being undermined. The mere moralistic expression of approval or disapproval, preference or detestation, is currently being used in our world as a substitute for observation and a substitute for study. People hope that if they scream loudly enough about "values" then others will mistake them for serious, sensitive souls who have higher and nobler perceptions than ordinary people. Otherwise, why would they be screaming? Anybody who spends his time screaming about values in our modern world is not a serious character. You might as well start screaming about a house that's burning down. To start announcing your own preferences for old values when your world is collapsing and everything is changing at a furious pitch—this is not the act of a serious person.

When things come at you very fast, naturally you lose touch with yourself. Anybody moving into a new world loses identity. If you go to China, and you've never been there before, you're a nobody. You can't relate to anything there. So, loss of identity is something that happens in rapid change. But everybody at the speed of light tends to become a nobody. This is what's called the "Masked-Man." The masked man has no identity. He is so deeply involved in other people that he doesn't have any personal identity.

It's why they have to kill in order to find out whether they're real. This is where the violence comes from. This meaningless slaying around our streets is the work of people who have lost all identity, and who have to kill in order to know if they're real or if the other guy's real. I suppose that one could even produce a theory of war to say that when a certain amount of technological changes happens very quickly to a whole community, they are so lost about who they are that they want a basic war to find out. It's another way of crashing through to find one's identity. Violence as a form of quest for identity is something the people who have been ripped off feel the need of. He's going to show who he is, what his credentials are, that he's tough. So anybody on a psychic frontier tends to get tough or violent and it's happening to us on a mass scale today. It might even be said that at the speed of light, man has neither goals, objective nor private identity. He is an item in a data bank—software only, easily forgotten—and deeply resentful.

The open society, the visual offspring of phonetic literacy, is irrelevant to today's retribalized youth; and the closed society, the product of speech, drum and ear technologies, is thus being reborn. After centuries of dissociated sensibilities, modern awareness is once more becoming integral and inclusive, as the entire human family is scaled to a single universal membrane. The compressional, implosive nature of the new electric technology is retrogressing Western man back from the open plateaus of literate values and into the heart of tribal darkness, into what Joseph Conrad terms "the Africa within."

The satellites changed the planet totally not into a global village, but a global theater. TV may have created a global village and other electric instruments like the telegraph, but with the satellite as a proscenium arch around the planet, the planet itself is now a stage on which everybody can do his thing.

The total-field awareness engendered by electronic media is enabling us—indeed, compelling us—to grope toward a consciousness of the unconscious, toward a realization that technology is an extension of our own bodies. We live in the first age when change occurs sufficiently rapidly to make such pattern recognition possible for society at large. Until the present era, this awareness has always been reflected first by the artist, who has had the power—and courage—of the seer to read the language of the outer world and relate it to the inner world.

Inherent in the artist's creative inspiration is the process of subliminally sniffing out environmental change. It's always been the artist who perceives the alterations in man caused by a new medium, who recognizes that the future is the present, and uses his work to prepare the ground for it.

All my recommendations, therefore, can be reduced to this one: study the modes of media, in order to hoick all assumptions out of the subliminal, nonverbal realm for scrutiny and for prediction and control of human purposes.

Claude T. Bissell

Herbert Marshall McLuhan

Herbert Marshall McLuhan was born in Edmonton July 21, 1911, and died in Toronto on December 31, 1980. He had been active as scholar and teacher until the fall of 1979, when he suffered a severe stroke.

McLuhan graduated from the University of Manitoba in 1934, and took an M.A. degree there in 1935. He spent the next six years at the University of Cambridge, where he took a Ph.D. in 1942. His thesis, "The Place of Thomas Nashe in the Learning of His Time," inaugurated a lifelong concern with the study of rhetoric. Just before his death, the thesis was being prepared for publication, and would no doubt have given essential clues to the development of his subsequent critical work. He was in Cambridge during the heyday of I.A. Richards and F.L. Leavis, who were advocating and demonstrating a disciplined and rigorous approach to the analysis of literary texts, and, at the same time, insisting that the critic should see literature in a broad social and cultural context. It was an environment that McLuhan found congenial and stimulating. During his Cambridge days he became a Roman Catholic convert, and he was throughout his life a devout member of the Church. In 1939 he married Corinne Lewis, who was a graduate of Texas Christian University and had done advanced work in drama at the Pasadena Playhouse. The McLuhans had six children, several of whom were to make their mark in literature and the arts. Marshall and Corinne were generous hosts. Gatherings at the McLuhan home were relaxed symposia, in which representatives from many disciplines, from within and outside the university, joined in free-ranging discussion.

After Cambridge, McLuhan taught English at the universities

of Wisconsin and Saint Louis, and at Assumption College in Windsor. He joined the Department of English at Saint Michael's College in 1946, and remained a member of the department throughout his subsequent career. His scholarly interests shifted from the Renaissance to the Modern, with a special interest in T.S. Eliot, Ezra Pound, W.B. Yeats, Wyndham Lewis, and, in particular, James Joyce. Although he did not publish extended studies of any of these writers, his books are full of shrewd critical comments on them, and his theories on the media and communication often have literary sources. To McLuhan, the great artist is also the prophet. "The artist picks up the message of cultural and technical challenge decades before its transforming impact occurs. He, then, builds models or Noah's arks for facing the change that is ahead."

During the forties McLuhan established himself as a fine literary critic who had a sensitive response to a wide variety of writers. He wrote about Poe, Keats, Hopkins, Pound, John Dos Passos, Tennyson, and Coleridge. (Critical articles on these poets and other writers were later collected in a volume: *The Interior Landscape: The Literary Criticism of Marshall McLuhan*, 1969.) But the key article of the forties was a discussion on rhetorical patterns in contemporary prose that, to McLuhan, indicated a basic division in attitudes toward the nature of man and society ("An Ancient Quarrel in Modern America: Sophists vs. Grammarians," which appeared in the *Classical Journal* in 1946). McLuhan contrasted the position of Robert Hutchins at Chicago with the popular ideology of liberalism. Hutchins, said McLuhan, stood for the Ciceronian ideal—a wide basis for learning, with the end of producing a citizen alert to the problems of man in society who would express himself with learning and eloquence. Hutchins emphasized the whole man, whereas the liberal spokesmen celebrated the individual as "a technological functional unit in the state" and opposed specialism to Hutchins' generalism.

Certain poets, McLuhan found, also celebrated an inclusive wholeness and sought to immerse the reader in a world of many levels. Such poets were T.S. Eliot and Hopkins and, supremely, Joyce, although he wrote technically in prose. They created worlds that were full of discontinuous sights and sounds that demanded the active involvement of the reader. They were symbolists who worked "backwards from the particular effect to the objective correlative or poetic means of evoking that precise effect."

At the end of the forties McLuhan had adopted a strongly moral, almost Swiftian, attitude toward industrial society. This attitude was embodied in his first book, *The Mechanical Bride* (1951), a study of the "folklore of industrial man." "Technology," he wrote, "is an abstract tyrant that carries its ravages into deeper recesses of the psyche than did the sabre-toothed tiger or the grizzly bear." But then, he reflected, the symbolist poets had found it easy to absorb into their work the effects of technological change, as expressed in the newspaper, radio and television.

At this time, McLuhan found in the later works of Harold Innis ideas that helped him to understand the kind of world that the symbolists had created. In these studies Innis was examining the relationship between forms of communication and political organization. He argued that the invention of the phonetic alphabet, and then the use of printing and paper, enabled empires to develop, ruling from urban centers through specialized groups of priests and bureaucrats. An oral culture, on the other hand, such as had flourished in the golden age of Greece, encouraged an intimate, tribal society with high participation. "My bias," wrote Innis, "is with the oral tradition, particularly as reflected in Greek civilization, and with the necessity of recapturing something of its spirit."

Here was a key to understanding the triumph of symbolism. The symbolists had recovered some of the spirit of the oral tradition—its inclusiveness, its sense of multiple perspective, its delight in color and sound. That had come, McLuhan argued, by their awareness and acceptance of the new electronic technology, which was an extension of man's entire nervous system, and returned him to a tribal world of instantaneous information and dialogue. They had thus broken away from, or at least modified, the technology that had been dominant for four centuries, and which had had the printing press at its very center.

The invention of the phonetic alphabet had made a break between ear and eye, "between semantic meaning and visual code." But as long as the means of spreading the written word was limited, man still lived in an auditory world. It was only with the invention of the printing press that speech was visualized and the principles of continuity, uniformity, and repeatability made the basis of our civilization. Print culture, by elevating the visual sense, broke up the balance of the senses, and created that dissociation of sensibility to which T.S. Eliot referred. Yet, it would be wrong to draw simple contrasts between oral and visual culture, to exalt the former and belittle the latter. The most vivid periods are those that come when one culture is about to yield to another, when we have the tensions of the interface.

This argument was presented in *The Gutenberg Galaxy* (1962) with copious illustrations of his thesis from literature. The very form of the book—short sections preceded by arresting and dogmatic summaries, long quotations from a wide variety of sources, puns and verbal play—embodied the qualities of discontinuity, simultaneity, and multiple association to be found in an oral culture.

McLuhan's next book, *Understanding Media* (1964), was the book that made him a central figure in the sixties. As Harold Rosenberg wrote: "*Understanding Media* is McLuhan's goodbye to Gutenberg and to Renaissance, 'typographic' man: that is, to the self-centered individual." As such, it takes its place in that wide channel of cultural criticism of the twentieth century that includes writers like T.S. Eliot, Oswald Spengler, D.H. Lawrence, F.L. Leavis, David Riesman, Hannah Arendt. In *Understanding Media* McLuhan seemed to embrace the new technology, whose watchwords were inclusiveness, identity, the dominance of the audile-tactile, and whose essential creature was the electric circuit. Technology was still a "tyrant," but it was a much more benign one. Indeed, at times McLuhan wrote as if the new technology would recover our lost paradise, which would not be a garden, but a global village. "The immediate prospect for literate, fragmented Western man encountering the electric implosion within his own culture is his steady and rapid transformation into a complex and depth-structured person emotionally aware of his own total interdependence with the rest of human society."

Understanding Media, written with verve and explosive wit, brought McLuhan great fame, but, among many academics, a kind of infamy. He had, they said, deserted the sacred word and allied himself with the infidels. He had become the sworn enemy of the book, a strangely learned exponent of pop culture. And his bias toward the oral and his questioning of the benevolent role of the printing press give some support for the cliché of criticism. Yet few writers are so persistently (often overpoweringly) bookish. When McLuhan talks about the individual book, it seems to transcend its medium—often triumphantly so in the symbolists—whereas for the favorite children of the electronic age—film, radio and television—the medium is indeed the message, a powerful, subliminal message, that can, however, be understood and controlled, especially if one diligently reads the dozen or so books that McLuhan has written.

The Gutenberg Galaxy and *Understanding Media* emerged from a seminar at the University of Toronto in the late fifties. The seminar was outside the formal academic structure, and was essentially a meeting between colleagues and graduate students with a common interest in communication. McLuhan was now sensationally launched on his career as the philosopher of communications, and he needed an academic basis. In 1963, the University responded to the need, created the Centre for Culture and Technology, and made McLuhan the director. The Centre had little need of "hardware." The physical center was an old coach house behind a nineteenth-century mansion on Queen's Park Crescent. Here McLuhan wrote, conducted seminars, and maintained by telephone his associations with kindred spirits throughout the world. There were occasional associates and collaborators at the Centre, but for the most part the Centre was McLuhan, and its program was reflected in a regular succession of his publications.

With the establishment of the Centre, McLuhan devoted himself to studies of the effect of electronic technology on the human community. In *From Cliché to Archetype* (1970) the concern is to follow the patterns of human cognition as they appear in language and in the arts. He examines the process by which worn-out and conventional themes and perceptions are habitually "flipped into resplendent new form." *Culture Is Our Business* (1970) and *Take Today: The Executive as Dropout* (1972) are studies of the impact of the electronic age on business. The world of simultaneous and instantaneous information requires that all business activities, particularly those of large multinational firms, be synchronized and interrelated. The administrative process no longer requires large centralized plants; there has been a shift from "hardware" to "software." Specialization has been outmoded.

> At electric speeds of information, whether telegraph or computer or telephone, specialism and compartmentalization, work and jobs have become impractical, and more and more people become aware of the work and function of other people around them, with the result that everybody becomes capable of a variety of functions and roles, and job-holding yields to role-playing.

Just before McLuhan's final illness, he was working on a study of The *Laws of the Media* and a preliminary manuscript had been prepared. In brief, the argument is that a new medium tends to intensify, enhance or promote something (radio, for instance, promotes an aural type of communication). At the same time, the medium tends to antiquate or obsolesce a previously intensified process (radio detracted from the importance of print). It also tends to retrieve yet another process (radio brings back the old oral, preliterate world), and finally, to reverse itself, or to engender a fundamentally different medium. (The "hot" medium of radio, concentrated on the aural, creates the "cool" medium of television, "an extension of the sense of touch, which involves maximal interplay of all the senses.")

No academic of our generation was more widely known than Marshall McLuhan. He believed that the engaged humanist had a broad social responsibility to carry his perceptions to a wide audience, and to do so with care and humor (jokes, he said, revealed the besetting grievances of today). In his last active year, he gave the Ezra Pound Lecture at the University of Idaho, a close study of Pound's rhetorical devices. That same year he presented a general discourse on the problems of the electronic age to a conference of bankers meeting in Monaco. He had many opportunities to take senior posts in the United States. (He accepted one: Albert Schweitzer Professor of Humanities at Fordham University, but only for one year, 1967–68.) He was, however, devoted to Canada and happy in his Toronto position, a member of a small college within a large federated university. He wrote amusingly and provocatively on the standard theme of Canadian identity. "Canada," he said, "is a land of multiple borderlines, psychic, social and geographic. Canadians live at the interface where opposites clash." Canada was then a good observation post, where one could early observe and appraise the mighty clash of opposites.

To many readers McLuhan's generalizations, although shakily founded, were enunciated with an irritating dogmatism. To McLuhan, however, they were "probes," designed not to give ultimate answers, but to shed light on dark places. He was unhappy, too, at the criticism that he had revealed a deterministic world in which man was at the mercy of his own technology. He maintained that, by understanding the effects of the media, we could control them, "even as the Greeks chose to alter the Dionysian fury with Apollonian detachment."

Marshall McLuhan was an informal, generous-spirited man, happiest in small groups at his coach house or in the living room of his home, which, if you blot out a few distracting high rises visible to the south, could have been an English country house on the southern downs. It was in his living room that I visited him during the last months. He sat close to the big fireplace, rising from time to time to make sure that the flames had not died down, as if he were at the same time rekindling the fire of his own spirit. Despite the sad deprivations of the last months, I believe that the inner forces always burned brightly, and that he continued to live in the glow of the ideas that had so powerfully illuminated his age.

Marshall McLuhan with Louis Forsdale

Technology and the Human Dimension

Forsdale: You often talk about the electric media as a kind of nervous system around the globe.

McLuhan: They are a very nervous system! The electric media are a physical extension of our own organic nervous system, which is literally constituted by electric impulses. When you put an electric system, or field, around you, you enlarge your own nervous system. Just as a wheel extends your foot, the "wired planet" now extends our nerves. All technology is a physical extension of man, and our bodies, said Emerson, are a "magazine" or storehouse of all past, present, and future innovations.

Forsdale: That is to say, the eyes are extended by photographs, television, film. The ears are extended by radio—

McLuhan: The eyes are also extended by such forms as print and microscope or telescope. The ear is extended simultaneously with the voice by telephone and radio and TV and other familiar means of communication. All the senses and body organs get their extensions by man-made means. Clothing is an extension of our skin. And clothing is also a weapon. For when you put on clothes, you put on power. Clothes are not worn merely to keep us warm and to protect our bodies. They are also worn to "speak," in the sense that theatrical costumes speak. All media, moreover, are weapons, as well as masks of power that are "put on," so to speak.

Forsdale: For instance?

McLuhan: Radio.

Forsdale: How's it work?

McLuhan: You can turn on or "put on" radio, or you can "go on the air," or you can get "radio coverage" (a kind of clothing) as a service, and you can also "put on" the illusion of an invasion of Mars, as Orson Welles did for us. It was terrifying!

Forsdale: Who puts it on? The creator?

McLuhan: The user, whether a child or the president. The language which we use is equally something which you put on. You speak, or wear, the language of your group. It's a corporate mask, a corporate insignia, that identifies you—you outer (utter) yourself. The traditional observation is, *Speak that I may see you.*

Forsdale: Back to radio. I'm a kid walking down the street and I've got a transistor radio up to my ear—

McLuhan: You're wearing several masks, one on top of the other. Kids love this sense of power. They're putting on English, putting on the radio network, putting on the game they're listening to, putting on music. The put-ons can be stacked layer upon layer, each resonating in the other. You've got to consider a lot of the meanings of "put on" here, and note that you can both put people on and also "take them off."

Forsdale: Why is radio a weapon?

McLuhan: Because it gives you enormous power of coverage over other people. Remember the secret radio in "Hogan's Heroes"? You can put people on by holding their attention as power, or they can put you on as power for them, as in Orson Welles's "Invasion from Mars" broadcast.

Forsdale: You mean you can know people's affairs with radio?

McLuhan: You can both know them and make them. The broadcaster shapes your thoughts and feelings while you listen. But the important thing is that radio makes you participate in somebody else's life. Suddenly you are beyond yourself. The new electric media involve you with other people. They are here and you are there. On the other hand, old visual media tend to make you detached.

Forsdale: What are the visual media as you think of them?

McLuhan: They're anything that depend heavily on the eye, like film and writing and print. TV, however, is only partially a visual medium, and that's tough to understand. It's audile-tactile.

Forsdale: But we use our eyes with television as well as our ears.

McLuhan: You use your eyes when you're looking at comics or cartoons, but cartoons aren't just visual. They, too, are tactile, because they're made of boundary lines which the eye must "handle" by scanning. Picasso leaves out the ordinary "fill-in," or connections, between spaces, and is called abstract. A child's drawing leaves out visual connections, and is called childish. Our sense of sight is given more importance as we become more grown up, as it were.

Forsdale: But tactile means touch. How can a medium like television, that we look at with our eyes, end up being tactile?

McLuhan: Well, the new physics tells us that touch is not connection but a gap where things rub, like the gap between the wheel and the axle. There has to be "play" here, if they are to "keep in touch." When the wheel and axle get too close together, they "seize up" in a bind. When they get too far apart, they collapse. When our eyes look at things on TV, they also behave as if they were handling or touching the image. They rub over it, so to speak. The television image, said James Joyce, is "the charge of the Light Barricade." TV is like a cartoon, consisting of lines that come at you. You view it as you must view an X-ray image, by using your eyes as hands, moving around the edges of the lines, just as your eyes explore a cartoon and fill in the spaces between the lines with your imagination or your other senses to make a picture.

Forsdale: How do you describe visual man?

McLuhan: Visual man, paradoxically, is detached, but he always has an aim or a goal. He finds it natural to isolate a special point on the horizon where he is heading, whether in travel or in career. He is en route, striving to attain. But under the conditions of the new electric service environment—which is not visual—you cannot have distant goals to aim at because you're already there. It doesn't matter which electric medium you select—you're there when you turn it on. And what can you do about this living at the speed of light? If you can't have goals, you can play roles. This is where the "put-on" becomes a new way of life like the international motley of hair and costume worn by the young. The new electric environment of simultaneous and diversified information creates *acoustic* man. He is surrounded by sound—from behind, from the side, from above. His environment is made up of information in all kinds of simultaneous forms, and he puts on this electric environment as we put on our clothes, or as the fish puts on water.

Forsdale: Do we all do this?

McLuhan: All electric media are service environments of information which are put on or worn as masks of subliminal power by the whole population. They are really the Emperor's invisible new clothes that look like the same old suit to the courtiers. Especially since Sputnik (October 4, 1957) the put-on has become planetary rather than regional. To say that these services of radio, telegraph, television, telephone are environments of information may sound a little bit metaphorical, but when you look carefully, you'll find that it's literally true, not figure of speech at all. You don't have to watch TV or listen to radio in order to have them put you on, because they're around you all the time—*physically* around you. Now, when you put on an environment or mask of power—a vortex of energy such as radio or telephone or TV—you are both extending your own ego and invading other egos to a fantastic degree. The ability to speak to Peking by telephone is the act of a superman, and we now take for granted that all people on this planet are supermen. What has thus happened to the "human scale" is very important to recognize. Can there be a "human scale" anymore? Or, under electric conditions, does everybody become superman? As far as I know, the answer is absolutely yes. Any child is superhuman today—on the telephone or radio or on any electric medium. The traditional human dimension hardly exists anymore.

Forsdale: Because man can extend himself so far?

McLuhan: No, because he has been extended. He accepts such universal extension as his "natural" environment now. Nature has disappeared and a new man-made "nature" has taken its place. When Sputnik went around the planet, the planet went inside an electric orbit and became the content of a man-made environment. The old planet and the old nature became art forms. The dominant art form now is our man-made electric clothing. Is there any other "nature" in our world now except the man-made environments of electric information?

Forsdale: You use the term art in what sense?

McLuhan: Making. That's what it means, and that is what we do in technology. We make artifacts. We make cars, languages, buildings; we make sense, when we are conscious.

Forsdale: What happened to nature?

McLuhan: It went inside the new man-made world of "pop" art. Renaissance man came to North America with gunpowder and printing, and he determined to conquer, or transform, or subdue nature. And, in our literature and poetry we show nature, consistently, as the enemy of man—whether it's Mark Twain or Thoreau or Melville or Hemingway. Nature appeared as the foe to be subdued. Ours was the first continent to get treated by the modern power technologies. Earlier, when men approached nature, they tended to come to terms with it, got as friendly as possible with it, and adopted a rather ecological relationship with nature. In North America, only, we conquered nature.

Forsdale: Did we?

McLuhan: We did. We broke it, smashed it to pieces. Now we're trying to put it back together again. We conquered nature, and it is no longer just an enemy, but a problem. It is now a broken enemy, like the Red Man. It's in flight, it's broken, and we're now using new technology to support the old nature. We're now propping up nature in North America and rebuilding the old environment as naturally as possible. Since ecology is the rebuilding of a broken nature, we're literally in the age of the garbage apocalypse. (Consider *garbage* and *garb* together.) It wasn't until we put the planet inside a man-made environment of new clothing that we realized what a mess we had made with the old technological clothing. Garbage (old clothes) everywhere. Suddenly the planet appeared as a hopeless confusion. But pollution was not a new or sudden thing: it was the awareness of pollution that was sudden. That came with the simultaneous patterns of the electric age, presented by instant replay, as it were.

Forsdale: Mother Nature is dead?

McLuhan: Yes, "the hand that rocked the cradle has kicked the bucket," to use another figure of speech. Nature has become as arty as Mother Goose. I don't think you'll find any scientist today who can talk about nature with a capital N. That's Newtonian language that belongs to another age.

Forsdale: You say this electric age is not a visual age but an acoustic age. Would you explain that further?

McLuhan: Acoustic space is created by our ability to hear from all directions at once. Electric information arrives from all quarters at once. Thus, in effect, acoustic environments were created by the telegraph and began to show up in the press as mosaics of juxtaposed and discontinuous items all under one dateline. Acoustic space is all touch and interplay, all resonance and sympathy. Acoustic space is like the relationship of a mother and child, which is audile-tactile, or sound and touch. The cooing and handling and touching—this is the kind of world the electric media put around us. The electric media are a mom-and-child or rock-and-roll relationship. Electrically speaking, there's nothing but nuzzling and cuddling and cooing, alternating with wild yells for love and food and help. It's always May Day in the global nursery.

Forsdale: You mean the relationship between a television set and a child is a cuddling relationship?

McLuhan: Entirely tranquilizing. Billing and cooing, rocking and rolling is the name of the game. It's an Archie Bunker love-hate relationship, if you like, but it is essentially love. It doesn't matter so much what the TV set says—that is, what kind of program is on—as long as it speaks to the child in us.

Forsdale: Television and viewers comfort each other?

McLuhan: And change each other. It's a changed world; yet, in the Western world especially, we have an inhibition about recognizing anything in the way of change. Visual man cannot tolerate structural change. He can only tolerate additions. You can add, add, add—as long as you don't change anything. The language of the computer men is *Garbage in and garbage out.* They do it by reducing the world to "bits" or bites. The computer is a two-bit machine, at heart.

Forsdale: But we keep thinking that we're always progressing.

McLuhan: Yes, but we are actually being *processed* when we think we are merely adding more of the same. We add to the same old things. The guy who is going to use a superhighway thinks he is the same man who used the dirt road it replaced. Of course, he may feel bigger with this new mask of power to put on as he drives down the superhighway, but still he thinks he's the same man. He doesn't notice that the highway has changed his relation to his family and his fellows.

Forsdale: You say visual man can't tolerate change. How about electric man who lives in this acoustic world?

McLuhan: In the electric world he finds that change is the only stable factor. He lives in a world where the criterion is *making,* not *matching.* Take the instant replay on television. It doesn't try to match the play, because the play is already gone. The replay is post-mortem, an instant post-mortem, not of a fact but of a process. It is not matching—which visual man would do—but making. Now, visual man was hung up on the idea of matching as a criterion of Truth. Under electric conditions, at the speed of light, there can never be matching, only making. The scientists discovered this forty, fifty years ago when they developed the "uncertainty principle," saying that no experiment could ever be repeated. You can't step into the same river once. This is now seen to be literally true. It had always been true, but electric speed made it obvious.

Forsdale: When this became obvious, what did it do to our goals?

McLuhan: Man's great visual goal had been competitive matching, which electronic man feels is a "drag." The pursuit of "objectives" had been his aim against all obstacles—the Western dream of conquest, one-upmanship. Now we have to say, *Cut nature down to size to match your limitations.* With electricity, when we found the old kind of conquest too simple, we suddenly realized that it wasn't a challenging goal after all. Now, when we can press a button and blow up the whole world, we realize that goals aren't really compatible with community. If that's all it ended in, it wasn't worth the bomb. So now we're beginning to ask, *But, what's the quality of life that goes with this easy conquest? What sort of human satisfactions are we developing in these conditions of endless rivalry? What sort of people do we want to be?*

Forsdale: So the young person now says, *I'm not sure what I want to do with my life.* He drops out of the old bind in order to get in touch?

McLuhan: He is rejecting those older values which were absolutely unquestioned for the past four centuries.

Forsdale: Is he drifting?

McLuhan: No, he is resonating. He's living in this new, nonvisual world of role playing. He has no goals, he's already there. It's just a question of enriching where he is, and where it's at, rather than wandering. And this is the new confusion. Of course, everybody in the older Western establishment still tends to look for goals and directions, like Mother Hubbard, and is constantly frustrated, since there now are none. The elders are still prone to be purely visual and directional. It's like the old hang-up that evolution had to be in one continuous path or direction. People have been forever trying to figure out where this evolution metaphor came from, since life obviously has never pursued any one direction. Natural selection and development go in all directions simultaneously. The kids today, in the electric world, are suddenly released from the fixed visual patterns of twenty-five hundred years of Western culture. The "missing link" has turned out to be a resonant interval because there wasn't any "chain of being" in the first place. I'm not saying this release is a good thing—

Forsdale: You're not saying it's a bad thing either, are you?

McLuhan: I'm simply saying that it has happened, and it happened because of our own *making* activities, our own innovations. Of course, we have brought incredible confusion and dismay upon the population of the Western world by electric innovation which reverses all the character of established society. Meanwhile, the Eastern world—much bigger than ours—has acquired the old Western technology and has decided to pursue outer visual goals and objectives of a Western kind. China, Africa, India, Japan are all pursuing Western objectives, while the West is going inward and abandoning Western objectives in order to meditate and reflect. So the West is Orienting and the East is Westernizing.

Forsdale: East is East, and West is West, and never—

McLuhan: That's Kipling at the end of the nineteenth century. It was a bad time to say it, just when the merger was taking place. He was just at the pivotal moment when East and West reciprocally switched directions.

Forsdale: What was that moment?

McLuhan: The moment when electric media came in. Telegraph and telephone. By 1830 there was commercial telegraph. The Civil War was a telegraph war, fought from the White House, putting the president on the front line—the first telegraph war, in which the head of state conducted the war from a distant point and became a world figure by the same electric means. Then telephone came in, and radio by the end of the century. So the new environments of information took over. What electricity does is like light itself: it is an environment made up of information. Electric light is pure information, and the user is the content—*I was illuminated. A great light dawned on me.* But there is the strange fact that the electric user is the entire world, rather than an individual.

Forsdale: How so?

McLuhan: Because electric information is a world environment that illuminates in all senses, mental and physical. We are now all skyjackers, as it were. We all can get world coverage, or spotlight, when we push a button. Notice, the electric surround of information that has tended to make man a superman at the same time reduces him into a pretty pitiable nobody by merging him with everybody. It has extended man in a colossal, superhuman way, but it has not made individuals feel very important. Our astronauts were real skyscrapers, but they don't seem or feel very important as private persons. Electrically, the corporate human scale has become vast even as private identity shrinks to the pitiable. The ordinary man can feel so pitiably weak that, like a skyjacker, he'll reach for a superhuman dimension of world coverage in a wild, desperate effort for fulfillment, or he will buy a private psychiatrist to be an audience. Violence on a colossal scale results from his feeling of impotence. The media tend to make everybody puny, while offering them the opportunity of being supermen. So there is a new desire to use the media to put on the colossal audience that today's media provide.

Forsdale: Once you told me that we live in a world today where nobody will study the effects of any medium. But don't some people think they are doing that?

McLuhan: Counting the number of TV sets or listening hours tells nothing of the changes that take place in people and in their relations to other people. It is a question of *figure and ground,* to use the language of Gestalt psychology. The car, for example, is a *figure* whose *ground* includes highways and industrial plants and oil companies. The effect of the car as *figure* is very small compared to the effect of the *ground* of the car. The *ground* alters everybody and also the times and spaces and interfaces of the entire community previously related to railway services. In the same way, the jet plane does not change the *figure* of the car, but surrounds and envelops the *ground* of the car, making the very *ground* obsolete by changing all the times and spaces of highways. The number of people who use the *figures* of electric media has comparatively little to do with the effects those media have on them. There is no more misleading approach to the actual changes than this quantitative concern with *figure* minus the study of the *ground,* and nothing about the quality of life. That's why many people were dismayed when I reported some of the things that happened with the printed *book* as a changer of human outlook and patterns of action. You have only to report the subliminal effects of any medium or *ground* at all to create panic in the Western bosom. Now, why should Western man be so terrified of anything that changes him? Because there has been no study in Western history of any media changes whatever. Innovations are reported, but their consequences have not been studied. When you look at all the changes that took place in Western science or philosophy or psychology resulting first from the written, and then from the printed, word, you have a revolutionary story of change which, of course, has now all ended suddenly with electricity. And people are just as terrified of these revolutions' having ended as of their having begun. If you ask me, *Why does Western man have no tolerance for the study of change?* I would be inclined to say it's because he still thinks as visual man, and visual man cannot tolerate change. Visual man lives in a world whose ground rules he perceives as static. Let me give you an example: visual or phonetically literate man will look at stars and cosmic forces and say they are changing things, but he will not say that he is himself changing. He passes this particular buck to the cosmic forces, to the universe.

Forsdale: You say visual man was afraid to study change. Did you find that looking at change was fun, or was it frightening?

McLuhan: It can be fun in the sense that it is itself a form of intellectual conquest, but it is frightening to find people ignoring these things. It gives you the reassurance, on one hand, that what you make, you can control—if you want to. On the other hand, you feel discouraged by the indifference of the users of technology to the psychic "rip-off" that is the price of the game. For example, we can turn radio off completely, and I think, if we were smart, we would try doing this to test effects, because the effect of radio on oral cultures is to drive them up the wall, as in the north of Ireland, and in Quebec. These people already have very sensitive hearing, and acoustic culture. As Edward T. Hall's work shows, they are very, very sensitive to each other in proximity. When you add the radio dimension of involvement to that hypersensitivity, they go wild. Radio can be an impulse to intertribal slaughter and genocide. Look at Hitler, who was a product of radio. Hitler could not have survived one hour on TV.

Forsdale: Why would Hitler have ended on TV?

McLuhan: Everything that sounded so important and earnest on radio would have been just comic on TV. Any process, pushed to its limits, flips. The specialized acoustic image of the demagogue on radio, or talking movie, is suddenly shifted into iconic or "cartoon" form on TV. Earlier I indicated why the TV image is a kind of X-ray mesh of lines and dots that comes at the viewer. It is an effect quite different from photo or movie, for these latter leave the viewer relatively detached and uninvolved. But to bring intensity to the TV medium is fatal, or at least comic, as witness Archie Bunker's earnestness. It becomes cartoon, like Bugs Bunny, because the TV image is so different in its structure from radio or film. Take President Nixon. He's somewhat untakeable on TV, but quite acceptable on radio or on film. The same man, performing in exactly the same way, is quite acceptable on film and unacceptable on TV because on TV he seems too intense, too much the specialist.

Forsdale: Marshall, you've often used the phrase *global village* in talking about the electric media.

McLuhan: It was just an accidental phrase that popped up. What it means, literally, is that, transmitted at the speed of light, all events on this planet are simultaneous. In the electric environment of information, all events are simultaneous. There is no time or space separating events. Information and images bump against each other every day in massive quantities, and the resonance of this interfacing is like the babble of a village or tavern gossip session. The absence of space brings to mind the idea of a village. But actually, at the speed of light, the planet is not much bigger than this room we're in. In terms of time and the speed of the event that are now programmed, they hit each other so fast that even a village is too big a thing to use for a comparison. The acoustic or simultaneous space in which we now live is like a sphere whose center is everywhere and whose margins are nowhere. Acoustic space cannot be cut into pieces, as visual space can. It is both compressed and indivisible.

Forsdale: If we live in a global village, does that mean that people are going to like each other?

McLuhan: Not likely, since proximity means there's more abrasiveness. Close quarters strain human tolerance.

Forsdale: So the fact that we're all interlinked doesn't necessarily lead to a peaceful world?

McLuhan: We're not so much interlinked as *interfaced.* That means intensive interface and loss of face as a result. This creates an enormous amount of irritation. When privacy becomes a problem, identity is threatened and violence is engendered by the need to recover identity. Electronic surveillance of every human being, every human action, is now a reality. 1984 really happened a long time ago.

Forsdale: So is privacy down the drain?

McLuhan: Yes. Totally. But we may recover community.

Forsdale: Can one adjust to loss of privacy?

McLuhan: All right, now tell me. What kind of changes do you make in your life in order to live minus all privacy—a life where everything has to be out in the open? What do you do?

Walter J. Ong

McLuhan as Teacher
The Saint Louis Years

Marshall McLuhan has influenced such a wide and diversified audience, from research scholars and scientists in dozens of fields to newspaper publishers, advertising agents, museum directors, poets, business executives, city planners, and computer designers, that it seems impossible to pull all of his activities together under one rubric. Yet I believe it is possible to do just that. Above all and in all and through all, Marshall McLuhan was a teacher.

All a teacher can ever do is get other people to think. Without a teacher, learners may be impoverished, may be unable to find much to learn. The teacher sets things up, whether by enlivening familiar matter or by providing unheard of things for the learners to think about. But, even with the most brilliant teacher, if the learners are to do any learning, they are the ones who have to do it. The pipeline information-transfer model does not really work for the teacher-learner relationship. It presents learners as passive recipients. Learners are not recipients but doers.

A good teacher is one who can encourage others to think actively about the things that he or she is dealing with. A superior teacher can make the thinking pleasant for the learners. A superb teacher can make the thinking an overpowering activity, delightful even when it is disturbing and exhausting. By these criteria, Marshall McLuhan was always a superb teacher. He could stir people's minds. Even those who found themselves baffled or exasperated generally found themselves changed.

I knew Herbert Marshall McLuhan first when I was at Saint Louis University from 1938 to 1941, in his early days of teaching. As I suppose is the case with most influential teachers, McLuhan had an inarticulate message that lay much deeper than the factual material he dealt with in his courses, which were mostly in English Renaissance literature and "Rhetoric and Interpretation," this last consisting of a brief historical survey of rhetoric in the West combined with interpretations of poems more or less in the *Scrutiny* fashion. It included some attention to Richards and Ogden's *Basic English.*

McLuhan was exciting in great part because for him the past and the present were matters of equal urgency. The New Criticism provided McLuhan's ground for considering them equally urgent. The New Criticism was the first serious academic criticism that developed after English became a major university subject in the early years of the present century. It was New, but there was no comparable "old" criticism it replaced. The New Criticism was hospitable to contemporary literature as well as to that of the past. As vernaculars had leaked into university curricula in the late nineteenth century, academic study of English had focused first on earlier periods, moving cautiously from Old and Middle English to later periods and pausing fearfully on the threshold of the twentieth century. Contemporary literature or art or contemporary anything had been officially a non-subject in schools from antiquity on until generations of print culture had accumulated and indexed enough circumstantial knowledge of the past to give the present by contrast a face of its own. (If knowledge of the past dries up, the present will become again, in a new way, faceless.)

McLuhan sensed and conveyed the excitement in the air. In literature grown out of one's own immediate lifeworld, contrasts between consciousness and the unconscious can be studied more confidently and in greater detail than in literatures more remote in time and culture. At this same time, and in a somewhat parallel fashion, the sophistication once reserved for the study of high culture was being brought to bear also on popular culture. The techniques used by anthropologists in addressing so-called primitive peoples were being used to study the societies in which the anthropologists had grown up.

The human mind needs distance when it first deals with a subject academically, but the need for distance was lessening. Some walls between past and present had broken down. McLuhan lived in the new spaces that the breakdown had created. He exhilarated his better students by his conviction that everything was related to everything else, past and present. At the same time he variously disturbed, annoyed and exasperated other students who feared the uncharted perspectives opened by this sweeping conviction.

One form the resistance to McLuhan took was expression of annoyance at or scorn for his "generalizations." It is true that his intellectual synapses leaped wide gaps. His formulations crackled, and they set nerves on edge. But a dismaying number of his "generalizations" turned out to be true.

Besides a sense of the interlocking of past and present, students also got from McLuhan a sense, less marked but inescapable, of the moral and social relevance of literature and of everything. F.R. Leavis, McLuhan's teacher at Cambridge, has been styled a moralist critic and this he was in the sense that he felt, intensely, that any literary work, if it is to be reacted to adequately, must kick up a storm in the reader that calls into action a deepened sense of values. Leavis felt that writing which fails to do this is beneath contempt, phoney, fraudulent, and psychologically, socially and even morally, corrupting. McLuhan conveyed the same feeling. He was more inclined to attend directly to the popular works that Leavis himself and his wife, Q.D. Leavis, rather scorned. When he did attend to such works, as in his first book, *The Mechanical Bride* (1951), it was to invest them with high seriousness by showing that such things as advertising and the comic strips were in their own way as deeply into certain cyclonic centers of human existence—sex, death, religious questions and the relationship of man to his technology—as was the most "serious" art, though they were into them both naively and meretriciously. However, awareness of the facts here was neither naive nor meretricious: it was upsetting and liberating.

McLuhan's courses in "Rhetoric and Interpretation" could be expected, because of the subject matter itself, to convey a sense of the moral and social urgency of literature as well as a sense of the interaction of past and present. His courses in English Renaissance literature did the same thing. In the late 1930s and early 1940s, English and other vernacular literatures were only beginning to mature as subjects of academic instruction. There was a lot of work to be done. Literary history and criticism were developing fast. Issues were often new and mobile, and excited the mind all the more because of McLuhan's irrepressibly diachronic mentality. You thought that if you were not keeping up on Renaissance scholarship—and on medieval and classical scholarship as well—

you were losing ground in understanding twentieth-century issues.

McLuhan's effect on the Department of English at Saint Louis University was massive and permanent. At a time when the New Criticism was just beginning to spread in England beyond Cambridge University, he made it an already overwhelming reality at Saint Louis University. The older pedagogy had mostly taught students about literature. The new was teaching them to read literature, forcing them to look closely at the text and to formulate questions never asked before. Opponents of the new way grumbled that, all too often, the approach was less open-minded than empty-minded. But empty or not at the start, minds were soon brimming with ideas.

Other developments abetted McLuhan's efforts. In knowledgeable circles, Catholic and other, it was becoming apparent that what had been passing for "Thomism" in the revival encouraged by Roman Catholic documents was not what you found if you read closely what Aquinas had written. In the Department of Philosophy at Saint Louis University, "Saint Louis Thomism," as it came to be known, had also become strongly oriented to original texts, rather than to commentaries. Other midwestern universities were into Thomism, too, most notably the University of Chicago, where the Great Books program also enforced studying major authors, in their own writings, rather than studying about them. In a way, what McLuhan was into had, for a while, the air of a Midwestern enterprise. It soon was in progress elsewhere, but Saint Louis University did not lose the momentum he gave it, even after he left.

The rest of the story of McLuhan's development after 1944, particularly after *The Mechanical Bride* in 1951, has often been told, especially with reference to the influence of Harold Innis, in pulling McLuhan's concerns more directly into the communications media. Anyone who knew the Saint Louis University milieu in the late 1930s and early 1940s can recognize the continued presence of the milieu in McLuhan's later work. Younger faculty members, and students in the very large Department of Philosophy, focused a great deal of interest and discussion on noetic processes, and McLuhan's continued concern with the accumulation, storage and circulation of knowledge, which matured in his media studies, owes a great deal to the Saint Louis University milieu. In *The Gutenberg Galaxy*, I could underline dozens of passages which echo the very wording that used to recur in our animated discussions. Out of this milieu Bernard Muller-Thym, one of McLuhan's closest friends, developed, first into a promising young scholar in medieval philosophy, and then, after the Navy in World War II, into a well-known management consultant, retaining all along his intense interest in the accumulation and use of knowledge. At Saint Louis University, he used to publish papers on the intellectual processes involved in listening to musical compositions. William Van Roo, S.J., has become a distinguished professor of theology at the Pontifical Gregorian University in Rome, publishing chiefly in sacramental theology and the nature of signs and symbols—noetic interests again. One could mention many other persons from the same Saint Louis University milieu still actively concerned with the problem of knowledge. I, myself, have developed my own lines of investigation into noetic activity. Peter Ramus, the French Renaissance philosopher and educational reformer, interested me, from the beginning, because of the way he handled knowledge. The dedication, in my *Ramus and Talon Inventory*, "For Herbert Marshall McLuhan, who started all this," refers to the fact that McLuhan had first called my attention to the work of Ramus, who had surfaced conspicuously in Perry Miller's work, *The New England Mind: The Seventeenth Century*, where McLuhan had discovered Ramus, when the book appeared in 1939.

For many years, large numbers of people believed and/or hoped that Marshall McLuhan was able to explain everything that was going on in the world. He, of course, never claimed this ability at all, but two factors I have discussed suggest why the impression might exist: his deep sense of the relevance of past to present, and his interest in knowledge-processes. When these were combined with his later concern with media, you had an exciting triad— especially if you remembered that, as I believe he has insisted, the future is a thing of the past.

The Saint Louis University milieu also developed, although it certainly did not initiate, McLuhan's familiarity with the Middle Ages. In the Jesuit tradition at Saint Louis University, scholastic philosophy bulked large. Shortly before he came to Saint Louis University, the *Modern Schoolman* had begun publication there. Scholastic philosophy was being seen in fuller historical and psychological perspective and was being joined with many main currents in American intellectual life, not only in Catholic-intellectual centers but also at other universities, notably, the University of Chicago, under the influence of Robert Maynard Hutchins. The American tradition of voluntary association had produced a network of Catholic institutions of higher education that allowed the Roman Catholic Church direct responsibility for intellectual development on a scale unknown in her earlier history—nowhere in the Church's life had there ever been a system of Catholic education so large, diversified and vigorous as in the United States. McLuhan, who had been received into the Catholic Church before he came to Saint Louis University, was perfectly at home in this milieu, and left his mark on it as it left its mark on him. He had absorbed the Catholic sense of at-homeness in the human lifeworld and the entire universe. He took for granted that everything in creation hangs together through all levels and that probing all connections is worthwhile. His ready familiarity with Catholic thought has given some people the impression that McLuhan himself is part of some vast Catholic-intellectual plot, although no one I have ever met has ever been able to tell me just who is plotting what, and why.

These reflections by no means account for the whole of Marshall McLuhan, but, I hope, they will help to make him understood and appreciated. One reason he is so hard to account for is the vast range of his knowledge, and his genius for spotting correlations between the most discontinuous phenomena. As I have earlier mentioned, his instant correlations have annoyed many and upset a few. But McLuhan would seldom argue over his point-of-view. If you didn't like one insight, he presented you with another. He always had plenty more. He himself called the products of his thinking "probes." Whatever they are, they have certainly been a way of teaching, if teaching means getting people to think. His observations create excitement. If as many of them were as wrong as some people would like to pretend, they could hardly have had the effect they did. Thousands of people have said that they don't understand what McLuhan is talking about and yet have argued over him and his message for years.

Among Marshall McLuhan's many admirable qualities were his unflappable good humor and Christian charity. He seldom if ever had any unkind word for anyone, even for his most virulent

critics. One of the reasons for his kind resilience was his ability to
hold his own ideas at arm's length, and another was the sense of
paradox, perhaps most strikingly shown in the title of his book *The
Medium Is the Massage*, a take-off on his earlier logion, "the medium
is the message." This book title suggests, to me, a deep suspicion
in his own mind that the term and concept "medium" is not
adequate for what he has been talking about. I do not think it is,
at least as applied to communication by the human word. I myself
now tend to avoid speaking of the oral, writing, print and electronic "media." "Medium," something in-between you and me,
suggests a kind of pipeline transfer of units of "information"
which, even with feedback loops, is hardly adequate as a description of verbal communication among human beings. I prefer to
speak now of oral communication and of the technological
transformation of the word by writing, print and electronics,
remembering that human beings interiorize their technologies
by making them a part of themselves. We have interiorized writing
and print so deeply that we are unaware of them as technological
components of our private thinking processes, and we are engaged in rapidly interiorizing the computer in a similar way.
Marshall McLuhan was part of the process of interiorization, and
we can thank God for that, and for him.

McLuhan Probes

Classification is not the beginning of the study of a problem—it's the end. For me any of the little gestures I make are all tentative probes. That's why I feel free to make them sound as outrageous or extreme as possible. Until you make it extreme, the probe is not very efficient. Probes, to be effective, must have this edge, strength, pressure. Of course they sound very dogmatic. That doesn't mean you are committed to them. You may toss them away.

World War I—a railway war of centralization and encirclement. World War II—a radio war of decentralization concluded by the "Bomb." World War III—a TV guerrilla war with no division between civil and military fronts.

The greatest propaganda in the world is our mother tongue, that which we learn as children, and which we learn unconsciously. That shapes our perceptions for life. That is propaganda at its most extreme form.

Discovery comes from dialogue that starts with the sharing of ignorance.

Money is the poor man's credit card.

Print would seem to have lost much of its monopoly as a channel of information, but it has acquired new interest as a tool in the training of perception.

Point of view is failure to achieve structural awareness.

The trouble with a cheap, specialized education is that you never stop paying for it.

Experience is play, and meaning is replay and re-cognition. Far from being normal, successful communication is a rarity. It requires not only repetition of a common language, but also demands participation of both author and audience in the process of remaking from their old components a pattern that only the author may have perceived. Communicating the new is a miracle.

Any highway eatery with its TV set, newspaper and magazine is as cosmopolitan as New York or Paris.

To act without reacting, without involvement, is the peculiar advantage of Western literate man.

Unlike the old specialism, contemporary forms of human employment demand the creative powers of design through pattern recognition and inclusive social awareness.

Marshall McLuhan

The Role of New Media
in Social Change

From the Neolithic Age until the advent of electromagnetic technology men have been busy extending their bodies technologically. The fragmentation of work and social action that results from specialized extensions of the body has been given close study by Lynn White, in his *Medieval Technology and Social Change.* He opens with a consideration of the stirrup as it modified social organization in the early Middle Ages. As an extension of the foot, the stirrup enabled men to wear armor on horseback. Man became a sort of tank. But armor was expensive. It required the work and skill of a craftsman for a year to turn out a full suit of armor. The small farmer could not pay for such armor. The result was a change in the entire landholding pattern. The feudal system was spurred into existence by the stirrup, the mere extension of the foot.[1]

The extensions of hand and arm and back that made up the industrial complex of the eighteenth and nineteenth centuries were meshed with Gutenberg technology to create the great team efforts of assembly-line patterns of work and production. But the industrial complex was based on specialist fragmentation of tasks and extensions of the body which carried to an extreme the division of labor that had begun in the Neolithic period in about 3000 B.C.

A totally different kind of extension occurred with the application of electro-magnetism to social organization. Electricity enabled us to extend the central nervous system itself. It is a biological kind of event that creates maximal involvement of each of us in the total social process. Electric speed tends to abolish time and space in human awareness. There is no delay in the effect of one event upon another. The electric extension of the nervous system creates the unified field of organically interrelated structures that we call the present Age of Information. With the reduction of time and space in the pattern of events there is not only a great increase in the amount of data for daily experience, but action and reaction tend to become fused. Whereas in the previous technologies of fragmented extensions of the body there had been typically a considerable gap in time between social action and the ensuing consequences and reactions, this gap of time has almost disappeared. We are confronted with a situation that invites simultaneous or configurational and ecological awareness instead of the older awareness of sequential and linear cause and effect. In the mechanical age of the wheel and the lever, acceleration had expanded and enlarged the sphere of action. At electric or instant speeds the same sphere contracts almost to the dimensions of a single consciousness. Listening to a concert with an eminent psychologist, I happened to mention the highly tactile character of orchestral strings as compared with the other instruments. He seemed quite surprised and asked: "Do you mean that an auditory experience can have a tactile component?" Discussing the matter with him later, it became apparent that many psychologists assume that not only is auditory experience merely auditory, but so with the other senses. Visual experience is merely visual, etc. Thus, in such a view, there would be little difference in the experience and effects of TV and movies. And indeed many students of the media assume that it is the content of media, whether of the sung word, spoken word, the written word, that really matters. It is this sort of assumption that has tended to divert attention away from the forms and parameters of the media themselves. The sensory modalities of the media as such have not been studied. The very idea of "content" which obsesses us, on the other hand, is unknown to nonliterate societies. Our Western divisions between form and content occur with literacy and because of literacy. Literacy is itself a work of intense visual stress in a culture. When men begin to translate the speech complex into a visual code they have already opted for a division of labor that affects the whole society. They have become settled and have begun to specialize. Writing is impossible for man the food-gatherer but it is inevitable for Neolithic man, the agriculturist.

In his monumental study of *The Beginnings of Architecture*,

Siegfried Giedion has many occasions to comment on the fact that before script there is no architecture. Until man intensifies the visual parameters of his life by writing, he cannot *enclose* space. Before writing, man resorts to hollowed-out spaces.[2] The parameters of hollowed-out space are mainly tactile, kinetic and auditory. The visual components of the cave are minimal. Such proprioceptive space is almost like that of clothing, an immediate extension of our bodies. In our own electric age, space for the physicist has become a nonvisual thing of complex stresses. It is no longer uniform and continuous but diverse and heterogeneous. On the other hand, when Newton's physics first entered the European ken, Pascal moaned: "The eternal silence of these infinite spaces terrifies me." Before Newton our Western space orientation had had a much smaller visual parameter but the auditory components of space-structure had been very high. With the advent of the printed word, the visual modalities of Western life increased beyond anything experienced in any previous society. The parameters of the visual as such are continuity, uniformity and connectedness. These are not the notes or modes of any of our other senses. Today, when our electric technologies have extended far more than our visual faculties, the parameters of sense experience in the Western world have been radically altered. Our new media —the telephone, the telegraph and radio and television—are extensions of the nervous system.

I suggest that the sensory typology of an entire population is directly altered by each and every new extension of the body or of the senses. Each extension is an amplification that in varying but measurable degrees, alters the hierarchy of sensory preference in ordering daily experience and environment for whole populations.

Thus, it is an ancient observation, that was repeated by Henri Bergson, that speech is a technology of extension that amplified man's power to store and exchange perceptual knowledge; but it interrupted the sharing of a unified collective consciousness experienced by pre-verbal man. Before speech, it is argued, men possessed a large measure of extra-sensory perceptions which was fragmented by speech technology.

Until electromagnetism over a century ago, all the extensions of man appear as fragmentary. Tools and weapons, clothing and housing, as much as the wheel, or letters, are direct, specialist extensions of our bodies that amplify and channel energies in a specialist and fragmented way. Today much study is being devoted to the micro-climates created for our bodies by clothing. Some measurements indicate that unclad societies eat 40 percent more than those that are clad. As a technology of physical extensions, clothing channels time and energies for special tasks. It also changes the patterns of sensory perception and awareness; and nudity has very different meanings in different cultures. So it is with all the other extensions of ourselves.

The problem of dichotomy between form and content, that troubles and confuses our Western perception of media today, is now beginning to yield to new awareness of structures, of total fields in interplay, and to ecological approaches in general. We still need to develop awareness of the pervasive visual parameters and assumptions that phonetic literacy had imposed upon Western culture for two thousand years. Today, even the physicist is often hampered by his unconscious visual bias. This bias is utterly inhibiting to the physicist since his data are almost entirely nonvisual. It is thus not at all accidental that physics is mainly cultivated by men from cultural areas in which visual values are at a minimum. The unfortunate effects of highly literate culture on the state of the physical sciences is a theme of Milič Capek's *The Philosophical Impact of Contemporary Physics*. In the West our intense visual bias and our habit of considering form and content as quite separate derives from the structure of the phonetic alphabet. There is only one such alphabet, among the many kinds of scripts. And the unique property of our alphabet that is unknown to the Chinese or to the Egyptian is its power to separate sound, sight and meaning. The letters of our alphabet are semantically neutral. They can translate the words of any language. But they translate them by semantically meaningless sounds into semantically meaningless visual symbols. This divorce between the visual code and the semantic structure has gradually permeated and shaped all the perceptions of Western literate man.[3]

We have long stressed content and ignored form in communication. But this visual and literate structuring of our perceptions has provided us with very little accompanying immunity to the effects of nonvisual form. We were amused in 1900 when the Chinese protested that vertical telegraph poles would upset the psychic equilibrium of their people. We still imagine that the effects of radio depend upon radio programs. Yet such literate assumptions were no protection against Fascism. When radio began in Europe it awakened the ancient tribal energies in their auditory depths, as radio does today in backward countries. The auditory form of radio has, of course, a quite different effect in literate societies from its effect in oral and auditory cultures. Intensely visual and industrial cultures like England and America had few remaining tribal roots and vestiges to be re-energized by the tribal drum of radio. Where such roots still existed as in Ireland, Wales and Scotland, there were marked tribal stirrings and revivals. In the more urban and industrialized England and America radio was mainly felt as a resurgence of the folk arts of jazz and song and dancing. In areas like Germany, where tribal experience had been retained by many linguistic and artistic means, radio meant a revival of mystic forms of togetherness and depth involvement that has not been forgotten.

In the same way, the effect of TV has been very different in Europe and in the U.S.A. The TV image or "mosaic" as it is named by the TV engineers, has a quite different sensory character and effect from the movie and photographic image. The mosaic of the TV image provides, structurally, an experience of what J.J. Gibson calls "active or exploratory touch" as opposed to passive or cutaneous touch.[4]

The TV mosaic created by the "scanning finger" is visually of low definition, making for maximal involvement of the viewer. The painters after Cézanne, in the 1860s, deliberately set about to endow the retinal impression with tactual values.[5] In order to involve their audience maximally they resorted to various low-definition visual effects, many of which anticipated the typical form of the TV image. They achieved an effect described by J.J. Gibson in his experiments when he reports:

> The paradox is even more striking, for tactual perception corresponds well to the form of the object when the stimulus is almost formless, and less well when the stimulus is a stable representation of the form of the object. A clear unchanging perception arises when the flow of sense impressions changes most.[6]

At the same time as Monet and Seurat and Rouault were dimming the visual parameters of art in order to achieve maximal audience participation, the symbolists were demonstrating the superiority of suggestion over statement in poetry. The same principle obtains on the telephone as compared with radio. The auditory image of the telephone is of low definition. It elicits maximal attention and cannot be used as background. All the senses rally to strengthen the weak sound of the phone. We even feel the need to be kinetically involved via doodling or pacing. And whereas we complete the strong auditory image of radio by visualizing, we only slightly visualize on the phone.

Dr. Llewellyn-Thomas has used the Mackworth head-camera to study the eye-movements of children watching TV. There is great significance in his discovery that the eyes of the child never waiver from the faces of the actors even in scenes of violence. Maximal involvement is experienced not in the actions of the scene but in the reactions of the actors in the scene. The result is the same as the one recorded by J.J. Gibson concerning tactual perception as most adequate when the stimulus was almost form-less. That is, exploratory touch comes into play as the visual parameter is dimmed. It is a normal feature of the comics. Cartoons and comics are visually very dim affairs. The amount of visual data provided is small. But involvement or exploratory touch is at a maximum. Leo Bogart's study "Comic Strips and Their Adult Readers" observes how comic strip humor seems to produce a grim, unsmiling kind of amusement for the most part. "Genuine hearty laughs seem to be few and far between."[7] Once more, the involvement is high in these forms just in proportion as the intensity of the stimulus is vague and weak. The same comic scenes projected in high visual definition on a movie screen would evoke much more overt response.

Most people were struck by the TV coverage of the Kennedy assassination. We were all conscious of great depth of involvement, but there was no excitement, no sensationalism. When involvement is maximal, we are nearly numb.

One of the notable effects of the TV image on those in the primary grades seems to be the development of near-point reading. The average distance from the page of children in the first three grades has recently been measured in Toronto by Dr. W.A. Hurst. The average distance is 6 1/2 inches. The children seem to be striving to do a psychomimetic version of their relation to the TV image. They seem to be trying to read by proprioception and exploratory touch. The printed page, however, is of high definition visually and cannot be so apprehended.

It isn't only the act of reading that conflicts with habits of TV perception. I wish to suggest that the depth involvement characteristic of TV viewing discourages the traditional habit and need of "seeing ahead." The TV child today cannot see ahead, in a motivational sense, just because he is so deeply involved. He needs a totally new pedagogy and a new curriculum that will accommodate his shifting sensory ratios and his natural drive towards depth participation since TV. This returns us to the theme that our Western preference for considering the content of media instead of their configurational features is itself a bias of perception derived from the form of phonetic literacy. I do not need to be reminded of how much we owe to literacy. It has given us our way of life. It separated the individual from the tribal horde. I suggest that if we value this legacy of literacy, we shall need to take steps to maintain its existence by a fuller understanding of the role of new media in social change. Autonomy and freedom are best secured by a grasp of the new parameters of our condition. I would meet you upon this exponentially, as the mathematicians put it.

T.W. Cooper

The Unknown McLuhan

The public image of Marshall McLuhan was misleading. *People* magazine and no less than thirty other national publications, transformed McLuhan from man to myth:

> At 9:30 a.m. McLuhan bounds up the spiral stairway to his office. . . . His secretary runs down the messages. Woody Allen wants him to act in a film. . . . Gov. Jerry Brown wants McLuhan to speak at a political conference in California. The vice-president of Televisa de Mexico asks McLuhan to a media conference in his country. Will he give hour interviews to Radio Quebec and the BBC?[1]

To the media myth makers, Marshall McLuhan seemed surrounded by a flood of media. Many visitors left his bustling center delighted to have wedged a few moments into his whirlwind of interviews for the mass media. A perusal of the deeper McLuhan, the private thinker, the family man, was quite impossible. First impressions were mythic, superficial, hit-and-run.

My own impression of Marshall McLuhan was startling; he sat on the floor, smoked a cigar, and chewed gum. In several years with McLuhan since our introduction, I had rarely seen him smoke cigars, seldom seen him sit on the floor, and never seen him chew gum. Moreover, he rarely appeared in movies, seldom used cameras, and never drove a car.

Of the hundreds of people interviewed about McLuhan, all appear to have crystallized their first impressions of the man. A majority of people have judged his books, if not by their cover, then by a few pages or paragraphs in between. Of those who had met McLuhan, few have engaged in prolonged, in-depth conversation. Fewer still had been keenly aware of his change in thought and manner during the previous five decades. Most of his critics attempted to tie small pieces of McLuhan's thoughts to previous masters of knowledge. Few scholars had come to terms with the unique qualities of his style and perception.

What of the unknown McLuhan? What of the terra incognita, the undiscovered continent of his particularly singular approach to language, literature and learning? The late Dr. W.T. Easterbrook, McLuhan's best friend since college, commented: "There's just no way of knowing McLuhan through his books or a few lectures. You have to spend a lot of time with him to see what an amazing individual he is."[2]

Who is the man behind the cloud of first impressions? To select details which make McLuhan *sui generis* ("altogether unique") is, in the first instance, to pinpoint McLuhan's own talent for discovering that television, James Joyce, and American advertising are *sui generis*. His was the capacity to isolate and identify distinctive essences. The unknown McLuhan was an intellectual detective.

Thus McLuhan is wrongly perceived as a social critic. His art is revelation, not condemnation, and his criticism, so-called, is not evaluation, but rather the unveiling of hidden structures and dimensions. In media studies he focuses the blur of mass technologies and points to the distinctive birthmark of each invention. Likewise, in literary studies, he was happiest ferreting out a poet's stylistic middle name. Alongside one of his shorter coauthors, the lanky McLuhan resembled Sherlock Holmes with Watson or Don Quixote with Sancho. His passion was the quest, the search, the act of discovery.

Throughout McLuhan's literary career, he discovered and described the unique fingerprints of his mentors. In his earliest published essay, "G.K. Chesterton, a Practical Mystic,"[3] McLuhan identified G.K. Chesterton's trademark texture:

Chesterton . . . is doing something quite different from . . . lulling the mind by alliterating woolly, caterpillar words. His energetic hatchet-like phrases hew out sharply defined images that are like a silhouette or a wood-cut. And these are of a piece with the clarity of his thought.[4]

Forty years after his tribute to Chesterton, McLuhan was no less likely to specify Martianus Capella's identifying contribution to organized insight: "Capella has succeeded in bringing the language arts to bear on the sciences and mathematics, creating that unified encyclopedism which characterizes the inclusive and acoustic approach to knowledge."[5]

After McLuhan *discovers*, he *appreciates*. For him the art of *appreciation* was not a matter of lofty adulation. Instead his early essays are the unwrapping of a gift, the exposure of hidden expertise, the appraisal of uncommon perception.

McLuhan "appreciated" few qualities more than "unified encyclopedism." An edited anthology of his research bibliography might be entitled "An Abridged Encyclopedia of Encyclopedists." The so-called "Sage of Aquarius" of the 1960s read the multidimensional Meredith in the 1930s, devoured such omnivores as Cicero, Augustine, Nash, Joyce, Pound and Innis in the 1940s and 1950s, and continued studying "omniscients" such as Bacon, Einstein, Eliot, and Quintillian in the late 1970s.

The continuity of in-depth appreciation within McLuhan's writing is especially directed toward those artists of broadest canvas, whether Erasmus, Shakespeare, or Innis. His inclination toward acknowledging encyclopedists was apparent at the outset of his academic career. In his master's dissertation, he portrayed George Meredith as a literary leviathan: "He is so wholly *sui generis* that neglect of him involves neglect of nothing else, implies no deficiency of taste, no literary limitation. He cannot be placed."[6]

What McLuhan admired in Meredith in 1934 and in Chesterton in 1936 (the power to focus a vast range of material into narrow compass[7]) was no less in evidence in his writing with Barrington Nevitt in 1972. "Adam Smith, a *doctus orator*, or encyclopedic mind, enchanted and awed the massive intellect of Edmund Burke, who declared that *The Wealth of Nations* was "probably the most important book that was ever written."[8]

Not surprisingly, McLuhan's strongest Canadian influence, Harold Innis, is described as ". . . *sui generis*, a man for all seasons, all schools, and virtually all social disciplines."[9] What McLuhan wrote about Innis characterizes both men's methods of absorption:

Instead of despairing over the proliferation of innumerable specialisms in twentieth-century studies, Innis simply encompassed them. Whether by reading or by dialogue with his colleagues, he mastered all the structural innovations of thought and action as well as the knowledge of his time.[10]

As *intellectual detective*, McLuhan discovered the footprints of escaped masterminds. As *encyclopedist*, he followed in them. As *aesthete*, he *appreciated* those capable of creating the perfect crime.

The greatly submerged aspect of McLuhan's *breadth* pertains to his search for *depth*. Rising at four a.m. to meditate upon five translations (Greek, Latin, French, German and English) of the Bible, he expressed a devotion to scriptural study rare among modern scholars. Though his prose proved too topical and iconoclastic to canonize McLuhan as medieval saint or modern Renaissance scholar, these are the neighbors from whom he borrows equal measures of breadth and depth. Even the McLuhan-directed Centre for Culture and Technology stood within a small community of saintly/scholarly hybrids—the Centre for Medieval Studies, Saint Michael's College, Saint Basil's Church, and the Pontifical Institute.

To fully acknowledge McLuhan's mode of "depth"—his "appreciation" for people and poems, artists and inventions, nature and culture—is to fully clarify the manifold meanings of the verb "to appreciate." "To esteem adequately" is an inadequate definition of the verb. More finely tuned definitions include "to be keenly aware of and sensitive to," "to perceive distinctly," and "to raise or increase in value."

In one sense, these three definitions indicate McLuhan's "appreciation" of the later writings of Harold Innis. At first, McLuhan "became keenly aware of and sensitive to" the later work of Innis. Later he began to "perceive distinctly" the especial qualities of Innis's thought. Ultimately, upon the publication of *The Bias of Communications* (1951) and *Empire and Communications* (1950), McLuhan wrote introductions or "appreciations." Consequently, the Innis books were "raised in value." Thus Innis, in three senses, was *appreciated* by McLuhan.[11]

The Cambridge scholar, George Steiner, has noted McLuhan's uncanny ability to uncover design hidden within a natural phenomenon:

"McLuhan's genius rests in seeing something . . . a tree, for example . . . in a brand new way, say, for example, as a bent-over peasant woman . . . as a poet or artist might see it. Once we had lunch together and the entire meal consisted of seeing everything in the restaurant, from the lighting to the menu, with fresh insight. He's quite remarkable at that kind of observation."[12]

As Steiner demonstrated, McLuhan's "appreciation" depends upon fresh observation from a well-chosen angle of interior viewing. No one has appreciated the painting of the Sistine Chapel or the engineering of a Rolls Royce so much as those who have studied at arm's length while lying on their backs. Like the painter's and the mechanic's, McLuhan's appreciation derived from his choice to work from the *uncommon* angle of observation. His seeing may be from "close up"—"long shot," from above or below, from Western or Eastern orientation. This multiplicity of perspectives distinguished McLuhan from the one-song fundamentalist theorist his image portrays.

How did the popular image of McLuhan begin? In Toronto, McLuhan's surface image as a pontificating oracle stemmed from his well-known evening seminars. On a given Monday evening, guests ranging from the university president to Malcolm Muggeridge might be present. The atmosphere became "electric." Late arrivals, whether executives, professors or students, sat cross-legged on the floor. McLuhan's six-foot–two-inch frame stretched across a chair as if his whole body were yawning. His left and right legs crossed above the ankles to balance his left and right hands joined behind the neck.

While absorbing aural intake McLuhan might close his eyes to think and even appear to be sleeping. Suddenly without warning he would interrupt a speaker to launch a ten-minute fleet of observations. As "king" of the seminar, McLuhan has been accused of being a "non-receiving transmitter" who fired impeachable proclamations. Although the allegation is, in part, true, when a provocatively brilliant guest did speak, McLuhan listened attentively.

Informal in posture, formal in speech, McLuhan symbolized the hybrid qualities of English-speaking Canada. Tweedy and traditional from neck to ankles, he suggested his Cambridge background until one observed the institutional aluminum chair upon which he was seated. His image depicted the "instant tradition" of Canada, a country equally populated by English parliamentary procedures and American hamburger chains. The Centre for Culture and Technology was likewise a nineteenth-century coach house exterior with an "interior" collage by American advertisers, poster producers, cartoonists and Xerox, Inc. The blending of American "instant" with English "tradition" typified McLuhan's culture, technology, seminars and personality.

A crank-out-the-concepts approach to thought was antithetical to McLuhan. His casual atmosphere for fireside probing allowed a family relatedness and friendships nourished over cider. Out of his seminar circle of graduate students, seekers, undergraduates, friends, guest scholars and interviewers came a relaxed form of communication which might be labeled "configurational learning": numerous individuals of diverse backgrounds threw assorted perceptual ingredients into the conversation before McLuhan himself "tossed the salad" or scrambled the components into a different pattern of insight. His books were written in a similar manner: quotations were selected from a multitude of exploratory thinkers before McLuhan stirred the scholastic stew and spiced the mix with "percepts."[13]

Both in seminars and in his writing McLuhan played moderator among his participants. If any contributor became too "serious," McLuhan lightened the tone with an ethnic joke or quip from a mimeographed list of one-liners. These jokes, cartoons, quips, and aphorisms, sent to McLuhan from around the world, were chaotically scattered throughout the two-story Centre. Prior to fertilizing future essays, books and articles were spread like compost atop other books and essays. The Centre's greatest storage center, however, was hidden within McLuhan's highly trained memory.

McLuhan's expert use of memory was initially due to the enthusiastic encouragement of his mother. Elsie Naomi (Hall) McLuhan, the traveling elocutionist, enacted solo productions which gave her sons an example of "rhetorical" memory. During childhood he was inspired to love and retain long poetic passages from highly refined cultures.[14] So great was Elsie's love of Brahmin, blue-blooded, Boston elegance that she expressed disappointment when Marshall attended Cambridge University rather than Harvard.[15] McLuhan's early erudition culminated in his absorption of thousands of books and a son who teaches speedreading.

Without a magnetic memory, omnidirectional associational powers and encyclopedic exposure to European erudition, McLuhan might have become "just another English professor." However, his unique talent enabled him to attach an encyclopedia of materials to his magnetic memory and to interconnect the material by structure rather than content.

Unlike the associational patterns of a specialist's mind, McLuhan's brain was cross-indexed, cross-referenced and cross-pollinated. Since the scope of his cataloged information was comprehensive, the word "Homer" mentioned to McLuhan triggers the response, "The Beatles." To him both Homer and the Beatles were "something of a tribal folk encyclopedia" of poetry to their respective audiences.[16] To thinkers whose minds reflect a Dewey decimal arrangement of knowledge, the words "Homer" and "the Beatles" would be unlikely companions; instead, literate minds associate "Homer" with "Greece," the "*Iliad*," "Hesiod," "blindness," or other conventional "closed-circuit" patterns of information.

McLuhan's trademark was pattern recognition. Associating the topical and classical, the occidental and oriental, the tribal and the literate, the philosophical and the technological, he provoked a restructuring in consciousness. New readers find his ideas either "fully liberating" or "utterly impossible."

Despite his status as one of the world's most widely sought lecturers, McLuhan preferred to think of himself as a "loner." He did not mean to suggest an estrangement from his wife and six children or a poverty of friendships; to be sure, he remained "happily married" until his death. Moreover, he is one of the few scholars who greeted learned friends from around the world. His "loner" image referred more precisely to his self-chosen position as mental maverick and independent iconoclast.

Frequently a creative cerebral eruption separates McLuhan from others. His mind may be active developing a line of observation or recalling a tetrad. During such intervals, as during his reading, McLuhan, like the literate people he loved to describe, became a "private" person, an absent mind, a "loner." As McLuhan himself observed, the acts of reading and writing academic material disengage one's mind from functions of human interrelationship: few people read and wrote more than McLuhan. A bibliography of his books and essays fills over forty printed pages.

The Canadian scholar never *appeared* to be a loner; he attracted friends throughout his career, dated girls during college, played with his brother and schoolmates as a child, rowed crew at Cambridge, traveled throughout England with a companion, wrote over half of his books in collaboration and worked closely with a secretary and assistant. Nevertheless, the *psychological* definition of a loner bespeaks Marshall's own disappointment at having very few, if any, friends with whom he could fully communicate. He sensed that he was widely misunderstood. Even his best "sparring partners" failed to follow his most penetrating insights.

One of the secrets of McLuhan's talent for self-education was close collaboration with coauthors who were expert in neighboring disciplines. From Edmund Carpenter, coauthor of *Explorations in Communication* (1960), he "learned a great deal about native peoples";[17] Barry Nevitt, coauthor of *Take Today* (1972), "provided quite a lot of experience in business and management";[18] while Harley Parker, coauthor of *Through the Vanishing Point* (1968), taught McLuhan "a great deal about space and painting."[19] Perhaps McLuhan's closest collaborator has been his older son Eric, coauthor of *The City as Classroom* (1977), whose combined acumen, alacrity, and speed-reading expertise have effected a second generation of encyclopedic erudition.

With such an array of specialists-turned-generalists upon his easel, McLuhan appeared to pick his colleagues' brains in the manner that Durkheim looted archives. Furthermore, with McLuhan's own ability to read with a mine detector, that is, to isolate explosive passages, he accumulated a gigantic warehouse of "signature" quotations from deceased "experts." From Eliot he fondly quoted, "The flowers had the look of flowers that were looked at"; from Thoreau he remembered, "Anyone who reads newspapers should be paid a salary"; from Joyce he would recite, "A Jung man is easily Freudened." Such a collage of "ear-raisers" gave ammunition to the critic who likened McLuhan to a grave robber: he picks the fillings from dead men's teeth and casts the booty into a likeness of himself. A less cynical commentator might suggest that McLuhan was a miner who chiseled nuggets from ancient ore to share with passersby.

That McLuhan was not weaving tapestries of secondhand quotations became apparent when one studied his relationship to friends and collaborators. Far greater than his mental virtuosity and his stored cornucopia of purple passages was his enormous capacity to absorb perspectives from other people. What McLuhan learned from his mother and teachers in Winnipeg, from Rupert Lodge and Noel Fieldhouse at the University of Manitoba, from I.A. Richards and F.R. Leavis at Cambridge, from Wyndham Lewis in Saint Louis and Windsor, from Eric Havelock and Harold Innis in Toronto and from Carpenter, Parker, Nevitt and other colleagues at the Centre for Culture and Technology includes a wide variety of materials, methods and scholarly skills. As early as 1929 in Winnipeg, McLuhan and Tom Easterbrook would "stand talking on the street corners 'til four or five in the morning" until they saw the milk wagons going by. "As far back as I can remember," Easterbrook commented, "Marshall's always needed a sounding board. He was always testing every new idea on everyone . . . even the dog."[20]

The chemistry of discussion, debate and, more recently, "probing" always provided McLuhan with a mirror and measure of his thoughts. He was never more at home than when conducting a seminar unless when bouncing a new "percept" off an old friend. The total number of his "sounding boards" and "sparring partners" sculpted the perimeter of his expression. Conversely the words of his more remote critics fell upon deaf ears. When G.E. Stearn asked McLuhan, "Are you disturbed by the sometimes harsh critical responses your work excites?" McLuhan replied, "Even Hercules had to clean the Augean stables but once."[21] To McLuhan, criticism is inevitable: "A superstar today is just another word for a sitting duck."[22]

According to McLuhan, what critics frequently failed to see is the satirical nature of his books. Being uncertain about how to read McLuhan has led many to believe that he is a bookhater, a critic of professionalized humanity and a camouflaged front for southern agrarian Roman Catholicism. Can this man who failed to give footnotes, facts, and figures, who never qualified his speech with "perhaps," "in my opinion," or "let me suggest that certain implications might point toward . . ." be taken seriously? Was he absolutely honest? Wasn't he playing a self-centered joke on the world?

Opposite those critics who pose such questions are the answers of those who knew McLuhan intimately. Victoria College Professor Bede Sullivan, for example, unveiled the hidden man not mentioned in the press. She cited McLuhan's generosity, his willingness to have visitors driven anywhere within the city, his loyal friendship, his desire to assist students of all backgrounds, his humility, his consistent love for his family and his colossal sense of humor.[23] Sullivan acquired an appreciation for the warm human being behind the image.

Frequently traveling abroad, McLuhan represented the talented tongue of the North American body. When he spoke, thousands of ears attentively focused upon every word of "the most important thinker since Newton, Darwin, Freud, Einstein and Pavlov."[24] Yet in Toronto, the world's largest small town, one heard of friends bumping into "Marshall" everywhere—on the subway, at a movie, at a public lecture, in Saint Michael's College cafeteria. Whatever his world popularity, the cultural virginity of Toronto provided McLuhan with a relative measure of anonymity.

McLuhan *did* grade student papers. But what is significant is *how* he graded papers. Although by profession a connoisseur of prose fabric, McLuhan had no preoccupation with correcting split infinitives or double negatives. On the contrary, a student might receive a "graded" paper with only the comment, "2 points," or "3 points," penciled next to his grade. McLuhan's real interest was with the number of truly creative ideas or "points" a student uncovered: if an impeccably well-written, thoroughly detailed and documented paper was submitted with mere conventional concepts at its foundation, McLuhan was not interested in the ingredients. Conversely, an unpolished essay of penetrating observation and new perspective might be marked "4 points" because the essay was fresh and illuminating.

One of McLuhan's best and least observed talents was acting, particularly his enacting of the role of classroom educator. As his paper grading indicated, he consistently encouraged students to think for themselves at a level they thought nonexistent. Whatever a student's amassed information within a particular branch of knowledge, McLuhan inspired the student to inspect the branch from the standpoint of the tree itself. Socratically, he cross-examined "experts" in special fields until they revealed their points of ignorance as an inauguration of fresh understanding.

By assembling bright graduate students from the various academic departments each year, McLuhan remained abreast of the latest thought in major disciplines. He simultaneously exposed his specialized students to a potpourri of perspectives. As the open-minded student heard complicated, mutually exclusive jargon fill the mouths of his colleagues, he became aware of his own specialized tunnel vision. Eventually, his classmates' insistence upon private terms and his own self-righteous belief in his own special field would melt into a larger vision.

When the need for a common tongue and overview appeared in the classroom, McLuhan provided the foundation for a new language. New perceptual sparks ignited spontaneously; thus each language was unique to the current seminar participants. The major breakthrough of these gatherings represented a flip in the current educational process. At the heart of McLuhan's pedagogy was a love for the shedding of worn concepts rather than their accumulation.

More traditional approaches to education attempt to propagate "ancient" or "modern" doctrine and consequently invest energy in proving or disproving theories, hypotheses, and arguments. McLuhan had little interest in building models or protecting intellectual structures. His was more the pure enjoyment of letting thought be changed rather than ossified. He was more infatuated by discovery's process than its content. His love of the catalyst-triggering realizations rather than their dogmatic routinization allowed education to inspire a transformation in consciousness rather than a transportation of information. To McLuhan real learning arose from the *unlearning* of clichéd conditioning.

Not all of McLuhan's students have assumed an appreciative pose in his classroom. The professional wordster's reputation drew a number of "whiz kids" (each seeking to be "the fastest pun in the east") who would challenge Marshall in clever wordplay. None ever survived more than a few moments of his follow-up questioning. However, when two of the truly expert verbal acrobats of this century, Proctor and Bergman, of the comedy team "Fireside Theatre," joined him for lunch, McLuhan relaxed and appreciated their routines. Aside from occasional comic observations, he was content to enjoy the entertainment of polished portmantologists.

A secret of McLuhan's character was revealed by his reaction to Proctor and Bergman. He *deliberately* sowed what he reaped. Those who came to challenge his thinking found their own beliefs put to the test. Those who came to destroy his arguments found their own favorite arguments destroyed. Those who came to share genuine friendship and ideas found him genuinely friendly and ideal. Proctor and Bergman visited McLuhan specifically to offer appreciation for his writing and found in him a highly appreciative audience. Less polite visitors who planned to pull the rug from under his assertions found him quite capable of pulling the rug from under the rug.

McLuhan mirrored his audience. If they were appreciative of individual style and performance, they found no shortage of nuance and personality to appreciate. If they were critical of unconventional scholarship and off-beat linguistic patterns, they discovered no lack of scholastic and verbal eccentricity to criticize. None of these reactions stopped McLuhan: he consistently contributed to the success of those who sought his attention. Whatever their reaction, he assisted literally thousands of students in their projects, gave interviews published by hundreds of journals and helped scores of friends by writing prefaces, reviews, comments or letters of recommendation. Throughout this tangle of activity he was always likely to employ "figure/ground" terminology, quote James Joyce or tell ethnic jokes.

This "damn the critics, full speed ahead" attitude made McLuhan, McLuhan. On a given Monday night every student in the seminar might feel emptied of new perception. But McLuhan, not to be influenced, would impart insights about the media (discovered while reading a biography of Oliver Cromwell) with the authority of Moses delivering the Ten Commandments. Measured by the structures of one's own consciousness, McLuhan's seemingly "off-the-wall" connection between the twentieth century and Cromwell had to be farfetched. Yet his words were spoken with such an unwavering conviction that one was always forced to think—McLuhan's prime intention.

By the time one's sleeping mind awakened, "maverick" McLuhan was galloping away to the next connection between the car-encapsulated motorist and the knight in shining armor. Footnoting his insights was like tracking a kangaroo. There was far more fun involved and far greater vision required in learning to jump with him.

Those who failed to appreciate McLuhan's kangaroo approach to exploration measured him by the tracks of the elephant. The great gaps between his footprints, his "down-to-earth" statements, led critics to believe that nothing transpired during the intervals, that no consistent logical development of "footnotes" occurred and, consequently, no significant conceptual movement appeared. Such attempts at understanding the uniqueness of species *mcluhanus* stand out like Western endeavors to analyze traditional Japanese music and theatre. New eyes and ears are needed.

Among those who have never seen a kangaroo, who are more accustomed to the "serious" approach to knowledge, the question arises "was he for real?" "Was this man putting us on?" To be sure, much of McLuhan seems a put-on, an entertaining mask designed to amuse visitors. After all, how many people create genuinely amusing, thought-provoking statements consistently throughout the entire day? How many people speak grammatically correct sentences as if they were reading? How many people seem always to be speaking before an erudite audience? How many people cite entire television programs as evidence about tribal vs. literate humankind? How many people . . .? And yet, this was Herbert Marshall McLuhan. He was no less the genuine article soliloquizing about Shakespeare before a class than eating Christmas dinner with his family.[25]

The question of identity arises: which was the "real" McLuhan, the relaxed family man who descended to the garage to bring up more beer to refrigerate or the sophisticated "sage" who wondered why the effects of refrigeration have not been studied? The two McLuhans were one: the "informal" and the "urbane McLuhan" were indivisible.

As a younger man the "urban McLuhan" often seemed out of place:

> He went through a stage of memorizing three new words from the dictionary each day and then using them in conversation. He didn't care whom he used them on. . . .
> When we returned from England we dropped in on an

Ontario farm where I had an old uncle who's never seen much school, and Marshall said, "*Sine qua non,*" and the old boy didn't know what he was talking about . . . only I knew that Marshall was just practicing.[26]

In other moments the "relaxed" McLuhan drew attention:

When we were visiting the beach and Marshall darted into the water and stubbed his toe on a rock, he acted as if he had nearly killed himself. As if this were not hilarious enough, he ran into the water a second time and stubbed his toe again. He could release loud maledictions upon such occasions. The incident was quite hilarious.[27]

Both aspects, the casual and the cultivated, were as much in evidence in the young student as were present in the sixty-nine-year-old professor. Dr. Claude Bissell noted that McLuhan was "Director of Culture and Technology of which he was both head and staff."[28] As head he was constantly dictating letters to secretary Margaret, asking son Eric to xerox articles and sending assistant George to the library for books. As staff he graded his students' papers and moved chairs for seminars. The same role switching took place at home where McLuhan was at one moment rolling a log through the doorway into the fireplace and in the next moment asking to be driven to the university.

McLuhan was master and servant, grandfather and child, teacher and student, jester and king. He was a citizen of the Old World and the New, from Cambridge and from Canada. His family roots were from the East and the West, from Britain and Nova Scotia, from Ontario and Alberta. His living was from the South and from the North, from Saint Louis and from Winnipeg. He was from the classical "Ciceronian" and the modern "McLuhanistic" world. He provided the greatest proliferation of *printed* material about *electronic* society. He was both sides of a weather vane pointing toward the social forecast.

Consequently, any attempt to define McLuhan is an oxymoron—the conservative revolutionary, the urbane domestic, the secular saint, the serious comic, the tribal literate, the Romanized anglophile, the prairie prodigy, the "loner" leader, the popular scholar, the avant-garde medievalist, the generalist-specialist. To many he represented the undisputed controversy, the anti-hero's hero, the counter-culture's culture, and the "*establishment* of a 'new age'."

McLuhan enjoyed quoting Mallarmé's words: "To define is to kill." To define McLuhan is to nullify "paradox," a word McLuhan likened to "the posture of the mind when, like a boxer balanced on two feet, it is feinting for an opening."[29] McLuhan, the verbal boxer, was always feinting for an opening, an interval, a paradox. His sparring partners could not pin down a kangaroo. They did, however, question whether McLuhan could pin down truth.

McLuhan, the wit, called Canada a "borderline case." He lived his life near midway borderlines. Across from the United States border, Toronto is the city equidistant from north and south boundaries of North America. McLuhan's former homes, Winnipeg and Saint Louis, connect eastern and western North America. The three cities are centers of trade, transportation and communication.

Like McLuhan himself, Toronto, Saint Louis and Winnipeg are prime crossover points, symbols of snythesis. "Toronto" is a Canadian Indian word meaning "the meeting place." McLuhan, too, was a one-man meeting place, an index of interface, the corpus callosum of contemporary consciousness.

Marshall McLuhan

Media and the Inflation CROWD

Today many literate people whose daily work requires much reading find increasing difficulty in covering the necessary ground. Facing the printed page, they find themselves, as it were, in a slow-moving center outside of which there is a very high-paced surround of data and images. In fact, they have long accustomed themselves to living with this accelerating environment of images and information so that the return to the "unpaced" environment of the page is a drag.

A great discrepancy of this kind has grown up in the public sector between the worlds of instant international information on one hand, and the much slower-paced movement of commodity transactions in the world of supply and demand, on the other. If we are to understand inflation it is necessary to recognize the principle of the dynamic at work in a new kind of situation—one in which there is an interface or abrasive action between two unconnected spheres. Ordinarily we try to explain events by seeking in them visually observable connections. With inflation via electric media, however, there is a kind of nonvisual order of echo and rumor and acoustic structure that bypasses all logic of connectedness; and this factor engenders new vortices of power quite beyond the range of pre-electric markets of commodity supply and demand.

Since inflation is an extreme form of social violence, or manifestation of crowd behavior, it would be well to recall that the presidential committee on violence was unable to find any connection between social behavioral activity and the fictional violence offered on media programs. Earlier studies of comic books as a possible cause for teen-age violence found many parallels, but the investigators were equally baffled by the absence of cause-and-effect connections between the fictional and the live events of our time.

Two obvious questions arise. First, is violence a meaningless and pointless activity, or is it a deep drive for re-establishing the profiles of lost identity? Second, is the gap or interval between the live violence and the fictional forms itself the hidden causal "connection"? In current physics and chemistry the resonant interval is where the action and abrasive interface is found. Between the wheel and the axle is an interval of "play" which is where the action is, but without this "play" there is no action at all.

In his study "The Emotion of Multitude," W.B. Yeats explained why the interface of parallel but unconnected actions creates the sense of universality in poetry and drama, the sense of the crowd. Between the parallel actions of Lear and his daughters, and of Gloucester and his sons, is an interface which renders the sense of the situations as indicative of the human condition in general. All this concerns the pattern of inflation. Today the fact of increasing prices has little or nothing to do with the old laws of supply and demand, but much to do with new media. Inflation presents a kind of media-crowd situation with all the familiar features of crowd emotions. There is the feeling of a great increase of scope accompanied by the panic sense of the loss of control and identity. The crowd emotion of suddenly imposed equality brings a deep sense of depreciation and diminution. The new kind of inflation "crowd" depends above all else on the cohesion created by instant information of the greatest scale. The "crowd," as it increases in scope, simultaneously develops the feeling of loss of identity as the very form of its cohesion. The greater the proximity and the greater the numbers, the greater the sense of loss of individual significance and control. It was Elias Canetti who (in his *Crowds and Power*) discerned this paradoxical yet essential feature of all crowds. As they grow they engender from within the emotion of depreciation and loss. As in all crowds, it seems necessary in the inflation "crowd" that there be created multiple kinds of scarcity.

Having encountered many media shocks about inflation and scarcity, women shoppers are often surprised at the abundance of goods on the shelves at noninflated prices. This gap between information and hardware, between the news and commodities, is a small instance of a pervasive conflict between the action of the media and the quieter motions of the shopping centers.

May it not be that inflation is engendered in this gap, in the resonant and abrasive interval between the rim spin of global credit and electric information, and the laborious motions and mechanisms of commodity supply and demand in the old markets of packaged goods and services? Between this system of instant information, on one hand, and a slow system of fragmentary transportation of commodities, on the other, is there not so great a disparity of action as to create the enormous noise and anarchy of sheer crowd dynamics? May it not be the very *lack* of connection between these two separate spheres that is itself the *cause* of the inflationary commotion? It is precisely where there is *no connection* that there will occur a resonant and potentially violent interface of mounting intensity.

The cause of personal and social violence is the threat to identity, even as the occasion of tragic suffering is a flaw or defect which impels compensating action. Is not inflation, as a form of crowd violence, an *effect* rather than a cause, a result of a defect in our means of interrelating old and new services of knowledge and social action? The older standards of information service which have constituted the ordinary levels of food and shelter, education, hygiene and employment in the Western world—these have long been maintained by complicated mechanisms of bureaucratic and private organization.

The images of goals of personal and national identity which have matured with these older services and disciplines are easily effaced by a great increase of speed in the operation of these same services. Even more destructive, however, is the advent of an adjacent operation of a faster system in proximity to the older one. Our electric information, global and spatial, is such a system of instant services, a system of "software" greatly exceeding in scope of both coverage and satisfaction the older hardware system of goods and services.

In 1896 Brooks Adams published his reflections in *The Law of Civilization and Decay*, noting:

> Nothing so portentous overhangs humanity as this mysterious and relentless acceleration of movement, which changes methods of competition and alters paths of trade; for by it countless millions of men and women are foredoomed to happiness or misery, as certainly as the beasts

and trees, which have flourished in the wilderness, are destined to vanish when the soil is subdued by man.[1]

Today in all areas of our establishment it is by virtue of a natural culture lag that specialist, nineteenth-century minds are in charge of major services. General Creighton Abrams put the matter clearly to the Senate Armed Services Committee:

> From a purely administrative viewpoint, this whole thing had become so complicated that I couldn't keep these things straight in my own mind. We have to have specialists to keep track of this thing and that thing.[2]

General Abrams is, like all old-style specialists, a centralist who depends on a hierarchy below him to keep him informed. It has not occurred to him to switch his perceptual activity to pattern recognition in a world of information overload.

By the same token, electric information provides instant data access equally to all the members of the organization regardless of their hierarchical positions. For the external action of an organization this fact of instant information spells total decentralization and calls for guerrilla warfare outside as well as civil war inside the executive structure of specialists. The new electronic man and preliterate man now see eye to eye. The organization man, the centralist, is caught between two ages, to our cost. He did wonders in the hardware age. Our entire business community is still arranged in the pattern of socialist forms of classified data and jobs and goals. But, now caught in the maelstrom of instant media, this still-fragmented group of specialist individuals begins to take on the patterns and dynamics of crowd behavior.

If bad money drives good money out of circulation, inflation drives traditional people out of existence by sheer depreciation and belittlement of their self-images. The ordinary functions of money in the exchange of conventional goods and services flip into an overdrive gear which moves directly to the crowd formation, with its survival obsession and impulse toward the ecstasy of power. Let me repeat: the crowd emotion in inflation is from two sources—first, from the sense of increase, and second, from the consequent fear of becoming much less meaningful via depreciation. Mere accumulation, whether of numbers or of money, diminishes the individual participant, making both the man of the crowd and the man of wealth a victim of intense paranoia. Paradoxically, then, loss of private identity attends both crowd and wealth, and inflation is thus the formula for both megalomania and fear, both greatness and littleness. These passions impel both high and low to the strategy of putting on the mask of corporate or crowd power and also to the need to rip off the mask of private appearances. In a word, inflation as a generator of crowd passion can consume the whole world and devastate the diverse wealth of this goodly frame, the earth.

One of the frustrating things about an inflation is that it keeps attention focused on a rapidly changing market of specific products and services while conveying the suspicion that the causes are elsewhere. At the present time the escalation of information services has provided an almost universal surround of awareness of specific world events and hardship. In fact, one obvious cause of inflation is the media-made *consciousness* of it. Everybody feels impelled either to grab some advantage or to take defensive action by direct intervention at the practical level. All these acts are themselves inflationary if only because they further agitate an already-existing exasperation. The main ground of the action remains hidden the more involved the participants become in the crowd dynamic.

Looking less at the economy then, and turning to psychology, it can be seen that inflationary depreciation of the human psyche—loss of identity—by rapid movement and changing environment has been an experience of many peoples in the twentieth century. For most people, movies, radio and television have brought entirely new worlds to replace their old ones, many times over. Information, packaged in these ways and moved at electric speed, has enlarged the experience of whole populations to the point where they have become nonstop tourists even in their own private lives. We now live in a man-made–information environment, especially since Sputnik which in 1957 put the whole planet inside a man-made environment, initiating a decade of ecological thinking and programming.

Today, money too has become part of the world information environment. Whereas formerly a dollar bill carried the promise to pay the bearer a dollar in gold, today the promise is to pay promise by means of another slip of paper. Perhaps the change from gold to paper also marks the change from the age of industrial production to the age of software services. "The soul of advertising," said Dr. Johnson, "is a large promise." Advertising is the garment of abundance, a massive put-on that is itself the source of many of the satisfactions we create for ourselves, as illustrated in the slogan: "You feel better satisfied when you use well-known brands." If money today acts mainly in the form of information and credit, credit exists by virtue of a pervasive system of espionage and interpersonal surveillance and "bugging" which turns us all into man-hunters. So intense has the "bugging" industry become (in the name of credit) it has bred a new industry of "de-bugging" services, whereby you can have your life and premises inspected for a removal of "leaks." That is to say, credit agencies have enormously depreciated our individuality in the process of propping up our egos. However, if actual money is indeed "the poor man's credit card" the good news is that it is now possible to get a special "credit card" that enables one to use cash without loss of face.

When money performs through information and credit, the wealth-making process becomes the exchange of information, so that even reading the newspaper serves a major transactional process in the community. The moving of information, however, is in transportation terms, only a very small part of the process of the transforming of men and institutions. For example, electric instruments from the telephone onwards do not so much transport data from person to person as they transport the user—the sender himself. On the phone you are in Tokyo at the same moment that Tokyo is here. When you are "on the air" with radio or television you are actually being transported around the world. The performers and the users alike are transported instantly everywhere. It is this transportation of the users and the audiences as electric information which has *transformed* the nature of man and society in the electric age.

In order to understand inflation in a world of instantaneous and universal information it is necessary to see the old hardware of products and prices as they now interface with the new hidden ground of worldwide and instant information. It is not only a new ball game; it is a new ballpark with new ground rules when the old industrial production of hardware technology is suddenly located inside an environment of simultaneous electric information. The phrase "making money" came in at the beginning of the twentieth century along with "making news." Both are aspects of the same information process. At electric speed, time and space are greatly abridged, if not altogether eliminated. Today, at electric speeds of information movement we have as it were encapsulated our planet in the form of what Peter Drucker calls a "world shopping center." Of course, any catalogue of the Sears and Roebuck variety is itself a world shopping guide, so that:

> "Back to the market" is becoming as nostalgic as "back to the land." In the age of the "military-industrial complex" the market place has already become an art form that no longer measures or motivates the main economic activity. . . . Rather, the bulk is to be found in the "consumption" of pure information, whether in entertainment or its opposite.[3]

In this century we have reached awareness of the unconscious itself as a major hidden resource available for the commercial and political manipulation of consciousness. Here is the area to which we assign all the components and factors that we cannot organize consciously, the vast reservoir of failures past and future to come. It is this great Sargasso Sea of forlorn endeavours to which we are now in the process of assigning inflation through our failure to understand its grammar and articulation. Inflation results from the action of the great resonating environment of information, as it reshapes and dissolves the hopes and dreams of the preceding world of hardware goods and services. Inflation is the pollution, or the dilution, of promises—a tribute levied on those who know by those who don't. It is hijack country.

Perhaps the best way to illustrate the complete flip from hardware to software, from products to information, that takes place at electric speed, is to point to the shift from the labor market to the stock market. Whereas the labor market offered the private services of individuals to corporate enterprises, the stock exchange offers corporate services of public enterprises to private individuals. The blue-collar worker now has the means to speculate in the stock market. The old hardware basis for uniform prices is gone with the advent of the new environment of electric information and the old flexibility of barter is back in our market place. "The stock exchange, which had originated in the world of the new dailies of the steam-powered presses, gradually became a major source of news."[4] This is as specific a description of the shift from hardware to software, from labor to information, from work to learning as I know how to make (but it is capable of much elaboration). Beginning as a product of news services, stocks came to dominate news and politics after the telegraph. Of course, by the 1960s the speed of stock sales was in excess of the means of transferring and storing securities. These latter, like the postal system, are a relic of old cumbersome hardware technology. If the postal system symbolizes obsolete hardware in the electronic age, it would seem that the very concept of a market of goods and services is being phased out at electric speeds of information.

Old hardware such as railways and the postal system tend to become charming art forms in the new software world, even as the new market in housing is "the atmosphere market" for history-hungry buyers. The new demand is for older houses with a feeling of character, of being lived in. Paradoxically, electronic man seeks roots and stability.

If ordinary technologies are extensions of the human body in the quest to create new service environments, Sputnik (October 4, 1957) and its successors may represent something quite different, namely an extension of the planet itself, creating a new ground for man in the sky and calling despotically for a new equilibrium and harmony of action and knowledge. The satellites have as it were transformed the planet itself into a work of art, inspiring a new need for programs and controls transcending all regional interests. One of the unexpected results of the information speedup, besides the transforming of the planet into an art object, has been the restoration of the significance of leisure and contemplation in the modern world, as old specialist markets and jobs alike disappear.

In hardware terms, however, the new hidden environment of universal information services represents a desperate depreciation of most exciting values with the accompanying decline of personal identity and worth. As pointed out in *Take Today: The Executive as Dropout*, "Nothing now is *in camera*: everything is *on camera*."

Human motives now stand out as starkly as factory chimneys did formerly. The "tapped wire" is programmed to mislead the secret observer. All actions are now "transparencies," featuring and filtering and infiltrating each other as diaphanous webs.

At this stage of interpenetration of goals and values, experts and monopolies of information sustain each other like a vocal refrain. Private monopolies yield to corporate involvement, and experts in the profession are obsolete before completing their training.[5]

In the past, for example, secret knowledge of trade routes has been made possible by monopolies of hardware treasure, for secrecy is a function of slow information movement, and monopolies of knowledge disappear in proportion to speedup. In the software world of instant information, secrecy is of brief duration. On the other hand, "Only puny secrets need protection. Big discoveries are protected by public incredulity."

And so it is with the invisible new service environment which bypassed conventional communism decades ago. So extensive a dissolution of established forms brings a universal feeling of outrage that calls for massive retaliation. The matter is stated memorably by Elias Canetti in his discussion of "Inflation and the Crowd."

No one ever forgets a sudden depreciation of himself, for it is too painful. Unless he can thrust it on to someone else, he carries it with him for the rest of his life. And the crowd as such never forgets its depreciation. The natural tendency afterwards is to find something which is worth even less than oneself, which one can despise as one was despised oneself. It is not enough to take over an old contempt and maintain it at the same level. What is wanted is a dynamic process of humiliation. Something must be treated in such a way that it becomes worth less and less, as the unit of money did during the inflation. And this process must be continued until its object is reduced to a state of utter worthlessness.[6]

The Watergate affair is precisely such a dynamic process of humiliation.

Gerald M. Feigen

The McLuhan Festival
On the Road to San Francisco

It took me a long time and a lot of work to begin to understand Marshall McLuhan, and it was worth it. He was a prime mover and a major force, and he was a threat to literary critics who spattered him with clever phrase droppings. People who are not themselves creative are puzzled by creativity and wonder how to manage it in someone else, especially if he might be right. Some were always down on what they were not up on; others tried to jump onto the bandwagon, as if this would neutralize any need to study. Literary figures stooped to feeble satire, enraged criticism, and a verbal reduction process designed to make McLuhan a pop figure.

I started *Understanding Media* in the winter of 1964 on my way to New York. A publisher-friend had sent the book thinking it was about advertising. I plunged into the introduction and the first chapter for the five hours on the plane. And what had started as refusal developed into doubt and then excitement. "The Medium is the Message." I said that phrase over and over, and almost got it. This was before the McLuhan explosion, before the phrase became a neologism. On the way back to San Francisco a week later, I read the book again, marking it up in pencil with furious objections, rhetorical asides, and other intrusions; finally, over Lake Tahoe, the first breakthrough! The message of TV is not what you see on the set but what effect TV has had on the culture, how it has changed people.

My partner, Howard Gossage, an organic thinker who wouldn't accept an idea without proceeding from structure to process, began to read the book. He read it slowly, painstakingly and with mutterings. He had fits and starts, exclamatory releases: "I know more about that than he does," and after all a recognition along with mine that Marshall McLuhan probably was something of a genius. Paragraph by paragraph we read and discussed the exasperating stuff, and it held up! Immediately we decided to use instant speed and call McLuhan on the telephone.

He was quite cordial. Gossage was no slouch when it came to projecting charisma, even on the phone. We were invited to Toronto. On the way we stopped at Carbondale, Illinois, where Buckminster Fuller lived. His comments on McLuhan were of meager help, but he was magical. John McHale, an associate of Fuller's and an old friend, provided us with some insight into McLuhan's work, giving it a substantive beginning and a kind of academic recognition. We had not read McLuhan's *Gutenberg Galaxy*, and what was the Centre for Culture and Technology?

We met McLuhan in the lobby of the Royal York Hotel, an ancient, elegant, tarnishing art form frequented by commercial travelers. We were a bit disheveled, depleted with jet lag when he marched up. There was a marvelous moment of inquiry. His eyes were clear, bright and accepting. We went up to our suite and began to talk. What later became habit was then a novelty. We discovered one talks only about McLuhan's subject, and during an ordinary conversation one remark would spark multiple responses from him.

In the curiously amorphous dining room we sat down to eat. The room seemed like most of Toronto — slightly out of focus, half American and half English with an overall gray coloration. The environment soon became invisible, however. We opened up on sensory ratios, then moved from *Finnegans Wake*, which McLuhan knew and loved, to puns and jokes which he relished. I've been collecting punch lines over twenty-five years, so I knew most of his jokes. He wasn't too good at timing, but he laughed at his jokes and ours, finding alternative meanings, and lead-ins to other stories or to his obviously vast knowledge of literature and technology. Gossage, an inveterate pun-hater, looked glum during the joke period.

There must have been some favorable chemistry going on; we found it most difficult to stop talking. When the waiter brought the check, unasked, Gossage was angry, until the waiter pointed out that it was after midnight and the restaurant had closed at eleven. McLuhan invited us to visit the Centre for Culture and Technology, and we accepted. We watched him leave, then went back upstairs to talk. We weren't sure. All the residues were good. He was honest, wide-ranged, and there wasn't a mote of phoniness.

I remember one set of statements that McLuhan made at dinner about sensory ratios. He had measured the relative use of the senses in a group of Toronto citizens. Apparently it was possible to measure eye utilization with special cameras attached to the face; what seemed important was that any change in the ratios of one's use of the senses—let's say the eye and the ear—produces a change in the culture, a change in people. The major change which took place among kids who watched a lot of TV was a relative increase of hearing over looking. That was because TV was an acoustic medium, as opposed to reading which was purely visual. The kids seemed to be perceiving differently from their parents and developing awareness in a less visual way. McLuhan said he wanted to get money to finance a trip to Greece which at that time did not have TV; he proposed to study the sensory ratios before TV and then measure them again after the advent of TV and demonstrate the change. He was having trouble finding money.

We met for lunch at the faculty club, which looked like a slightly worn illustration of what it was. We sat in the main sitting room and ordered drinks. A young reporter from *Mclean's* magazine came up, apparently on appointment. He didn't seem to figure out who we were and obviously wasn't sure of his man. In his piece which was published in 1966, he described Gossage and me as "important visiting professors from California," but on the whole it was a creditable article for that time.

The lunch was what you would expect, but the talk was heady; we had gotten hooked on the totem and were on a first-name basis. McLuhan, as always, acted a bit rueful that there was so little time; that accounted for his urgency and his impatience with interviewers whose egos required value judgments, but whose knowledge of McLuhan's writing was a synopsis—born without careful preparation or concern.

Marshall began to talk about environments. At this date everyone is vaguely familiar with his theories, but we were impressed with the crispness and freshness of his perceptions. He spoke as he ate, relishing his food without paying attention to it. The chicken croquettes were gritty and plain, but it made no difference to him. I have eaten dozens of meals with him since, in high-priced restaurants in New York and San Francisco, in college cafeterias and in private homes. He had a first-class appetite, but didn't seem to care what he ate. He talked and ate and talked.

After lunch we walked across the literary lawns of the university getting a peripatetic description on a straight line to his office. The office looked like a second-hand bookstore. Walls, desks not yet old enough to be antiques, a few chairs, all were covered—cluttered—with hundreds of books. Tables were lost in books and papers. He introduced us to his son, Eric, a tall, good-looking man who favored his mother. He had just come out with a book on the meaning of the "ten thunderclaps" in *Finnegans Wake*. Eric's thesis was that each thunderclap accompanied major changes in environment, the last one being television.

We met McLuhan's wife, Corinne, who did most of his typing on an old, tired machine; she was a warm, gracious Texan with a musical voice—a helpmate of the old school—committed, dedicated and a lot of other adjectives, all in Marshall's favor.

He was full of his new projects—the book on environment, the study of sensory ratios, the prediction of the future of education, work, language and mankind in general. He recommended books and more books—Edward Hall's *The Silent Language* and his later *Hidden Dimensions*, Thomas Kuhn's *The Structure of Scientific Revolutions*, Harvey Cox's *The Secular City*, and Owen Barfield's *Saving the Appearances*. It was as if he wanted us to get busy and learn enough so we could communicate. I have bought and read all the books he suggested. In retrospect, I think he wondered just who we were and what we were doing there, but he liked us and seemed certain that it all would work out.

Years later he expressed delight with Martin Gardner's *The Ambidextrous Universe*, Pierre De Latil's *Thinking by Machine*, and Albert T. Simeon's *Man's Presumptuous Brain* which I sent him.

There was a satisfying lack of conceit or egotism in his approach to discussion. The day produced a marvelous intimacy, a confirmation, a validation of the trip and an expression of ideas. Gossage and I exchanged long, heavy analyses that evening. We had surrendered our initial rejection of his stuff as "fake" and recognized the real. We had misgivings, still, but mostly about specific ideas. McLuhan was for real, and we suspected he might be a genius. We were elated. We liked the man. He was not the kind of genius who took infinite pains, but the kind who breaks through with a new way of looking at things. We made plans: he would be the first "find" of our genius-scouting.

The next day we left for New York with McLuhan's promise to meet us there in a few days. He was a little reluctant because he had to grade his students' papers. That really knocked us out! We already suspected it wouldn't be long before McLuhan would be able to forget about that kind of tiring routine. Later on when we proved it, he said, "Do you mean it can be all fun?"

A few months later, in the famous firehouse in San Francisco, we held the first McLuhan festival: six days of roundtable talks from 9 to 5. We invited those whom we thought would enjoy the challenge. There were adventurous lunches and great dinners, and McLuhan emerged as the champ. But that is another story.

Marshall McLuhan

In 1901 a message was read to a group at the gate of Windsor Castle:

> "Her majesty the Queen breathed her last at 6:30 p.m., surrounded by her children and grandchildren."

Pandemonium broke loose. A yelling stampede of journalists on bicycles hurtled down the hill to Cowes to be first with the telephones, bawling as they went, "Queen dead!" "Queen dead!" The famous "hush" which had always surrounded the "The Widow of Windsor" was shattered at a blow. A new age had begun.[1]

At the moment of Sputnik the planet becomes a global theater in which there are no spectators but only actors

Declining to write for the *Revue Européenne* in 1831, Lamartine said to its editor:

> Do not perceive in these words a superb disdain for what is termed journalism. Far from it; I have too intimate a knowledge of my epoch to repeat this absurd nonsense, this impertinent inanity against the Periodical Press. I know too well the work Providence has committed to it. Before this century shall run out journalism will be the whole press—the whole human thought. Since that prodi-

gious multiplication which art has given to speech—multiplication to be multiplied a thousand-fold yet—mankind will write their books day by day, hour by hour, page by page. Thought will be spread abroad in the world with the rapidity of light; instantly conceived, instantly written, instantly understood at the extremities of the earth—it will spread from pole to pole. Sudden, instant, burning with the fervor of soul which made it burst forth, it will be the reign of the human soul in all its plentitude. It will not have time to ripen—to accumulate in a book; the book will arrive too late. The only book possible from today is a newspaper.[2]

Perhaps the largest conceivable revolution in information occurred on October 4, 1957, when Sputnik created a new environment for the planet. For the first time the natural world was completely enclosed in a man-made container. At the moment that the earth went inside this new artifact, Nature ended and Ecology was born. "Ecological" thinking became inevitable as soon as the planet moved up into the status of a work of art.

Ecological thinking and planning have always been native to preliterate man, since he lived not visually but acoustically. Instead of having external goals and objectives, he sought to maintain an equilibrium among the components of his environment in order to ensure survival. Paradoxically, electronic man shares much of the outlook of preliterate man, because he lives in a world of simultaneous information, which is to say, a world of resonance in which all data influence other data. Electronic and simultaneous man has recovered the primordial attitudes of the preliterate world and has discovered that to have a specialized goal or program merely invited conflict with all other specialized enterprises. "All the arts aspire to the condition of music," said Walter Pater, and under conditions of instant information the only possible rationale or means of order involves us in the musical structuring of experience.

Gutenberg man, in the sixteenth century, had achieved a new kind of detachment, thanks to the new intensity of visual experience deriving from the innovation of the printed word. This new visual stress impelled the men of that time to follow their individual goals, whether of learning or of travel and discovery, to the utmost extremes. A new race of visually oriented explorers of space and time emerged from the "caves" of the Gutenberg technology. The Gutenberg innovation enabled men to retrieve antiquity as never before. The new speed of the printing press created vast new political spaces and power structures based on the creation of new reading publics. The matrix of the press, with its assembly lines of movable types, provided the archetypes of the industrial revolution and universal education.

The typical virtues of industrial and typographic man are radically revised and reformed when information moves at the speed of light. Whereas visual man had dreamed of distant goals and vast encyclopedic programs of learning, electronic man prefers dialogue and immediate involvement. Since nothing on earth can be distant at the speed of light, electronic man prefers the inner to the outer trip and the inner to the outer landscape.

Simultaneous man is, paradoxically, traditional and simple in his tastes, preferring the human scale to the ancient grandeurs which are no longer difficult to achieve. Simultaneous man is acoustically rather than visually oriented, living in a world whose center is everywhere and whose margin is nowhere. Not for him the spirit of geometry or the spirit of quantity; instead of distant goals, he seeks pattern recognition, and instead of specialized jobs he prefers role-playing, with its flexibility and diversity. Indeed, at the moment of Sputnik the planet became a global theater in which there are no spectators but only actors. On Spaceship Earth there are no passengers; everybody is a member of the crew. These facts do not present themselves as ideals but as immediate realities.

To give both sides tends to ignore the possibility that there may be many more sides than two.

It is noteworthy that the popular press as an art form has often attracted the enthusiastic attention of poets and aesthetes while rousing the gloomiest apprehensions in the academic mind. Let us look at the image of the newspaper as it still is today after a century of the telegraph. That image is organized not according to a story line but according to a date line. Like a symbolist poem, the ordinary newspaper page is an assembly of unconnected items in abstract mosaic form. Looked at in this way, it is plain that the newspaper had been a corporate poem for many years. It represents an inclusive image of community and a wide diversity of human interests. Minus the story line of the connected narrative, the newspaper has long had an oral and corporate quality which relates it to many of the traditional art forms of mankind. On every page of the newspaper, in the discontinuous mosaic of unrelated human items, there is a resonance that bespeaks universality even in triviality. Robert Louis Stevenson said, "I could make an epic from a newspaper if I knew what to leave out."

The telegraph press was born in the age of symbolist poetry, the age of Edgar Allan Poe. Poe had confronted the poetic process in a way entirely consistent with the new electric speed of events and reporting. He simply pointed to the possibility of writing poetry backwards, starting with the effect desired and then proceeding to discover the "causes" or means for the desired effect.

Snyder and Morris pointed to the same structural revolution in news writing that Poe and the symbolists had discovered for poetry:

> Over the past hundred years the structure of the news story has undergone drastic modification. It is today a commonplace of American journalism that a news story must illustrate hind-to-end writing. Unlike other literary forms, the climax is at the beginning. The lead, or opening paragraph or paragraphs, gives the reader the essential facts. The body of the story is merely detailed expository material, its paragraph structure a series of separate units without transitions connecting them with what went before or what is to follow, and arranged in decreasing importance.[3]

Symbolist art is the art of the rip-off. It is the experience of this active stripping that is the effect of symbolism. Merely as classified, separate items, things do not achieve symbolic status. It is so in the newspaper.

In the past decade there has come a recognizable change in the styles of reporting, now referred to as the "old journalism" and the "new journalism." The "old journalism" had sought objectivity; in presenting people and events it tried to achieve this by giving "both sides" at once. To give the pro and the con, the good and the bad, has been, for a century at least, the approved way of

attaining judicial balance and fairness. To give both sides, however, tends to ignore the possibility that there may be many more
sides than two, and as the means of access to information im-
proved and as the means of processing information speeded up,
the mere chiaroscuro of the light and the dark, the pro and the
con, has tended to yield to nonvisual and subjective patterns of
depth involvement by immersion in total situations. However, if
the "old journalism" tended toward the salience of *figures* in men
and events, the "new journalism" can be discerned as a preference
for *ground* rather than *figure*. The "new journalism" offers not so
much a view of men and events but a means of immersion in situations which involve many people simultaneously. Thus, Norman
Mailer's account of the 1968 political conventions in Miami and
Chicago is less concerned with the policies and the parties than
with the experience of the hurly-burly of the conventions.[4] After
all, the "you are there" immersion approach in journalism is only
natural in the new surround of TV imagery: for TV brings the
outside into the intimacy of the home, as it takes the private world
of the home outside into the forum. The bounding line between
the old and the new journalism seems to have been the popular
line: "A funny thing happened to me on the way to the forum."

Xerox comes as a reverse flip as the end of the Gutenberg cycle;
whereas Gutenberg made everybody a reader,
Xerox makes everybody a publisher.

Without trying to look ahead one hundred years—without
looking even one year ahead, if we merely *Take Today*[5] for a look
at the changing nature of human organization as reflected in
things and in newspapers—it is possible to see some striking new
patterns. The release of the Pentagon papers and the Ellsberg
investigation point to one of these patterns, one directly related
to the matter of Xerox. Xerox, as a new service in connection with
printed and written materials, is so decentralized, accessible, and
inexpensive that it results in making the ordinary person a
publisher, if he so chooses.

Quite apart from its threat to the publishing business and to
copyright regulations, Xerox has two other features. On the one
hand, it has created the large committee as a new means of
decision making, because it permits uniform briefing and *position*

papers for all. On the other hand, it has created, also on a large scale, *the underground press.* [In passing, it might be helpful to mention apropos the underground press that its relation to the public, or above-ground press, is somewhat similar to the old and new journalism. Speaking in gestalt psychology terms, the press can be seen in relation to *figure* and *ground,* and in psychology as well as in journalism, the *ground* is usually subliminal, relative to the *figure.* Under conditions of electric simultaneity the *ground* of any *figure* tends to become more and more noticeable. Perhaps it all began with cubism and the discovery that by eliminating the merely visual or rational relations between services, by presenting the inside and the underside at the same time as the outside, the public became totally involved and aware in a multisensuous way. As new media continue to proliferate, the nature of "news" will naturally change too, along with the perpetually renewed revolution in information speeds and patterns.]

Position papers are secret or confidential documents for the attention of committees, and any office boy can publish these, no matter how top secret they may be. The Pentagon Papers were position papers which may or may not have been studied or discussed by a congressional committee. They are "the news behind the news," which used to be considered muckraking but has now become an ordinary dimension of journalism, such as nourishes the underground press and which, in turn, affects the forms and publics of the regular press. What has happened since the old muckraking days of the 1920s is that espionage, whether political or commercial, has become the largest business in the world, and we take it for granted that the modern newspaper depends on "bugging" the whole community. In fact, we expect the press to "bug" the world and to challenge and penetrate all privacy and identity, whether private or corporate.

Among the unexpected features of the information revolution are the extraordinary diminution of private identity and egotistic conviction, as a result of major involvement in the lives of other people, and the extra-ordinary enlargements of the public sector. We have moved into an age in which everybody's activities affect everybody else, and therefore the whole matter of privacy is suspect, even as it is impractical. One result has been a relaxing of private morals (sometimes referred to as "permissiveness") and at the same time an extraordinary new intensity in public morals. This change is well reflected in the Watergate affair. In Washington, as elsewhere, laxity of private standards is expected, but the same private standards no longer extend to the image of the president. Under electric conditions it is not possible to extend the laxity of private life into the public domain; rather, a new absolutism in the public domain is felt to be mandatory.

The United States happens to be the country in which the private and specialized had been allowed the utmost development. Quite dramatically, therefore, the "bugging" of private lives, long taken for granted in the commercial, the political, and the military establishments, has suddenly become the means of revealing the bankruptcy of public morals.

A spectacular paradigm of the information revolution has been developed for the world at large by the Watergate affair. While it seems to specialize in matters of political espionage and image-building, it also draws attention to the fact that the entire educational and commercial establishments, as much as the political and military establishments, depend on data banks of total information concerning both producers and consumers, both the governors and the governed. The Watergate affair makes it quite plain that the entire planet has become a whispering gallery, with a large portion of mankind engaged in making its living by keeping the rest of mankind under surveillance. The FBI includes among its responsibilities keeping under surveillance individual members of the CIA. We thus have a complete scheme of baby-sitters for the baby-sitters—chaperones for chaperones— and it is the business of every commercial establishment to keep all other commercial establishments under surveillance as a minimal condition of survival.

Xerox is a new kind of decentralized service which dissolves privacy and creates many new forms of human association, whether in the classroom or in the legislature or in the press. Whereas Gutenberg had created a service that extended to whole nations, he had at the same time invented a form of hardware that fostered new forms of central organization, including a price system and the markets that came with it. What Arnold Toynbee had discerned as "etherealization"—the tendency in our time to do more and more with less and less—is part of the electronic information revolution of "software," which has the opposite effect of decentralizing. While hardware requires uniformity of product to pay for a centralized operation, the electronic form of information service permits not only decentralizing of organizations but a wide diversity of products without additional expenditure.

If book and hardware sales need to be large to defray expenses, electronic publishing by Xerox can dispense with large-scale publics and markets almost entirely. Even more easily than by hand press, a writer can publish a few copies of his work for his friends by simply multiplying the typescript. In fact, Xerox completes the work of the typewriter. A poet composing at the typewriter is "publishing" his work, as it were, while composing. Xerox gives to this fact a new meaning.

Electric speed may already have violated human scale, tending as it does to transport man instantly everywhere.

In the early days of the book, Montaigne thought of printing as a kind of flip from the confessional to the expressional:

> Letter writing . . . is a kind of work in which my friends think I have some ability. And I would have preferred to adopt this form to publish my sallies, if I had had someone to talk to. I needed what I once had, a certain relationship to lead me on, sustain me, and raise me up. . . . I would have been more attentive and confident, with a strong friend to address, than I am now, when I consider the various tastes of a whole public. And if I am not mistaken, I would have been more successful. . . . Amusing notion: many things that I would not want to tell anyone, I tell the public; and for my most secret knowledge and thoughts I send my most faithful friends to a bookseller's shop.[6]

Montaigne here draws attention to the book as a kind of message in a bottle: secretly dispatched, to an unknown public of potential acquaintances. His thoughts on this subject help to reveal an aspect of the newspaper as well, because there is a special meaning in publication as a form of "put on"; the writer, whether of a diary or a newspaper column, is engaged in a very special way in putting on his public as a mask.

The most secret diary, even that of Samuel Pepys, written in a code which remained unbroken for centuries—even such a diary is for the writer a mask or a vortex of energy which increases his power over the language; for our mother tongue is itself a corporate mask of energy which is stepped up by the act of writing and, once again, by the act of publication. In the early days of printing, Montaigne saw this action as both putting on the public and taking off his privacy:

> I owe a complete portrait of myself to the public. The wisdom of my lesson is wholly in truth, in freedom, in reality . . . of which propriety and ceremony are daughters, but bastard daughters. . . . Whoever would wean man of the folly of such a scrupulous verbal superstition would do the world no great harm. Our life is part folly, part wisdom. Whoever writes about it only reverently and according to the rules leaves out more than half of it.[7]

Montaigne had discovered the paradox that the larger the public, the greater the premium on the self-confessional.

There is something rather mysterious about the process of the "put on" which is inseparable from communication. Baudelaire's famous phrase "*hypocrite lecteur mon semblable, mon frère*" captures the entire process. The reader is *hypocrite* in the very act of putting on the author's poem as his mask, for in reading the poem he is perceiving the world in a very special way, using what another poet, S.T. Coleridge, called "a willing suspension of disbelief for the moment." When we put on any man-made mask such as painting, poem or music, or when we read a book or a newspaper, we are looking at the world in a very special way, altering our own perceptions by an artistic act of faith in the process in which we are engaged.

The second part of Baudelaire's phrase, "*mon semblable, mon frère*," draws attention to the reciprocal part of the action. Whereas the reader or the user of any form puts it on as his mask, as an extension of his own perception and energy, the author or maker has also to put on his public, the potential reader or user of whatever he has made. The maker tends to project his own image as the mask of the user or reader which he endeavors to "put on." This complex process of communication, by which the medium is "put on" by its users in order that they may experience some alteration and extension of their own perceptions or powers, includes the "putting on" of the user by the medium. Commercially, this latter operation is referred to as "giving the public what it wants" or "the customer is always right." The complexity of this process is such that even literary critics have despaired of ever unraveling it. Critics of the press, on the other hand, are accustomed to labeling the whole thing as degrading, even as Shakespeare did with his own profession of acting.

One thing that needs to be noted in both connections is the great increase of the sense of power on the part of both the maker and the user. Since the process in question is at the very heart of the communication activity, it is certain to remain central to the issue so long as readers are human and not merely robots. Since "human scale" is indispensable for human satisfactions, the future of the press must inevitably retain this dimension. At present, electric speed may already have violated human scale, tending as it does to transport man instantly everywhere. When you are "on the air" you are simultaneously here and in many other places in a manner that is discarnate and angelic, to say the least.

*At instant speeds . . . the public begins to participate directly in
actions which it had previously heard about at a
distance in place or time.*

It is time to ask ourselves: "What is news?" When a visitor stepped into an antique store, he asked: "What's new?" His jocular query draws attention to the fact that we live in the age of the fake antique, which is itself a form of the replay. Is not "news" itself a replay in the newspaper medium of events that have occurred in some other medium, and does not this replay quality in reporting urge us to narrow the margin between the event and the replay? Does not this make us define news as "the latest"?

However, in the new age of the instant replay, news takes on a totally new dimension that is almost metaphysical. A ball game or a horse race can now be replayed for its meaning, as it were, minus the experience. During the actual experience the issue may have been in doubt, but, as the poet explains, "we can have the experience and miss the meaning." In fact, such is the nature of experience that it is almost inevitable that we do miss the meaning. The "meaning," or the relation to ourselves of a particular event, may not come home to us until much later. However, with the instant replay of our own or others' experiences, it is now possible to have the meaning without the experience. Referees and judges may wait for the replay in order to render a decision. They have had the experience and are merely waiting for the meaning or the relation of the experience to themselves and to others.

The quality of the instantaneous in the replay of experience is somewhat like the difference between cognition and recognition. Recognition may come somewhat after the event and is a form of awareness in which we say: "Oh, I didn't realize it was you" or "Oh, now I see what it's all about." Recognition is an altogether higher order of awareness from cognition, and yet it is now taken for granted as a normal feature of daily life in the electric age. Newspapers have long used this instant dimension in experience, at least since the time of the telegraph and the telephone, which have been with us for many decades. The mysterious thing about this kind of speed-up of information, whereby the gap is closed between the experience and the meaning, is that the public begins to participate directly in actions which it had previously heard about at a distance in place or time. At instant speeds the audience becomes actor, and the spectators become participants. On Spaceship Earth or in the global theater the audience and the crew become actors, producers rather than consumers. They seek to program events rather than to watch them. As in so many other instances, these "effects" appear before their "causes." At instant speeds the cause and effect are at least simultaneous, and it is this dimension which naturally suggests, to all those who are accustomed to it, the need to anticipate events hopefully rather than to participate in them fatalistically. The possibility of public participation becomes a sort of technological imperative which has been called "Lapp's Law": "If it can be done, it's got to be done"—a kind of siren wail of the evolutionary appetite.

Matie Armstrong Molinaro

Marshalling McLuhan

I became Marshall's agent in 1968. From our very first telephone conversations I liked the underlying spirit of fun that was always present. No matter how difficult the problems, or how odd Marshall's requests, I always treated them seriously . . . for a while at least. Some of his worst problems involved liberties taken in radio and TV programming, as well as with films. McLuhan had not been too careful about protecting his copyrights in print but, while this was bad, his film experiences were total disasters for the most part. A great part of my work involved the constant waging of campaigns for the retrieval and protection of his copyrights. To protect Marshall, I first arranged for his membership in ACTRA and AFTRA, the Canadian and American television, radio and film performers' unions. I hoped to organize and regulate this important aspect of his work. Marshall went along with this but, in a discreet aside, said to me, "Matie, I have a little idiosyncrasy about the number three. Do you think you can get me membership numbers that are divisible by three?" We were able to arrange this. I also learned never to book anything for Marshall on the thirteenth of any month, during full moon or on Corinne's birthday.

Often I was asked to attend meetings with foreign visitors who might want to arrange for radio, TV or filmed interviews. One year McLuhan was listed in some tourist publication as a resource of the Province of Ontario. Several times that year, Margaret Stewart, Marshall's wonderful and efficient secretary, called my office. "Matie, there are two busloads of Japanese visitors here at the Centre. Can you come down here and sort this out? They *all* have a great assortment of cameras!"

Usually Marshall telephoned me every morning and began the conversation either by reading me the "Morning Smile" or by telling me that it was no good. This would be followed immediately by the latest joke he had heard or made up. Starting off thus, in a happy frame of mind, we moved right along to review each day's agenda. There were meetings about books, translations, TV programs, feature films, telephone conferences and guest lectures around the world. If McLuhan declined an invitation, Margaret Stewart looked after it. If he accepted, our office and his then had a lot to do to assure the best possible preparation for Marshall as well as for his hosts. Never did he visit a foreign country without the most careful advance study, and we made certain that never did he move into a circle of sponsors or audiences who were unmindful of his work and his views. As the years wore on, he had more and more friends the world over so that usually lectures could be combined with the renewal of friendships begun on some previous occasion.

In the mid-seventies McLuhan was asked to help solve various "communication crises" around the world. He was wary of these invitations and, while he accepted some, it was arranged in a few of the more complicated situations for me to precede him and Corinne by a day or so. This was to give me time to find out what problems Marshall would be asked to solve. At the Acapulco Conference in the fall of 1974, President Echeverría desperately wanted Marshall to state that there was a causal relationship between the violent U.S. TV programs shown on the independent Mexican network and the kidnappings in Guerrero Province. Marshall would not do this, of course.

In 1975 we had strong suspicions about the crises connected with the Barcelona Conference. I had a most difficult time getting hosts to admit there were *any* problems at all. After about a day and a half of questioning they finally admitted to me that their 400 radio stations jammed half of Europe after sundown and the International Communications Commission had ordered them to reduce their number of stations to 200. By the time Marshall arrived, I had done a media check on their TV and print so that he could make a suggestion about shifting personnel into other areas. At the close of this conference there was a warm and happy farewell luncheon at the very elegant Via Veneto restaurant in Barcelona and the newspaper and magazine people were exceptionally happy to hear Marshall emphasize to them the continuing importance of print.

On this same occasion Corinne was hoping to buy a leather coat. The only available time for shopping was an extremely short period between meetings. Unable to get a taxi at our hotel, the four of us, Marshall and Corinne, Barbara Rodrigeuz (our Spanish translator) and I, tore off on foot from the hotel to Las Ramblas to the special store Barbara recommended. On the way we had a very close call in traffic that nearly ran the four of us down. Marshall flinched slightly but kept on racing, only calling over his shoulder to us, "This is what's meant by 'hell bent for leather'!"

Everyone knows how wide Marshall's range of interest was, but it never failed to fascinate me as I watched him shift from one level to another as required. He and John Lennon and Yoko Ono all interviewed each other one day in late December of 1969. After this I warmed up greatly to the Beatles. Accompanying Marshall on a small book promotion tour also changed my views about Frost and Newman and only confirmed an already high opinion of Dick Cavett.

In the early seventies ABC News sought McLuhan's advice about the way its news was presented on television. Marshall pointed out that, unlike radio news that could be read efficiently to listeners in a very straightforward way, television newspeople were visible, after all, in everyone's den or living room or family room, and this intimacy, artificial as it might be, required that the news be shared with the viewers in a more natural way. Thus was born the term "Friendly Teamness." This expression and the recommendations shocked the ABC News executives at first, but as they gradually saw the rightness of it, they accepted the concept and as this principle was applied all across the United States, ABC News's ratings soared.

Marshall loved jokes and cartoons, collected them avidly and shared them just as enthusiastically, often sending them to colleagues here and to friends all over the world. He was a great celebrator of birthdays, his own and all of his friends', a most genial host at champagne breakfasts (instituted to celebrate just about anything), a sharer of joys and a comfort in sorrow; truly a very, very good friend.

There were many happy occasions that often included unexpected encounters such as an Irish Night program at Saint

Michael's when Marshall asked me to help look after W.H. Auden. I moved on into the room chatting briefly to Corinne and Marshall while also keeping an eye out for Auden. I went back to the reception area to find him pinning something on his jacket. I introduced myself and asked him if he was expecting a friend to join him. When he replied negatively I suggested that we switch his tags around. He was wearing the "Friend of W.H. Auden" tag. I took it off and pinned the "W.H. Auden" tag on him. The "Friend of W.H. Auden" tag went swiftly to my pocket and into my archives! Auden was suffering from a very bad cold and so was not at his best in the preliminary social exchanges. When he took his place on the panel, however, the ensuing game of intellectual tennis between Auden and McLuhan was [a match of giants].

In late summer of 1976 Woody Allen, a McLuhan favorite, asked Marshall to appear in a cameo role in *Annie Hall.* (This incidentally was the name of one of Marshall's forebears in the early nineteenth century.) Marshall wanted to do this, subject to the requirements of the film, as we had been told at the outset that Marshall would be playing himself. On arriving in New York, I found Marshall's "script" in my letter box at the hotel. A quick perusal indicated Marshall could not say those lines. When Corinne and Marshall arrived, we discussed the difficulties but had to wait to see Allen on the set the next morning. The "set" was the New Yorker Theater at Broadway and Eighty-fifth Street, and the sidewalk in front of it. On arrival, we were ushered into a large Winnebago parked on Broadway and were soon joined by Woody Allen and assistants. Allen said the lines were not unchangeable and that Marshall could say whatever he felt comfortable with as long as it emphasized how little a character in the film (a so-called communications professor from Columbia University) really knew about Marshall's theories. In a little run-through, Marshall listened to the Columbia professor's lines, followed by Woody Allen's lines and then said something we'd all heard many times before, "You mean my fallacy is all wrong?"

The crowd of extras fell apart, and the laughter was spontaneous, genuine and sustained. Allen looked very surprised. A further discussion with Allen indicated that he did not want the word fallacy used. He said he'd prefer focus or something they could lip-sync into the fallacy frame. I immediately said that fallacy was funny, focus was not. How ridiculous for Marshall to say his focus was all wrong. It would have been academically unsound and stupid . . . and not true. It was also not funny. New York suffered a hurricane that afternoon and evening but we were ordered to wait so that Allen could see the rushes of Marshall's scene. On the third day, Marshall had to re-record sound and neither Corinne nor I was allowed to go with him. We kept reminding him, up to the very last minute, not to say focus at any cost. When the film was released the scene was as Marshall played it, with one notable omission—the laughter had been erased.

In June of 1979, Marshall and Corinne and I were in Los Angeles for several projects. One was the planning of some PBS programs with some young people from the University of California at Irvine. Marshall and the young men tossed all sorts of programming ideas about and towards the end of the morning the students had reached an all-time high of excitement. One of them fairly shouted, "I've got the perfect title for this series. It's got to be AT THE SPEED OF LIGHT." Marshall surprised them mightily by saying, "No, no, no, that's too slow! It's the speed of the MIND that really matters! Nothing can beat the speed of the mind!" The programs were never made because Marshall was not able to help.

Very elaborate and complicated arrangements had been made for Marshall to address one of the largest international communications conferences ever organized. The figure given us was 40,000 delegates over a period of seven days. This was to take place in São Paulo, Brazil, at the beginning of October 1979. Because Marshall suffered a stroke on September 26, his son Eric filled the gap immediately. The morning Eric and his wife left for Brazil, Marshall was operated on to relieve an occlusion. When he regained consciousness in the recovery room, he asked Corinne haltingly, "Eric went Brazil?" She assured him that he had. "Good," Marshall said. Following this Marshall experienced a severe aphasia which lasted until his death fifteen months later.

On her way home from the hospital, at the time of the stroke, Corinne regularly stopped in to see us. It was impossible to believe that the prognosis was so poor. Family and friends adopted the most positive attitudes about Marshall's recovery, and bravely continued to collect jokes and cartoons for his amusement. He seemed to understand all of us well enough but had great difficulty responding. Suddenly, we all realized how much his daily dependable wit and wisdom had meant to us. People close to him had become quite used to this very rich and abundant diet, and to be deprived of it suddenly brought upon many of us the most hideous withdrawal symptoms.

I did not see Marshall until about five weeks after the stroke. Corinne, George Thompson and I had been to the King Tut exhibition and on the way back, while we were stopped in traffic, a large truck backed into us and caused some damage to the car and some delay in our progress home. Corinne, who had a few more errands to do, sent me on first to keep Marshall company and to let his regular nurse leave for the day.

On my arrival, I found the nurse had gone and Elizabeth was there reading poetry to her father. I explained about the accident and Marshall expressed great concern about all three of us and the car. I then produced a box of chocolate Sphinxes I had brought him and we all laughed at how ridiculous they were, even as an art gallery fund-raiser. This first meeting wasn't as difficult as I expected but, nevertheless, I felt very depressed.

Throughout the next year, we managed to work and communicate and get quite a number of problems solved. Corinne was magnificent about treating Marshall in a "business as usual" way, at the same time making sure that all bases were covered all the time, thus preparing for any eventuality. She had even prevailed upon the powers at the University to keep the Coach House intact for a while so that Marshall could go back to the office. This, it was hoped, would be therapeutic.

At the end of one of the taped series edited by Derek de Kerchove for "IDEAS" on CBC radio, Marshall said, "Don't let the Juggernaut roll over you!" When the program was over I telephoned Marshall and launched into a monologue about how we were all ready to help him take his own advice. He only replied with sighs and pauses, "Yes . . . yes."

Over the years it had worked out that Corinne and Marshall usually visited us on Boxing Day and we went to their place on New Year's Eve. So it was on Boxing Day 1980. Corinne knew Marshall was concerned about starting a new year with several unfinished projects, so we talked about everything and planned for the future. Even though Marshall had been too ill to travel to receive the many academic honors that were bestowed upon him in those last fifteen months, he was pleased that he had not only not been forgotten, but that he had been remembered and recognized for a great body of work. We talked about all this in a positive way and had a wonderfully happy visit. When we said goodbye, it was with anticipation of another happy year of working together. Since I had never thought of Marshall's condition as life-threatening, I never suspected he'd be gone by New Year's Eve.

Corinne called me New Year's Eve morning and said that Marshall had died during the night. She and Eric had worked out a press release and they just wanted to review it with me. It was simple and perfect.

Many friends and colleagues were interviewed by the press and asked to comment on McLuhan's death. Northrop Frye is reported to have said that henceforth life would not be as much fun. This was very similar to what Ezra Pound is reported to have said on the death of his friend T.S. Eliot. "With whom will I share a joke?" This seemed a very appropriate comment and one that Marshall himself, I'm sure, would have liked.

Margaret Stewart for years had been the dedicated custodian of McLuhan's files and papers. When she became ill and then Marshall fell ill and the Centre was closed, the papers were moved around to several repositories and in the course of these disasters, the indexes and inventories were lost. To put everything back together again became a task that Corinne McLuhan and I undertook in July 1981. This was not the first time that Corinne and I had worked closely together. We'd been doing it for years, as she virtually ran McLuhan Associates, Ltd. alone. As we sorted through his material day after day we both regretted that we had not begun this task while he was alive. This would have allowed us to demonstrate our genuine interest and, more important, ask him from time to time what he meant. While he was alive, of course, the idea of examining his papers never occurred to me. To be realistic, while he was alive he kept Marg, Corinne and me so busy with the day-to-day problems of the present, there was no time left to investigate his past!

In addition to the personal material that Marshall kept at the office, there were boxes and boxes in the closets of the study at Wychwood that had not been looked at for many years. Going through this material was especially painful for Corinne because most of it was written during the early years of their marriage. Nevertheless, we persevered and after three years produced a respectable inventory of some 800,000 pieces of paper. I completed the sale of this material to the Public Archives of Canada in February 1984.

Along with the old records of Marshall's we discovered Elsie McLuhan's treasure of letters from her son. This gave Corinne and me a fresh insight into the importance of his mother in Marshall's early years. There were more than four hundred letters to her. This cache showed the transition from boy to unsophisticated young man, to mature literary critic, to original thinker. All of this is dealt with very fully in the book Corinne and I edited for Oxford University Press: *Letters of Marshall McLuhan* [published in 1987]. Marshall speaks for himself throughout that collection more eloquently, of course, than any of his followers can speak for him.

The dozen or so years I worked with Marshall are totally unforgettable. I found him to be enormously generous with his time in dealing with colleagues and students, and with his money to good causes. Spiritually and intellectually he bestowed so much on his friends and the people who worked closely with him. The research of the last three years has shown us that, even in death, McLuhan is still giving. I can see the framework for the task at hand but I dare not contemplate all the other possibilities. My association with McLuhan's work has most certainly been my longest intellectual adventure . . . and it is not yet over. I only hope that before it comes to an end we'll find some way to put back some of the laughter. Our purpose in editing the correspondence is to remind his followers (once referred to as McLunatics) of the excitement in the studies and probes that dominated four decades of Marshall McLuhan's writing, and to capture the attention of new readers and students so that they too can share the enriching insights of this truly remarkable scholar who became the most widely recognized figure in the field of international communications.

McLuhan Probes

When mechanical industry separated home and work, women too became fragmented, mechanical brides. Unmatched, mismatched, rematched.

Heidegger surfboards along the electronic wave as triumphantly as Descartes rode the mechanical wave.

Life at these speeds obliges everyone to discover a new career for himself every ten years, a new job and even a totally new personality. At electric speed it is not wise to try to be one and the same person and have the same job for more than ten years.

The unique innovation of the phonetic alphabet released the Greeks from the universal acoustic spill of tribal societies.

Games are the mask of the crowd. Their dynamic is towards increase. They drive to *win*. Each nation's popular games project the image of its central dynamism.

The print-made split between head and heart is the trauma which affects Europe from Machiavelli to the present.

The phonetic alphabet is a unique technology.

All media are extensions of some human faculty—psychic or physical.

There is a great tradition that women are much more integral in their life and men much more specialized, fragmentary, and that's why women are thought to be intuitive. The world of insight is primarily one of touch rather than sight, and so the woman's intuition means the use of all the senses at once, a response to which is touch-active touch, that is, not just passive touch. Touch is our primary and deepest experiential mode of relating to the world.

Guilt and remorse are retrospective by definition and exempt the guilty party from any redeeming act of expiration or creative renewal. Guilt and remorse are forms of despair and sloth.

It's always May Day in the global nursery.

No medium has its meaning or existence alone, but only in constant interplay with other media.

Literate man naturally dreams of visual solutions to problems of human differences.

The nuclear bomb is not hardware. It ends war as a means of international powerplay.

Literacy, in translating man out of the closed world of tribal depth and resonance, gave man an eye for an ear and ushered him into a visual open world of specialized and divided consciousness.

War is never anything less than accelerated technological change.

Marshall McLuhan

Violence of the Media

"The Kingdom of Heaven suffereth violence." Violence against the Kingdom of Heaven proceeds by prayer and petition, prayer being one of the more extreme forms of violence, since it is conducted by superhuman force. It should not be surprising, therefore, that the ages of the utmost physical violence have also produced the greatest exemplars of heroic sanctity, as in the sixteenth century, and also today. Violence means the violation of territories, whether political or psychic, physical or moral. *The Listener* records a discussion on pornographic violence under the head: "No victim, no pornography."

> How, in the age of Marxism, socialism, liberation, have we all come to be landed with de Sade? There's another very important thing to say here. To you and me, sexual meaning is meeting and entering the body of another person in the closest creative intimacy. The pervert—that is, the person to whom this has no meaning, who needs pornography—doesn't understand the meaning of sexuality. He needs to penetrate the body of the other person in order to find whether there is any meaning in there, just like a child sticking its needle in a teddy bear.[1]

To invade the private person, or to invade a group with teaching, with doctrines, with entertainment, all these are alike forms of violence. To assume the right to program the sensibilities or thoughts and fantasies of individuals or groups, has long been taken for granted as a viable form of personal or social action. The private educator, as much as the college of propaganda in Rome, assumes a mandate to shape individuals and societies in any age.

Today, however, there is a new dimension in all of these activities. Electric media move information and people at the speed of light. It is this instant and total quality that constitutes the condition of mass man and the mass society, an effect that occurs not so much by virtue of size as speed of involvement and inclusiveness. Moreover, the hidden dimension in all electric media, whether the telephone, TV or radio, is that *The Sender Is Sent.* When you are on the phone or on the air, you can be anywhere and everywhere at the same moment.

The violence that all electric media inflict on their users is that they are instantly invaded and deprived of their physical bodies and are merged in a network of extensions of their own nervous systems. As if this were not sufficient violence or invasion of individual rights, the elimination of the physical bodies of the electric media users also deprives them of the means of relating the program experience to their private individual selves, even as instant involvement supresses private identity.

The loss of individual and personal meaning via the electronic media ensures a corresponding and reciprocal violence from those so deprived of their identities; for violence, whether spiritual or physical, is a quest for identity and the meaningful. The less identity, the more violence. Violence exerted by private individuals tends to have limited results, whereas the violence exerted by groups knows no bounds. Media are always and necessarily corporate or group activities, whether they are the mother tongues or the father images of big corporations. With the proliferation of multimedia in our time, there is a new consensus that some manner of media ecology and control be put into action; but against this proposal there is a negative and hidden factor in the Western world. Edward Hall, the anthropologist, has drawn attention to this negative attitude in the Western world in a recent study, *The Fourth Dimension in Architecture: The Impact of Building on Man's Behavior.*

> The most pervasive and important assumption, a cornerstone in the edifice of Western thought, is one that lies hidden from our consciousness and has to do with man's re-

lationship to his environment. Quite simply the Western view is that human processes, particularly behavior, are independent of environmental controls and influence.[2]

The obsessional concern of Western man with "content" and the correlative indifference to hidden environmental or side effects stems from the very character of Western literacy. This is easy to observe by contrasting our skepticism about general or environmental effects with the attitudes of preliterate or nonliterate societies of the Third World. In his *The Savage Mind*, Lévi-Strauss discusses the pervasive feeling of nonvisual cultures that every kind of change effects everything else, adding that this kind of awareness is pure paranoia. Literate, or visual man, in contrast, has to be *shown* every kind of relationship. Visuality favors quantification and exact measurement and is not inclined to listen to the protests of the Chinese that telephone poles deeply disturb their entire psychic balance. It is true that Plato at the end of *The Republic* mentions that any change in musical rhythms could cause a political revolution; but jazz and rock and jets are accepted as national phenomena which could not disturb the psyche or sanity of a literate man. The "content" of any work, philosophical or physical, is the *efficient* cause in the situation. The *formal* cause concerns the effects proceeding from the total structure of the situation, which includes the public and the users. It is the *formal* cause which constitutes the environmental violence, the side effects of the media.

Harold Innis was one of the very few people since Plato to show serious interest in formal causes and the effects that result from the formal structures of total situations. The numerous commissions on violence that have marked our violent time have, without exception, paid attention only to the *efficient* cause, the program content of the media. The effects of the media themselves represent a form of violence so vast as to be unnoticed. It is a situation not unlike that in the old rhyme.

You hang the thief
Who steals the goose from off the common,
But leave the larger felon loose
Who steals the common from the goose.

In *Identity, Youth and Crisis*, Erik H. Erikson observes:

In Jung's "persona" a weak ego seems to sell out to a compelling social prototype. A fake ego identity is established which suppresses rather than synthesizes those experiences and functions which endanger the "front."[3]

In *The Nuremberg Mind*, F.R. Miale and Michael Selzer, in search of understanding how the Nazi leaders could seem to be ordinary, well-intentioned people, encountered the fact that "values, and behavior of individuals are shaped by social forces beyond our control—and often, indeed, beyond our recognition."[4] The forces which are typically "beyond our recognition" are the environmental or diffused forces, what we ordinarily take for granted as the existing social services of the media, whether they be highways or airways. Since visual, rational man can find no "connection" between such forces and their victims, he throws up his hands in mystification. Radio had a fantastic and profound effect in retrieving the ordinary tribal consciousness of Germany in the twenties and thirties. TV, which is an addictive inner trip (regardless of program), sent American youth in pursuit of the occult and group awareness. Since there are no visual or quantifiable *connections* between radio and TV and their effects, Western man humbly and dumbly submits to their magic. What Miale and Selzer found by way of analogue for the monstrous behavior of the Nazi leaders relates to the case of the psychological study at Yale, undertaken by Stanley Milgram: "Milgram sought to discover the extent to which human beings will obey commands which come increasingly into conflict with their consciences."[5] The teachers chosen for the job proceeded to demonstrate experimental shocks to subjects as part of a memory test.

Sweating, trembling, and in other ways indicating their extreme reluctance to continue administering the punishments, *65 percent of the teachers nevertheless obeyed orders all the way to the end of the scale on the shock generator!* Not a single teacher disobeyed the experimenter's orders before reaching 300 volts—marked INTENSE SHOCK—and only 12.5 percent of them stopped at this point.[6]

Milgram concluded:

> When the individual is *on his own*, conscience is brought
> into play. But when he functions in an organized mode,
> directions that come from the higher level component are
> not assessed against the internal standards of moral judg-
> ment. . . . The psychology of obedience does not depend
> on the placement within the larger hierarchy. . . . The
> social psychology of this century reveals a major lesson:
> often, it is not so much the kind of person a man is as the
> kind of situation in which he finds himself that determines
> how he will act.[7]

Since the kind of situations in which twentith-century man exists
are almost entirely products of the mass media, we have to face the
further fact that these situations are beyond the ken of Western
awareness. Western literate man is easily inclined to make moral
protests, but is seemingly incapable of recognizing the formal or
"acoustic" structure of situations which are disturbing and destroying him.

The group, or the crowd, has minimal identity and exists in a
state of paranoic anxiety about any threats to its precarious
pattern. In his classic work *Crowds and Power* Elias Canetti explains
that all kinds of crowds experience a need to get bigger, and also
fear that they are getting smaller. This passion can extend to
money (one kind of crowd), as much as to the mindless group.
The formal effects of the electric media in invading individuals
and groups are in no way limited by the content or the programs
so purveyed. The effects of the car are felt in the highways,
factories and oil companies, or the service environment. The
service environment constituted by electric networks acts as a kind
of *formal* cause, or hidden *ground*. That which appears or is noticed
is only the efficient cause. The Greeks gave no heed to the effects
of the phonetic alphabet which transformed their inner and outer
lives, ending the bardic colleges which had long served as their
educational establishment. Like ourselves, the Greeks had a
strong visual bias toward efficient causality and ethics and applied
knowledge. Efficient causality is the world of logic and connectedness, and of specific goals and directions. In a word, it is the

province of visual man. Until visual man, or alphabetic man, the pre-Socratics lived and thought in the acoustic or multi-directional world.

Today, the Third World, which is eager to resemble and to surpass the First World, is still in the elder province of intuitive experience which precedes the advent of phonetically literate or visual man. From his beginnings, phonetically literate man assumed it was his right to invade other cultures and to impose his discoveries wherever possible. Whereas the Greco-Roman world, constituted by the phonetic alphabet and by techniques of visually applied knowledge, assumed a mission to extend itself and its institutions to the "lesser breeds," electronic man, on the other hand, has re-entered the world of acoustic experience, thereby losing all confidence in his right to impose the old visual culture of the West on people who have not yet been invaded by the phonetic alphabet. From the first, identified with the Greco-Roman culture, Christianity had at the same time brought the hidden Word and the new visual culture to the "lesser breeds." Today, a crisis in Christianity emerges with the possibility of propagating the hidden Word directly without the benefit of the written word, or Greco-Roman culture. The patterns of Western civilization are as incompatible with simultaneous or acoustic culture as the pre-Socratic Logos was incompatible with the alphabetic innovation.

The violence of dominant culture consists in the assumption of the right to invade and to shape groups and individuals with the preferred norms of one's choice. In the electronic world we now take for granted the coexistence of all cultures and their immediacy of access, while sheer diversity and range of cultural choice daily brings into doubt the rights of any one culture to impose itself on another. We have begun to doubt our own rights to mold and shape our own children. Women's Lib is by comparison a side issue, yet one that is essentially electronic in offering power to all participants.

Without exception, then, the activity of media, old and new, as invaders of both public and private space, raises the question and image of violence at every turn. At the speed of light, American political institutions are trembling and quaking in this bicentennial year.

Writing on "pre-election blues" in the *Globe and Mail* on March 16, 1976, James Reston observed:

> The more this capital fusses and agonizes over the election, the more it seems to long for fundamental change. It would never admit as much in public, but the truth comes out in private: from the top of the Administration and the Congress to the critical levels of the civil service, it is almost yearning for new faces and new beginnings. This may not be logical or even rational, for all the devilishly complicated problems will remain after the election, but there it is—an intuitive feeling that something is deeply wrong here and probably won't be corrected by the old cast of characters or the old ideological arguments of either party.[8]

He adds that "This is not a partisan but a general feeling that Washington is not at the beginning of something but at the end of something."[9]

In the February 1976 issue of *Atlantic*, David Halberstam has some observations on TV and politics:

> Television not only changed the balance of power, but it became a vital part of the new balance of power. Presidents knew the advantage they had in gaining access to the air and the difficulties any competing politician or institution had. Presidents had used or suffered press conferences for a variety of reasons, including a chance to listen to the country. Kennedy seized on live television as an opportunity for political theater. He used reporters as pawns to help make him look better, smarter, shrewder, more capable, and in control. Indeed, mastery of the press conference became a kind of substitute for mastery of the political scene.[10]

He continues:

> In that sense John Kennedy changed the presidency more than any recent predecessor with the exception of Fran-

klin Roosevelt, who had slipped so naturally into the radio presidency. Kennedy's ascendancy, like Roosevelt's, was a confluence of a man and a technology, of a new political force and a politician with the skills and instincts to exploit it. The television audiences were acutely aware of style now. The President came not just into their towns but into their homes.[11]

The last sentence points to the violent invasive character of radio and television. Representative government had belonged to a period of communication by rail, when the representatives were at a considerable distance from the home. Both radio and TV restored the character of the tribal chieftain:

At the same time that television was granting immense and almost unchallenged power to the President, it was granting less and less power to anyone else, particularly its own people. The role of reporter and commentator was diminishing. There was less time for serious analysis, and fewer explanations of complicated stories. As the role of the reporter diminished, the role of technology grew.[12]

As the primacy of the image increases, the role of parties and policies recedes, as is the case with all media "content." This is not to say that content and program have no function on TV. Indeed, their function is to assure that TV will be turned on so that it can perform its work of obliterating all individuality and all privacy. Mr. Eliot observed long ago that the chief use of the content of a poem is "to satisfy one habit of the reader, to keep his mind diverted and quiet, while the poem does its work upon him: much as the imaginary burglar is always provided with a bit of nice meat for the house-dog." Likewise, the function of a program is to keep the users occupied by some diversion while the medium itself does its work upon him.

John Culkin

Marshall's New York Adventure
Reflections on McLuhan's Year at Fordham University

It was in 1963 at a seminar at Brandeis University in Massachusetts that I first met Marshall McLuhan. By then I had been a closet scholar of his work for five years. His first words to the group were: "Of course, it's very difficult for a naked person to learn how to read." It is still as good an introduction to his thinking as there is. This was all back in the early sixties before there was a "McLuhan." The articles were still signed "H. Marshall McLuhan" and it was a year and a half before *Understanding Media* would turn his name into an *-ism* and an adjective (*-esque*).

Four years later Marshall would be joining me for a year at Fordham University. Eighteen years later I would be giving a eulogy at his funeral. These are the numbers which bracket my relationship with Marshall and his family. This account, which of necessity will be freighted with some unwanted autobiographical detail, will focus on his year in New York.

At the end of the Brandeis seminar, Marshall and I sat down for a drink and a chat. We had been corresponding and communicating by telephone for the previous two years and we already felt as though we knew each other pretty well. At the time I was a Jesuit priest and I was finishing up a doctorate at Harvard. Marshall asked me to do a favor for him. He requested that I write a letter to the president of the University of Toronto assuring him that Marshall's work was important. At first I was stunned. It was as though Babe Ruth had asked me for a few batting tips. But in ten seconds, my memories of the academic world and of the history of prophets in their own countries had put the request in a very understandable context. The letter was written and graciously acknowledged.

While at Harvard I was striving desperately to incorporate some work on communication into an otherwise tedious degree program in education. My own interests lay in helping young people to process and control the new media culture by getting some training in being smart and selective about all the media in their experience. One of my major projects at Harvard was a series of papers which attempted to present McLuhan's ideas in an orderly and reasoned fashion. At the time there wasn't a great deal of material to work with. Marshall's first book, *The Mechanical Bride*, was to me "pre-McLuhan." It was the work of a brilliant literary mind having at the world of advertising, but it contained none of the insights which would later set his work apart. *The Gutenberg Galaxy* was published in Canada in the middle of my first year of study. But mainly there were articles and reprints of speeches scattered in fairly arcane and specialized magazines. The probes were distributed all over the neighborhood. And there weren't "experts" whom one could consult on the topic.

Gertrude Broderick to the rescue. She was a friend in the U.S. Office of Education and she told me that Marshall had written a report for them in 1960. She sent it. I read it. And now I could cause serious trouble. It was called "Report on Project in Understanding New Media." It had been funded by the government under a contract with the National Association of Educational Broadcasters, whose president, Harry Skornia, was an early admirer of Marshall's work. The author was our old friend "H. Marshall McLuhan" and the fourteen chapters of the report dealt with "the languages and grammars of the media." It was all there, right from the beginning. This mimeographed report had all the freshness, breathlessness and roughness of a journal by a traveler in a new land. It was telegraphic in style. It was punctuated by charts and lists of questions. Even today it stands as the best codification of his thinking.

The last two paragraphs of the introduction catch the scope and flavor of what in four years would become *Understanding Media.*

Today it is axiomatic that we live in a global space fed by information from every point on the sphere at the same time. What possible relevance to the student of media could a point of view be in such circumstances? He must adopt the mosaic approach. He must deal with all media at once in their daily inter-action, or else pay the price of irrelevance and unreality. He must deal with each medium as it affects all of our senses, not as it makes an impression on one sense. Because any medium which singles out one sense, writing or radio for example, by that very fact causes an exceptional disturbance among the other senses. Speech is the only medium that uses all the senses at once, and therefore in the multi-media electric age the structure of speech probably holds the orchestral clues for cultural control and equilibrium. We may be forced, in the interests of human equilibrium, to suppress various media as radio or movies for long periods of time, or until the social organism is in a state to sustain such violent lopsided stimulus.

Nothing could be more unrealistic than to suppose that the programming for such media could affect their power to re-pattern the sense-ratios of our beings. It is the ratio among our senses which is violently disturbed by media technology. And any upset in our sense-ratios alters the matrix of thought and concept and value. In what follows I hope to show how this ratio is altered by various media and why, therefore, the medium is the message or the sum-total of effects. The so-called "content" of any medium is another medium. So that the concept of "content" naturally begins with writing, whose "content" is the medium of speech. But the *effect* of writing is not at all the effect of speech. The content of radio is usually speech also, but the effect of radio is neither that of speech nor of writing. Such are the relationships and discoveries which I seek to demonstrate and clarify in the sections which follow.[1]

McLuhan had still not been "discovered." I recall being at a meeting of 200 communications professors and professionals in Washington. Someone mentioned McLuhan's work and a poll of the room indicated that fewer than ten people had heard of him. In those days we few card-carrying McLuhanites would seek each other out at such gatherings to swap anecdotes, ideas and self-congratulation. But increasingly he was being invited to lecture at conventions and to write for a wider range of periodicals. He made annual trips to New York to lecture for Lou Forsdale at Teachers College, Columbia, and for me at Fordham. I recall one Media Studies conference at Fordham which featured Paul Newman and Marshall and an audience of only forty people about half of whom were nuns. Marshall had still not been "discovered."

It would not be long. *Understanding Media* had been accepted for publication by Frank Taylor at McGraw-Hill. Marshall was getting invitations to consult for American corporations. The band of disciples was growing. Two of the most fascinating of the breed were a couple of San Franciscans who had offices in a refurbished firehouse. Howard Gossage was something of a legend in the advertising business and Gerry Feigen was a medical doctor. Inventive, creative, quixotic, maverick are the kinds of words that come to mind in thinking of them. They had read and understood and respected Marshall and they looked on him as an idea whose time had come. He spent time with them in San Francisco and through them he met the journalist, Tom Wolfe, whose later article for the *New York Herald Tribune*—"What If He Is Right?"—caught the spirit and wonder associated with the rapidly emerging McLuhan phenomenon.

Gossage, Feigen and I spent a lot of time together on both coasts discussing Marshall and his work. I recall one evening at dinner at the Plaza Hotel when we conspired to hasten the process of Marshall's inevitable rise to public attention. Gossage arranged a small reception for Marshall in New York with a group of magazine editors and writers. The event certainly helped to get out the word on Marshall but it was in no way "the packaging of a star" type of thing which the later mythology would often prefer to interpret it as. Both Gossage and Feigen disclaimed any such causality and they were right. They were merely pointing to a star which was already well above the horizon.

Then *Understanding Media* hit the bookstores and people who couldn't spell McLuhan's name felt obliged to have some kind of opinion about his work. Marshall became a body of theories completely surrounded by interviewers. You couldn't avoid references to him in the press and we all discovered that we were living in "The Age of McLuhan."

Back to the road to Fordham. In 1965 I finished my sentence at Harvard and was appointed Director of the Center for Communications at Fordham. It was a catch-all title which made me sound important while freeing me up from any administrative duties so that I could plan the future of the communications program for the Lincoln Square campus of Fordham. The chairman of the undergraduate Department of Communication Arts was Father William Trivett, S.J. He had come to know Marshall through the annual summer speaking assignments Marshall had taken on for us at Fordham.

A year before, the Board of Regents of the State of New York had begun an ambitious program to attract major scholars to New York State universities. They created ten endowed chairs, five in the sciences (named for Albert Einstein) and five in the humanities (named for Albert Schweitzer). Fordham applied to the program and was awarded an Albert Schweitzer Chair in the Humanities. The Chair and I arrived at Fordham at about the same time and I had no doubt about whom I thought should find his way into that chair.

The mid-sixties were heady days at Fordham. An experimental college was opened under the aegis of Elizabeth Sewell. A college for women, Thomas More College, began accepting students in 1967. The new campus in midtown Manhattan at Lincoln Square was under construction. Three new schools were to be part of that campus: Arts to be directed by Livingston Biddle, Social Sciences to be directed by Margaret Mead and Communications to be directed by the writer. The new president of Fordham, Father Leo McLaughlin, possessed a blend of vision and courage rarely to be found in *homo administrator*. I made my recommendation that Marshall be offered the Chair. I laid out all the reasons for and against the idea, spelled out the arguments and controversies surrounding his ideas and assessed our chances for having the offer accepted. The administration said: "Go." And I went.

Inevitable as the decision may seem in retrospect, the fact was that I knew there were a lot of reasons why Marshall and his family might not want to be uprooted for a year and come to New York. Marshall was very comfortable in the working conditions afforded by his home and office in Toronto. He knew where all the books were and he was also geographically buttressed against the increasing demands on his time. His secretary, Mrs. Margaret Stewart, knew how to deal with the details of his somewhat frantic existence. In addition, he hated noise and litter; New York specialized in both at world-class levels. And finally, there was the family to consider. Four of the children were still living at home and the youngest, Michael, was still in high school.

We did, however, have a number of things going for us. The prestige of the Chair in its own way would serve to validate the academic solidity of Marshall's ideas at a time when many didn't think it quite respectable to be dealing with the new media and the popular culture. The Chair also carried with it a stipend of $100,000 to pay the visiting scholar and his staff. Fordham was offering $40,000 of that total to the holder of the Chair. Besides, the contract was just for one year and Marshall had been at University of Toronto for twenty years. Eric would be able to work with the Schweitzer team at Fordham. Teri would be able to complete her final year of college at Fordham. Liz would be able to join the first class at Thomas More College. And Michael would be able to continue his high school work in Bronxville. My friendship with Marshall was also important, as was the fact that I was a priest who understood and appreciated his ideas. Marshall's conversion to Catholicism was central to his life and it counted that Fordham was a major American Catholic university.

My personal concern was for Corinne and the family. I knew this was no small decision for them. Ralph Baldwin, a writer and business consultant, who had known the McLuhans for many years, was most helpful to both the family and to me in working through this aspect of the decision. Late in 1966 I visited the family at their home on Wells Hill Avenue in Toronto to lay the proposal out before them and to discuss any of the difficulties which it might entail for them. The first and lasting impression I had from that visit was of books and beautiful women, not necessarily in that order. I met Mrs. McLuhan earlier on one of her trips to New York and I was most taken by her handsome good looks, gracious ways and concern for Marshall and the family. I was pleased to note that the daughters of the family favored their mother. Perhaps that is the reason why I don't recall any of the business details from that meeting. But nonetheless, the process had started that would bring Marshall and Corinne and four of their children to Fordham the following September.

The Fordham administration was helpful at every step of the way. I could just presume that there would be a solution to any problem that came up. One of the new vice-presidents, Robert

Kidera, and his wife Helen were particularly helpful in giving of their time on a personal level. They had just gone through a move themselves and they were sensitive to all the details involved. They found a beautiful house with spacious grounds which was available for a year's lease. It was large and elegantly furnished and, as a result, took a lot of the curse off the physical process of moving. It was located near Sarah Lawrence College in Westchester County and, as we later found out, had Jack Paar as the next-door neighbor. (Ironically, Marshall had used Paar's TV show to make a point in his chapter on television in *Understanding Media*.) I think it was the house that finally clinched the deal. It meant that Marshall could have a quiet and commodious living and working space among the trees in Bronxville and then commute to the Bronx where Fordham had a handsome sprawling campus standing like an island in the midst of a changing neighborhood. The decibels and debris of Manhattan lay far to the south. The decision was made. The game was on.

Since the budget for the Chair included salaries for two other scholars, Marshall and I consulted and decided to invite Dr. Edmund Carpenter and Harley Parker to join the conspiracy. Carpenter was an anthropologist who had been a longtime colleague of Marshall's at the University of Toronto and who had edited the magazine *Explorations* with him. Parker was an artist who at the time was a curator at the Royal Ontario Museum and who was collaborating with Marshall on a book project. I had met Carpenter before and I flew to California where he was teaching at San Fernando Valley State College and at UCLA. Ted signed on and I then met with Harley and completed the team. I consulted with Mrs. McLuhan about the qualities most desired in a secretary for Marshall. She said: "Just like Mrs. Stewart. Efficient and low key." The Fordham grapevine went to work and delivered the perfect candidate for the job in Mrs. Betty Lewis. We were ready.

The official announcement was made early in 1967. The New York press gave it plenty of space and requests for information started pouring into Fordham. In March I did a cover article for *The Saturday Review* ("A Schoolman's Guide to Marshall McLuhan") which became their most heavily reprinted article. One of the faculty at Fordham announced that he was writing a pamphlet to be called "What to Do until Marshall Comes." We devised an academic program in which twenty seniors would work full time with the Schweitzer group and there would be a large lecture hall course featuring three classes a week. Interest and enthusiasm were high.

At this time Fordham was engaged in continuing discussions with the New York State Department of Education about its eligibility to receive state funds. There was strong feeling among some that as a Catholic institution it should be precluded from some or all public funding. The Schweitzer Chair was one of the areas under discussion. Fordham had assured Marshall and the others in the Schweitzer program that the university would honor all the commitments even if the state did not provide the funds. It didn't take long to test their promise. Marshall and the others had just about arrived at Fordham when the attorney general, Louis Lefkowitz (a Fordham graduate, by the way), announced that Fordham was ineligible to receive the Chair because it was a Catholic institution. More press. More TV cameras. Much comment that it wasn't a very nice or equitable thing for the state to do to a bunch of guys who were running a pretty good school and who were adventurous enough to lure "The Oracle of the Electronic Age" to the Bronx. Fordham lost the Schweitzer Chair and picked up the bill for the year, but the incident triggered a series of decisions which led to a change in the structure of the Board of Trustees so that Fordham was no longer legally a religious institution. Once this happened, the Chair was also restored to the university.

The day after the attorney general's first decision, I received a call from Mr. Walker Buckner who told me he was distressed about the turn of events and would like to meet with me to discuss the situation. I met with him in his office the next day and learned that he was a stock broker, a major investor in IBM and Sony and an avid fan of McLuhan. He showed me his well-used and annotated edition of *Understanding Media*. He also gave me a check for $10,000 to help support the program. He and Marshall became close friends during the year and he continued to support Marshall's work when he returned to the University of Toronto.

Meanwhile the creative academic chaos went on. Marshall, Ted and Harley shared the lecturing duties for the large class which included a number of media professionals who made the pilgrimage to the Bronx to sit in on the classes. The requests for interviews and speeches were interminable. We did a special issue for *Harper's Bazaar* with Ted Carpenter on text and Ken Heyman on photographs. In a memorable speech sponsored by the Fordham Ad Club, Marshall told the New York advertising community that they did their job so well by communicating the thrill of owning the advertised product that they made it unnecessary for the consumer to actually buy the product. They laughed. . . . sort of. Perhaps the most creative collaboration developed during the year was between Marshall and Tony Schwartz, the award-winning sound artist and maker of commercials. They were made for each other. Tony was doing what Marshall was talking about. Marshall was providing the theories for Tony's work. Visitors kept popping in to confer with Marshall. On one occasion, he and Corinne were invited by Stanley Kubrick to a personal, private screening of his unreleased film, *2001.* After ten minutes he told Corinne it was time to leave because he could see which way this one was going. He was coaxed into staying by Teri and he did, if not always in a waking state. The other thing which drove him out of rooms were the words of some of the avant-garde, multimedia artists who would say they were inspired by him to do some eight-track, forty screen, screaming commentary on contemporary existence. "What has this got to do with my work?" said the fleeing oracle.

But all was not well. Over the years a number of us who were close to Marshall noticed that occasionally he would undergo brief dizzy spells or blackouts. After a minute or two he would pick up again as before. It had been diagnosed some years before in Toronto as "a touch of epilepsy." Ted Carpenter and I were at this time giving a series of lectures to doctors at Downstate Medical Center in Brooklyn. Ted mentioned Marshall's symptoms to one of the doctors who said: "The first thing I would check for is brain tumor." This was in late October. Two days later Marshall had a particularly bad spell in front of his large class. I sat down with Marshall and Corinne and told them about the doctor's suspicion of tumor. Marshall was no lover of doctors or hospitals and we knew that we were in for some delicate negotiating. Our research indicated that the best hospital for us would be Columbia-Presbyterian in New York. Marshall entered the hospital for a series of three tests. He checked himself out after completing two of them. By then we knew that he had a brain tumor, that it was benign, that it was operable, that he was fortunate to have discovered it at this time before it caused irreversible damage. Marshall gallantly went back to work but his energy was flagging and the spells recurred.

By now it had become a matter of public knowledge that something was wrong and reporters were starting to pester students and family members with questions. Whether they knew it or not, they were interfering with our getting Marshall back into the hospital to complete the tests and to undergo surgery.

Marshall reluctantly went back into the hospital for the final test, but he was still fighting the idea of an operation. For the next ten days or so, Corinne and I were constantly at the hospital. When Marshall and I were alone we did all the things friends do to pass some tense time; we talked about ideas, told bad jokes, read to each other, sat in silence and occasionally talked about "it"—the operation. We had more than one of those conversations which reveal so much that you find it difficult to look at each other the following morning. Finally, just before Thanksgiving, Marshall agreed to the operation. The date for surgery was set for the Saturday after Thanksgiving Day. The surgeon would be Dr. Lester Mount. He informed us that it would be a long procedure, lasting perhaps as long as five hours. On Thanksgiving Day Marshall somewhat sheepishly asked me: "Do you think that Dr. Mount drinks?" I reassured him about the sobriety of his sixty-two–year-old surgeon.

We set ourselves for the operation. Corinne stayed at home with Teri, Liz and a number of family friends. Marshall's son, Eric, and I went to keep vigil at the hospital with the promise that we would report to Corinne every hour. Marshall went into the operating room at about 11:30 a.m. and the hourly reports from the nurses were relayed to the home in Bronxville. It started getting tense after the fourth call. After five hours a second team of assistants and nurses joined Dr. Mount. The hourly reports got harder and harder for me to make and yet the news remained the same—"All is proceeding well." After ten hours a third team of assistants took its turn with Dr. Mount. At 5 o'clock on Sunday morning, they called and told me that the operation had been a success. My call to Corinne was the happiest I had ever made in my life. Marshall had been on the table for more than seventeen hours. Later I heard that it was the longest neurosurgical operation in the history of American medicine.

When Marshall awoke just before 6 a.m., he looked at the clock on the recovery room wall and thought it was 5:30 p.m. on Saturday. Corinne came to the hospital and we were having a lively conversation with Marshall by 8 a.m. The more than 200 news media representatives who had been in touch with the hospital during the time of Marshall's hospitalization went home with something less than front page news—"McLuhan survives surgery." The front page story which had already been prepared by the *New York Times* would not be used that day.

Marshall and Corinne vacationed in the Bahamas for a couple of weeks and he went back to the classroom before Christmas. Apart from the fact that he had to ration his energy more carefully and get some extra rest, he resumed a full schedule of activities at Fordham and gave several lectures around the country. Needless to say, the second semester was a less exciting time in the Bronx. The year was topped off with a gala fifty-seventh birthday party for Marshall at the McLuhan's Bronxville home. The experience of living in that spacious house carried over into their choice of a new home in Wychwood Park in Toronto. It had been a year of living dangerously, but more importantly—it had been a year of living.

Marshall was back in Toronto but the influence of the year in New York continued, although not at Fordham. The keepers of the flame cashiered the visionary president and brought in a tidy type to run the ship. The very exciting and very possible dream was over. I resigned from Fordham and founded a not-for-profit organization to carry on the work in media. Naming it was easy—"The Center for Understanding Media." Within three years we had founded a graduate school program in Media Studies based entirely on Marshall's ideas. It is at the New School for Social Research in New York City. As far as I know, it is the only school with such a lineage with Marshall's thinking. Recently the president and trustees of the New School approved the establishment at the school of the Marshall McLuhan Chair of Communications. We are now in the process of seeking endowment funds for the Chair. His New York presence is really the story of two chairs.

This is the twenty-fifth anniversary of the publication of *Understanding Media.* I remember the excitement of reading it in galley form on a plane to Tokyo. My own feeling is that McLuhan hasn't been read by most people even for the first time. The media blitz obscured the seriousness and scope of his thinking. To me his ideas are more relevant today than ever. Interestingly, his last book, the still unpublished *Laws of the Media,* is the most direct and logically organized of any of his published work. It is as though he wanted to make sure that we wouldn't be distracted by anything but the pure ideas. On the last occasion on which we met I read the book in manuscript form and told him that I thought it would stand with the *Gutenberg Galaxy* and *Understanding Media* as the best examples of his work. Although he couldn't speak at the time, he nodded his head enthusiastically.

He was a nonesuch.

A McLuhan Symposium

Norman Mailer

He had the fastest brain of anyone I have ever met and I never knew whether what he was saying was profound or garbage. It was perfect for McLuhan to come up with a couple of famous phrases like—"the medium is the message" or "global village"—because he thought associationally. Some of his perceptions are actually startling and remarkable. "The medium is the message" is one of the most useful remarks uttered in the twentieth century.

Martin Esslin

It is a mistake to deal with McLuhan on the pedantic level. There are scientists and philosophers who deal with points of detail, and there are other people like Nietzsche, who are prophetic philosophers, whose function is not to produce a system, but to open up a whole new way of looking at things, a whole new field of knowledge. In the course of this, they tend to exaggerate things. This kind of innovatory prophetic philosopher is on a higher level, more important culturally than the person who produces a system where every actual fact fits. This detailed carping is vacuous. He will be remembered as a great discoverer, as the founding father of a new field of knowledge.

Barry Day

For most people, the trouble with McLuhan was that he refused to sit still, would never quite fit into the pigeonhole we had available for him. In time, that became disconcerting, even threatening. After all, philosophers are supposed to incubate their pet theory and then fuss with it *ad infinitum*.

McLuhan could not or would not oblige. It was as if he liked to tease us, as if his statements were a form of intellectual catharsis conducted primarily for his own benefit. (How do I know what I think until I hear what I say?)

His "insights" sprang from his passionate involvement with the process of communication and his conviction that the particular circumstances we were living in were conspiring to create a context which was no longer passive. We were being actively changed by what we beheld. The *way* we received information was now more important than the information itself. Only the beginnings of knowledge of what was now happening to us could provide survival, let alone wisdom.

Where he succeeded, he helped us put the pieces of the puzzle together to make a coherent pattern for the first time. Things you had been vaguely aware of in isolation suddenly made collective sense. You felt you had made the connection for yourself and no teacher could ask for more.

Corinne McLuhan

He was completely different from anyone I had ever known. His reactions were different, he was more self-contained. His head was working twenty-four hours a day. Often he'd get up in the middle of the night and scribble down something, or read. It wasn't a choice, he just couldn't help it. He was intellectually driven. He was always so sure of what he was, and who he was. Never any doubts. He was a very religious man and, as a matter of fact, that was the only thing that helped him through the fifteen months after his stroke. That was the core of his being—his religious strength.

Arthur M. Schlesinger, Jr.

Marx used to say changes in the modes of production determine the movement of history. What Marshall McLuhan in effect was saying was that changes in the modes of communication determine the movement of history. The point he was making was revolutionary, he made it in a faddish way. I once wrote somewhere that he seemed to be a very intelligent, very serious man who, for reasons of his own, preferred to masquerade as a charlatan. I do think that the passage from the era of print to the electronic era is going to have all sorts of reverberations on our ways of seeing, perceiving, feeling, and behaving. Marshall McLuhan was the first man since Henry Adams to call the world's attention to that in a vivid and arresting way.

William Kuhns

Since McLuhan's death there have been no major re-assessments, nor have his ideas found any serious expansion, deliberation, or exegesis. To my knowledge no one has set to work finding experimental proof for any of his hypotheses. The growth industry that McLuhan helped initiate—writings in communication theory—has for the most part roundly ignored him, preferring to distance itself from that quaint, perplexing, probably totally errant figure of a bygone time whose name carries a stigma of academic embarrassment. Most of McLuhan's writings have lapsed from print.

Meantime, our world changes, and what it changes into seems increasingly, inexpressibly confounding—as if no one, anymore, could chart, or even clearly discern, what is going on. How can a United States president achieve an incredible psychic equilibrium between Pershing missiles and jelly beans? How can the opinion polls about that president berate, bemoan and wholly sack his actions while expressing high approval of him? How can a canny, megalomaniacal Libyan despot utterly convulse sensible world opinion with acts of naked terrorism? We should miss McLuhan today: we are living in a time he would have understood.

Pierre Eliot Trudeau

Our correspondence led to an exploration of ideas. He asked questions, and I threw back questions asking him to reconcile this with that. When we began to meet he would say, don't worry about contradictions, look at them as probes, don't try to put me into conflict with my own thoughts. I found it a freeing experience. His thoughts were not essentially political, but they were an effort to explain human behavior under the impact of a new technology, and I think some of his intuitions were those of a genius. He explained to me why inflation was so dangerous politically. Because each person was somewhat diminished by inflation, his value, his worth, was less than it had been.

Like all Canadians, he was brought up in a society which was looking for its identity. That may have conditioned him to experiment with his ideas about new technologies. Canadians' distaste for heros and for successful thinkers may have also given him a certain freedom. He didn't become a celebrity in Canada first. He probably became famous in the United States or in France.

George Thompson

His mind, and his whole attitude, was that of a giant scanning machine, continuously searching the universe for the *significant idea*. He scanned everywhere—in music, education, the arts, sciences, business, industry. But of course his chief source would be literature. That's why he read so avidly and why he could pick up a book and scan it. I was going to say *skim* but Marshall never *skimmed*. He *scanned* for the significant idea. If it was there, he would grab it.

When Mrs. Stewart (McLuhan's secretary) typed something, he wouldn't reread it, he wouldn't even let her reread it, or proofread her own typing. He assumed that everything she did was perfect. She would say, "But I might have made a mistake." "No, no, no," he'd say. "It's quite all right, that's good enough. Let it go." "But I think I made a mistake!" "No you didn't." He would pull the paper out of her typewriter, stuff it in an envelope, stamp it and go marching to a post box. It had to be mailed then. His business was communicating the written and the spoken word.

We who lived on the razor's edge with Marshall, in the so-called twilight zone, stumbling, falling toward the future, experienced a peculiar sense of living that wasn't available to most people.

Charles Weingartner

In a curious way, McLuhan illustrates O.W. Holmes (Senior)'s point about the "hydrostatic paradox of controversy," one of the most relentless sources of problems in human communication. Briefly, he knows too much, at least for most who hear or read him. He speaks in highly compressed metaphors, and unless his audience is familiar with all of the discrete items compressed in his metaphors, confusion, not communication, results. It is analogous to the problem of trying to read James Joyce without having some deep familiarity with all of the things Joyce was compressing in his writing. . . . The hostility which greeted many of McLuhan's "probes" is simply an illustration of the fact that most of us regard anything different from what we already know as "weird" or "crazy"—by which we hope to symbolically reduce it to insignificance so that we can dismiss it rather than deal with it.

John Wain

McLuhan worked by sending up a shower of comparisons, analogies, wisecracks, sudden satiric jabs at people and attitudes he disliked, and equally sudden excursions into scholastic philosophy or modern advertising practice (both these last were subjects he had studied attentively), all in the service of illuminating, or preparing for illumination, whatever book or writer he was discussing. It was like riding on a roller-coaster; it also reminded me of Johnson's description of the practice of the Metaphysical poets: "The most heterogeneous ideas are yoked, by violence, together." In McLuhan's case, the violence had nothing sullen or offensive about it; it was the natural outcrop of a geniality, an impatience with conventional categories, and a willingness to have a go, and try anything for size. Most critics make an *aperçu* serve them, as theme, for a whole essay, or even a whole book; McLuhan provided an *aperçu* in virtually every line, and if they were not all equally good, if indeed some of them were unconvincing to the point of absurdity, well, there was always the interest of seeing what the man would say next; and there was a large, gusty breeze of fresh air blowing through the whole enterprise.

Tom Wolfe

I pay attention to every one of Marshall's insights, no matter how implausible they seem at the time, because he has been proven right over and over again.

In 1967, he said two wars can no longer be waged at once in the world, because journalists would only cover one. After the Arab-Israeli War, he noticed that the War in Viet Nam came to a halt because AP and UPI and all the other news services immediately packed up all of their people and sent them to the Middle East. This was followed by a remark that he made in Italy, about the Aldo Morro kidnapping. Approached by an Italian journalist who asked his opinion about the whole business, he said, "You can end the Morro incident any time you want, by just ceasing to cover it. Terrorism is an ingenious invention by which any two or more armed people can take over an entire billion-dollar industry with the complete cooperation, not only of its workers, but of its owners."

Every time I saw him, he was the same person, still exploring, always exploring all the questions anew. His stock in the world will return as people look back with a little more detachment. The insights, the aphorisms, the sayings, have forced people to reinterpret the world that they live in.

Robert Hittel

Something of great importance took place in the sixties. McLuhan gave us a glimpse of ourselves as creatures who resented the implication that we were pawns moved by environmental forces. We didn't like that glimpse and we took it out on McLuhan.

He was deeply concerned about the psychic pollution that confused our perceptions. His development of the *Laws of the Media* was a quiet attempt to construct a foundation for the understanding of technological effects that would help us explore the limits of our freedom without despair.

Pierre Emmanuel

No artist will remain indifferent to McLuhan, the only "socio-anthropological" thinker who has fully understood the prime importance of art, not only as a foretelling of the forms which roughly sketch themselves out in man, but in their role as safeguards against brutal changes in our sensory and psychic balance.

Edward T. Hall

Marshall was brilliant, but then a lot of people are brilliant, so what was it then that made the difference? He had a tremendous insight when he tied up the "media is the message" metaphor with the altered sensory mixes associated with media changes. The message of *The Galaxy* has yet to be read and understood. *The Galaxy* was a breakthrough.

Marshall represents one of the many tragic results of PR. Though famous, I would venture that he is less understood now than he was before, when a few of us were exchanging ideas in a less frenetic atmosphere. To be both successful as well as famous takes more than most people have to offer. You have to be a Shakespeare to digest this one. Marshall is a tragic lesson in the consequences of over popularization of very complex and subtle ideas. He was a great man. Much too great to be famous.

Margaret Stewart

There was a wooden plaque that hung in Marshall's Centre which bore the following inscription: *"In taberna quando sumas non curamus quid sit humus."*

Although I can neither read nor write Latin, I have always loved the sound of that language. One day I asked Marshall if he would read the words to me. After he read it to me, I said, "Marshall, that sounds *so* beautiful and soft! What does it mean?" He replied, "Well, let's see—this would have been a toast in ancient taverns, and it means—well—a quick translation would be: Here's mud in your eye!"

Hugh Kenner

Instances of his prescience multiply. Once brushed off by the *New Yorker* as a "pop philosopher," the author of *Understanding Media* is starting to look like a prophet.

So obsessed was his readership by "content" that detractor and disciple alike tended to think he was talking about the effect of the medium on the message it carries: TV is highly visual, for instance, hence its fondness for crowds and confrontations. But that barely concerned him. (He said TV was "tactile.") What obsessed him is clearer after twenty years: the effect of the mere *availability* of new media on people's sense of who and what they are.

Patrick Watson

His writings were filled with images that came to life later in my mind. I found, when I began working in the television medium, ideas such as hot and cool, linearity, the tactile nature of television, had a great effect upon my thinking and my actions as a director.

He came up with phrases which stick in the mind. They make you angry because they seemed over-simplified, but when you think about them, they're right. When I came back from France, Marshall said, in that grand way he had, "Well of course you do know that the Frenchman goes out to be social and goes home to be alone where a North American goes out to be alone and goes home to be social." He had that nice ability to do reversals when he set up a pair of lines like that.

Harold Rosenberg

Instead of discovering menace in the chatter of the disc jockey and the inanities of the commercial, or relief in New Wave films or in Shakespeare and ballet on TV, McLuhan probes beyond the content of the media to the impact of each medium itself as an art form. What takes place at any moment in the rectangle of the comic strip or on the screen of the TV set may not be worth serious reflection. But as you look, or look and listen, in the particular way demanded by the comic strip or the television image, something is slowly happening to one or more of your senses, and through that to your whole pattern of perception—never mind what gets into your mind.

As an artist working in a mixed medium of direct experience and historical analogy, he has given a needed twist to the great debate on what is happening to man in this age of technological speed-up. Other observers have been content to repeat criticisms of industrial society that were formulated a century ago, as if civilization had been steadily emptied out since the advent of the power loom. As against the image of our time as a faded photograph of a highly pigmented past, McLuhan, for all his abstractness, has found positive, humanistic meaning and the color of life in supermarkets, stratospheric flight, the lights blinking on broadcasting towers. In respect to the maladies of de-individuation, he has dared to seek the cure in the disease, and his vision of going forward into primitive wholeness is a good enough reply to those who would go back to it.

Walker Percy

The most valuable contribution—to me—of Marshall McLuhan is that he almost single-handedly laid hold of what seems obvious now but what was then invisible to everybody else. This is the subtle yet pervasive impact of the manifold media upon us who, until then, thought we were receiving the "content"— whether in print, radio, TV—without a second thought about how the "content" was transmitted and how the transmission affected it. I am not so sure about the specifics of his analysis, i.e., his "hot" and "cool" media, but I am sure about his main thesis.

His achievement is all the more impressive for coming at the very time when conventional notions about a book and what a book is "about" were being challenged by "information theory," which sought to understand communication by messages coded and sent through channels and being decoded—a theory which purported to be revolutionary but which was as naive as the popular ideas about books, TV, radio and such-like.

It occurred to McLuhan to take a look at the channel. The medium may not *be* the massage, but something is going on in its message parlor and McLuhan opened the door. He was the real revolutionary.

George Steiner

A McLuhan too fastidious or ironic to make use of the advertising power of the mass-circulation magazines or the television interview would be negating his own principal argument. He sets his readers a perpetual, irritating problem: that of reading any further. But that is his master stroke: by making of his manner a close representation of the anomalies which he observes in the act of reading, in the essential nature of human communicating, McLuhan draws us into his argument. To put him down is to let that argument pass unchallenged.

Nothing is more Blakeian in quality of vision than the notion, hinted at in *Understanding Media*, of a world falling silent as electronic means of storage and appropriate selection replace the spendthrift chaos of traditional writing and human speech. Like Ernst Bloch, like Lévi-Strauss, McLuhan has the capacity to materialize his theoretic arguments in sudden myth. He too is one of those shapers of the present mood who seems to mark a transition from the classic forms of Cartesian order to a new, as yet very difficult to define, poetic or syntax of experience.

Bruce Powers

He considered a cliché to be a form of mental paralysis, symptomatic of a society which must have a neat network of commonly accepted explanations for why things are the way they are, for stability's sake. But stability all too often leads to stasis. Like Ezra Pound's poet—an "antennae of the race"—Marshall forged a psychic sword to broach single-mindedness, what he liked to call the "probe." But here we have to be careful. The probe is not really a technique; that would be too much like a statement, an abstraction. It is not quantitative, for then it could be too easily contained and memorized. It is rather like a posture, an attitude of constant mental inquiry.

Gerald O'Grady

His critics seemed obsessed with deriving a theory from his writings, coming to them with the academic expectancy for the definitive treatment of a field called communications. They never grasped that his meaning was merged with his method, and that the method rested entirely and completely on metaphor, that every word, sentence and paragraph he wrote was part of a process to generate insight, not to establish classifications.

John Cage

I am today as indebted to McLuhan as I ever was. He was a creative critic, probably the only one there ever was. His observations of art, media, society in some cases corroborated the independent actions of artists, in other cases suggested what their next ones might rightly be.

Bruce W. Powe

McLuhan believed he had come to an understanding of the modern world. He saw himself as a "mediator," a translator of the *Zeitgeist*'s manifestations into popular and poetic terms. His aim was to alert audiences: "In a period of rapid change you have to wake up. We are all sleepwalkers, but when you're changing from one element to the other, you must be completely awake."

There was a sense in which he allowed his message to be distorted. His refusal to make clear value judgments alienated ideologically inclined thinkers, particularly Marxists and most liberal humanists. He had said: "I want to understand everything, then neutralize it. Turn off as many buttons as you can. I am resolutely opposed to all change and innovation, but I am determined to understand what's happening." Yet as McLuhan himself taught, each electronic medium imposes its bias on the receiver *beyond* the rational value judgments of those users. The misunderstandings of his insights were, as he later realized with some horror, a sensational part of the mass-age.

Jane Jacobs

Making a Movie with McLuhan

I first met Marshall McLuhan in 1969, when we had lunch together at the Faculty Club at the University of Toronto. I found him interesting and kind, but I hardly knew what to make of him as a thinker because of the way his conversation jumped about. He would say something interesting or outright brilliant which I would have liked to pursue with him and test out a little bit, but instead he would flit—or so it seemed to me—to a different idea, and from that to still another.

But although this was bewildering and a little frustrating, I found the lunch enjoyable and knew that I'd met a really remarkable man. Then Colin Vaughan called up one day and brought McLuhan over to where I lived at the time on Spadina Road. They were concerned about a tract of land just south of Wychwood Park where they both lived, which was going to be developed into hideous highrise slabs. Colin Vaughan, who is an architect, had figured that the same number of people could be housed in a decent, human way. Marshall had become involved because he saw how horrid those slabs would be right on their border. We talked about how to fight it; of course I was on their side.

Sometime later Marshall got in touch with me again. In his wonderful energetic and optimistic way, he said:

"We need a movie about the Spadina Expressway! You and I can do the script."

I said, "But I don't know a thing about scriptwriting. I won't be any use."

"Oh, I've never written one either," he said, "but we can easily do it together. Come on down to my office and we'll get to work."

I was dubious about this, but I was carried away by his

enthusiasm. We really did need a movie about the issues involved. It was a good idea, so I went to his office in the Coach House, and McLuhan called in his secretary, introduced her, and said, "She'll take down what we say."

So we talked. Both of us were enthusiastic and much of our conversation consisted of, "Hey, what about this?" followed by some notion, and "Hey, what about this?" followed by another. After we had talked for about an hour, Marshall asked the secretary, "Have you got it all down?" Then he turned to me and said, "Well, that's it. We've got the script."

"No, we don't!" I said. "It's all just 'Hey, what about this?'"

"Oh, that's immaterial," he replied.

He made a date for us to see the filmmaker, who was Christopher Chapman—the man who made "A Place to Stand." When we arrived at his studio I was handed a typed copy of the script. I started looking through it, and it was even more garbled and unreadable than I expected. It was not the secretary who had garbled it—she had done an excellent job—it was just that what Marshall and I had said was so garbled. All the "Hey, what about this's" were in there. The thing jumped around, without beginning or end. This did not bother Marshall but it did bother me. I thought we needed a thread.

Chapman also had a copy of the script in his hand, but to my mingled relief and alarm he didn't seem exactly to read it. He flipped through it, back and forth, and said congenially that it was fine; it was something to go on. He asked us a lot of questions about the issues, Marshall went off and I remained a while longer to answer some more questions. That's all I did.

Once in a while Marshall phoned and said everything was going fine, and in due course invited me to a viewing. I couldn't have been more astonished that there even *was* a film. Marshall had obviously done lots more work on it. The name of the movie was "A Burning Would." The title was, of course, Marshall's.

There was a shape to it. It had music. It did have a thread and raised a lot of important issues. Colin Vaughan provided an excellent narration. It was a good movie; furthermore, it was shown a lot, especially in the United States. For a long time I would get an occasional letter from this or that group in California saying that they had shown the movie. However, the final product bore no relationship at all to our original script.

That was my experience of writing a script with Marshall McLuhan. I'm still as bewildered about scriptwriting as I was when I began. It's a mystery to me that something tangible, coherent and constructive could come out of that mess. I'm still bewildered about Marshall too. I used to think that if I had his brain I'd go nuts, living with all those skittering thoughts not put into order—chaos and confusion. But of course it wasn't awful for him. He relished it. He was at peace with those dazzling sparks and fragments. He was not a disintegrated man, but the opposite. I saw that his brilliance swiftly opened up whole avenues of thought even if you had some suspicions about them. Like our movie, Marshall really got somewhere.

Another movie experience of mine had an analogous relevance here. In 1941, when Orson Welles's *Citizen Kane* was released, I went to see it and was both entranced and puzzled. *Citizen Kane* was radically different from any other movie I'd seen. It jumped around without warning or explanation. You had to provide the order, or so it seemed, and you weren't always quite sure just what you had seen. Decades later when I went to see *Citizen Kane* again, I wondered how I could have felt that way about it. The movie now seemed so straightforward. What had changed in the meantime was that other filmmakers had learned from *Citizen Kane*. We had become accustomed to its swift, fragmented style.

McLuhan's work may now strike people as *Citizen Kane* did its early viewers. I suspect that Marshall was ahead of his time, and it may be that his work will assume an order that people don't yet easily see.

Marshall McLuhan

Why the TV Child Cannot See Ahead
The Unconscious Bias of the Visual Mode:
A Note on the Meaning of *Mosaic*

One reader of the *Galaxy* made a comment to the author that he found quite startling. It was also a very helpful remark, and had it been possible to have heard it when the book was being written, there would have been a little preface to explain the nature of the "mosaic" approach used in the book. The reader's remark was simply this, "You obviously expect your readers to have read a great many books." On the contrary, the writer of the *Galaxy* intended to spare his readers the task of reading a great many books. The quotes and excerpts that are arranged in mosaic form from many sources are themselves the material that it is needful to know from these books. These excerpts are not just references. They are structures that embody special kinds of perception and awareness. Each is a kind of example or anecdote. Each is a kind of little world that needs to be apprehended in depth. For this reason it is not at all necessary to read them in any special sequence. They are, however, a mosaic, and, like a mosaic, they are not just to be seen, but to be perceived by all our senses. Highly literate people in our Western world are naturally confused whenever they move across the boundaries of visual order and arrangement. But mosaic form, although it can be seen, is not visual in its organizing principle.

It will be well to clarify this matter as far as possible since it concerns not only the habitual modes of visual awareness in literate society, but even more does it concern the nonvisual modes of awareness and organization of experience in the new electric age. Phonetic literacy is an extension of the body in the way that wheel or clothing are extensions of the body. Electricity, however, is not an extension of any position of the body but rather of the central nervous system itself. That is, the instant character of electricity introduces the principle of interrelation that is antithetic to all earlier technologies which in effect had fragmented and extended the body by way of specialism and amplification.

The effect of phonetic literacy in extending and amplifying the visual component in Western experience and social organization was to create a sort of hypertrophy in our visual lives at the expense of the other senses. This situation exists even among our scientists who make assumptions about the natural order of things as if this order were primarily visual in respect to uniformity and continuity and connectiveness. The same situation can be tested in the ordinary inability to discriminate between the photographic and the TV image which is not merely a crippling factor in the learning process today; it is symptomatic of an age-old failure in Western culture. The literate man, accustomed to an environment in which the visual sense is extended everywhere as a principle of organization, sometimes supposes that the mosaic world of primitive art or even the world of Byzantine art, represents a mere difference in degree, a sort of technical failure to bring their visual portrayals up to the level of full visual effectiveness. Nothing could be further from the truth. This, in fact, is a misconception that has impaired understanding between colored and white societies. There is a very large stake in proper understanding of the differences in our sense orientations effected by technological extensions of our bodies and our nervous systems.

Unawareness of the specific modalities of the senses is a great disadvantage, especially when one encounters artistic extensions and amplifications of the various senses. The traditional arts of dance and song and sculpture, iconography and celatura extend, heighten, and orchestrate the human senses, as indeed does human speech itself. The arts of any culture in expressing the preferential bias of the culture also channel the perceptions of the culture, providing a basis for the observation that "nature imitates art."

Unlike the arts, the technologies of a culture specialize in extending one sense at a time, whereas the arts involve all the senses at once, like speech. The wheel extends the kinetic movement of feet in a specialized way. The tribal drum extends hearing in a specialist mode. Clothing extends skin and heat control in a specialist way. Each of these extensions or amplifications, in turn, involves all the other senses, modifying their relation to each other. While, like the arts, the technologies of a culture involve all the senses, like technology, the arts appear to have a sense bias. For example, painting at first glance is a visual art, poetry an auditory one. However, this casual interpretation of the sense bias of the arts does not stand up to scrutiny. Painting can have a tactile stress as is evident in the reified images of iconography. Poetry can have a visual rather than an auditory bias as in the poetry of Wordsworth. Technology, because of its drive toward amplification, is quite explicit in its separation of the senses. Radio is an extension of the aural, high-fidelity photography of the visual. All forms whether of art or technology, if not for their impact, then in our reactions, involve all the senses, as does that initiator of the mode of specialized extension, speech itself.

For Western man, however, the decisive extension occurred by means of phonetic writing which is a technology for extending the sense of sight. By making both sight and sound semantically meaningless, phonetic writing was able to provide a visual means of reducing the characteristics of speech to a visual code, which also made possible the extension of speech in time and space in a way quite unlike any pictographic or ideogramic form of writing. All nonphonetic forms of writing are, in effect, artistic modes that retain much variety of sensuous orchestration and, indeed, much of the original speech mode. They include much of the semantic complexity as well. Phonetic writing has, by comparison, the power of separating and fragmenting the senses and of sloughing off the semantic complexities.

It is the visual stress in phonetic writing that makes it primarily an extension of the visual faculty, and makes it necessary for literate people to understand the modality of the visual sense. Alex Leighton once said: "to the blind all things are sudden," drawing attention to a dominant characteristic of the visual. To the seeing man nothing is sudden. To the phonetically literate, the extension of the visual power in space and time endows him with a sense of continuity, of sequence and of transition, of causes and effect quite beyond the power of him who lacks this amplification of the visual power. The phonetically literate acquires detachment and noninvolvement that applies not only to his sense life but to his psychic and social life. He has, in fact, through literacy, the means of de-tribalizing himself, of becoming progressively less deeply involved in all situations. In literate societies, most people are unconsciously involved in the attitudes of detachment. They are apt to be aware of the assumptions and structures of all societies save their own.

The visual stress on continuity and sequential transition, as it relates to literacy, confronts us with the great technological means of implementing continuity and lineality by fragmented repetition. The ancient world found this means in the brick, whether for wall or road. They also conceived of phonetic letters as "the dragon's teeth." For the only part of the animal body that has a lineal character of sequential repetition is found in the jaw with its teeth. It was an apt observation to note phonetic letters as extensions of the teeth, both visually and functionally, for literacy confers the power of reducing and homogenizing whole cultures as the Hellenic and Roman empires testify.

The repetitive, uniform brick, indispensable agent of road and wall, of cities and empires, is an extension, via letters, of the visual sense. The brick wall is not a mosaic form. The mosaic form is not a visual structure. The mosaic can be seen as dancing can, but is not structured visually; nor is it an extension of the visual power. For the mosaic is not uniform, continuous or repetitive. It is discontinuous, skew and nonlineal. To the sense of touch all things are sudden, counter, original, spare, strange. The "Pied Beauty" of G.M. Hopkins is a catalogue of the notes of the sense of touch. The poem is a manifesto of the nonvisual. The nonvisual mosaic structures of modern art, like those of modern physics and electric formation patterns, permit little detachment. The mosaic form demands participation and involvement in depth, of the whole being, as does the sense of touch. Literacy had, by extending the visual power to the organization of time and space, psychically and socially, conferred the power of detachment and noninvolvement. Phonetic literacy liberated the individual from the tribe and even from the state. It gave the power to act without reacting, the power to transform cultures and environments in a spirit of indifference. Electricity (the extension of the central nervous system) by contrast permits no detachment. In the electric age, all is involvement, touch, mosaic and reaction in depth. The spirit of ecology and unification supplants the habit of specialism, of fragmentation and detachment.

The visual sense when extended by phonetic literacy fosters

the analytic habit of perceiving the single facet in the life of forms. The visual power enables us to isolate the single incident in time and space as in representational art. In visual representation of a person or an object a single phase or aspect is separated from the multitude of known phases and aspects of the person or object. By contrast, iconographic art uses the eyes as we use our hand in seeking to create an inclusive image, a moment made up of all the phases or aspects of the person or thing. This is not visual representation, nor the specialization of visual stress as defined by viewing from a single position. The tactual mode of perceiving is sudden, but not specialist. It is total, synesthetic, involving all the senses.

In a very real sense the icon form is a mosaic, even as the mosaic tends to be iconographic. That is, the icon form is a composite of discontinuous spaces and experiences, not unlike a paneled narrative in a medieval saint's life. The visual or representational mode selects a salient moment in the life of a form or a situation. The mosaic necessarily uses a multiplicity of salient moments—moments that are discontinuous in experience, but able to include a lifetime of individual awareness or the unified insight of a whole community. The mosaic unity can manage a diversity of experiences gathered in a single life, or a traditional awareness developed in a communal life. The extension and specialism of the visual sense, developed in literate societies, stresses an individual point of view that precludes traditional and communal "overview."

Such "overview" is inherent in the very mode of mosaic as it is in the vision of the airmen. From the air the space below is flat and discontinuous, as in a mosaic. The patterns of stress and action in the total field of vision are revealed ecologically, in depth. Paradoxically, a point of view in its specialist intensity excludes depth, even as it omits the interplay of forces. The visual demand for lineal connection in sequence cannot cope with the simultaneous interplay of diverse forces. Literate man expects that he can reduce such diversity to uniformity of action in space and time.

The problem of distinguishing between the inherent nature and the psychic and social consequences of such different images as the photograph and TV can be mentioned by way of a footnote. Technically, and structurally, the photograph possesses in an extreme form all the features of the extended visual sense. The photograph is a repeat on hi-fi of the visual fact without any intervention of the other senses. It is the hi-fi repeat character of the photograph that minimizes participation of the other senses. The TV image is a low-fi mosaic (coarse screen) of the visual world. It is achieved by a scanning finger that ideally follows contours and requires very much participation and involvement of the viewer. The TV image is to the photograph what the handmade manuscript was to the printed page. The manuscript was a non-uniform mosaic, very close to tapestry in its sensuous effect and involvement. The TV image, that is to say, even more than the icon, is an extension of the sense of touch. Where it encounters a literate culture, it necessarily thickens the sense-mix, transforming fragmented and specialist extensions into a seamless web of experience. Such transformation is, of course, a "disaster" for a literate, specialist culture. It confuses many cherished attitudes and procedures. It dims the efficacy of the basic pedagogic techniques. If for no other reason it would be well to understand the dynamic life of these forms as they intrude upon us and on one another. The young people who have experienced a decade of TV (to cite only the most obvious mosaic form of our electric age) have naturally imbibed an urge toward involvement in depth that makes all the remote visualized goals of usual culture seem not only unreal but irrelevant, and not only irrelevant but anemic. It is the total involvement in all-inclusive nowness that occurs in young lives via TV's mosaic image. This change of attitude has nothing to do with programming in any way, and would be the same if the programs consisted entirely of the highest cultural content. The change in attitude by means of relating themselves to the mosaic TV image would occur in any event. It is, of course, our job not only to understand this change but to exploit it for its pedagogical richness. The TV child expects involvement and doesn't want a specialist *job* in the future. He does want a *role* and a deep commitment to his society. Unbridled and misunderstood, this richly human need can manifest itself in the distorted forms portrayed in *West Side Story.*

The TV child cannot see ahead because he wants involvement, and he cannot accept a fragmentary and merely visualized goal or destiny in learning or in life.

Footnote

It was the assassination of President Kennedy that first brought home to many people the extraordinary change that TV has brought into all of our lives. Few people would have predicted how profound a response we all made to this event. Ten years of television have created a great degree of involvement, even for Canadians, in the role and office of the American presidency. The same event prior to TV would have had an altogether more sensational character. By press and radio, the coverage and effect would have been violent. Covered by TV, the event became numbing and profound. There was no excitement. There was a depth of numbness as in grief itself. People were moved, but not excited. Such is the pattern and structure of this unique medium. It involves people in a degree of communal participation for which we have had no example, save in human speech itself. It is this kind of effect of depth and total involvement that is being felt by all levels of thought and feeling, as of learning and action in the electric age. Specialized and fragmented patterns of perception and experience cannot hold up against the dynamic pressure of electric awareness.

Fred Thompson

Monday Night Sessions

Marshall McLuhan's return from Fordham brought with it a great surge of curiosity, and for some an opportunity to study under him. It was as though his analogy that "water probably wasn't discovered by a fish" had worked itself in reverse. Instead of the fish discovering water by jumping out of it, Canada had discovered McLuhan when he left for the United States.

The curious were allowed to listen to him. Some twenty or so were privileged to study under him in his Monday evening seminars on media and society. The classes however were not the normal classes where knowledge is to be picked up, stored and retrieved from the proper places in the textbook. A textbook didn't exist. In its place there was a large reading list from which the students were to choose three books in preparation for the final examination. This and a paper to be delivered in the second term of the course were to make up the final mark.

The first seminar was held in an old building on the Saint Michael's College campus at the University of Toronto. A crowd of people standing, sitting, crowding in the hall and doorways was met by McLuhan saying, "Let's start with an A and see what we can do about it." These were the first words spoken to a packed house of people still wondering which were students and which were spectators. It was the start of a series of seminars whose pedagogical base turned out to be similar to the original meaning of the word "encyclopedia—a circular or complete education." An education by example, an education by role playing, it was quite different from the later meaning of "encyclopedia—a work containing information on all branches of knowledge, usually arranged alphabetically, 1644."

McLuhan had no sooner started the seminar than his sense of wit came to the fore with the comment that "the reason universities are so full of knowledge is that the students come with so much and they leave with so little." An immediate burst of laughter revealed that many people had been caught off guard. They knew it was funny, but they didn't know why and McLuhan wasn't about to tell them. He was merely pushing people to discover the hidden ground which surrounded them. He hadn't invented the joke, he had merely uncovered it. And so the evening continued, "so far so good as the suicide victim was heard to say as he passed the outside of the fortieth floor of the Empire State Building on his way down." For many, there was a sense of bewilderment, and for the remainder who stood as spectators there was curiosity as to what might happen to the victims. Yet McLuhan, although he was witty and often intense in his attacks on ignorance, was a kind man whose generosity was such a part of his hidden background that few chose to dwell on the man in any other role than that of a media critic.

McLuhan's role was that of an educator, who, by example, begins to affect the way his students perceive things. He forced them to make their own realities rather than to match his. You remembered something because it struck a note. The note was internalized. Those who wrote down what they heard found themselves with notes which stuck well to the paper, but had little meaning after the event. Instead of facts there were aphorisms and probes which by themselves had little meaning until they were used as sounding boards for what you had already experienced in one form or another.

One or two weeks after the beginning of term, the classes were moved to the Coach House on Queen's Park and McLuhan was to sit in his chair and carry out his act for two hours every Monday night for the rest of the year. To describe the contents of the seminars would be a disservice to McLuhan whose intent was to observe process patterns rather than to frame ideas. McLuhan the actor reminded me of James R. Brandon's remark about Kabuki actors in the Japanese theater, "Recognition of the actor-as-actor is made explicit . . . of course it is a joke for an actor to refer to himself or any other actor by name, but the Japanese spectator considered it a perfectly reasonable joke. After all, an actor is an actor, even when playing a role." (The Western "realistic" convention of pretending that actors do not exist on stage but only characters do is much more fanciful.)[1]

As the seminars went on, participation became clearer. The audience could call upon the actor and encourage him. Sometimes this ploy would break down. Someone would try to raise a debate and as Johan Huizinga has implied in *Homo Ludens* playing by the rules and cheating are acceptable, but a spoiled sport ruins the game.[2] When this happened, there was chaos. The teacher would turn to Barry Nevitt and say, "Who is that guy?" Barry, of course, was such an integral part of the McLuhan seminars that he would topple the situation back to play again rather as a clown might distract the spectator from a shift in scene.

All went well for the first term with students and audience mixed together in one rollicking chorus. The blow came after Christmas. McLuhan's first seminar of the winter term followed the normal pattern. A guest was present. One of McLuhan's colleagues had invited a friend of his, a Cree Indian, to the seminar. McLuhan started in his usual way by giving some witty remark and then turned to his colleague and asked him if he would like to introduce his friend. The Indian put his hand on his friend's arm and said, "You shouldn't have to introduce me to Mr. McLuhan. If I am your friend, that is enough." That was not the blow I meant, it was merely a matter of getting the act together and it took a Canadian Indian to demonstrate what tribalism was all about. The real blow came at the end of the seminar when McLuhan said, "Well, . . . who is going to give the first paper next week?" There was a silence in which even the carpeted floor could be heard. The new tribe was being called together and separated from the spectators. The pause seemed everlasting until McLuhan said, "Well, . . . I told you last term that we would be having papers this term—what about it?" Finally, after what seemed an endless passage of time, Derrick de Kerckhove said, "I'll volunteer to go second." With that remark, confidence was restored and yours truly, sitting on the floor beside McLuhan, piped up with, "Well, if he will go second, I'll go first." The looks of amazement on the faces of the spectators and disbelief on the faces of my friends was enough to make me laugh. After all, McLuhan had said, "Let's start with an A and see what we can do about it," and so far nobody else had set the standard so why not take the A and run with it? It's rather like academic tenure—until you have it, you don't have to worry about defending it.

My topic was to be the Japanese sense of space known as MA[3] so I was dubbed "the Japanese Sandman" and was followed by Derrick de Kerckhove. The variety of topics chosen by the remainder of the group and the ways of presenting them were uniquely fitted to the way McLuhan had chosen students to work with him. At one seminar a medical doctor presented a stack of manila folders of agencies studying cancer, the point being that solutions to cancer probably existed, but there was inevitably no way of coordinating the material available in order to confirm the proposition. One seminar on planning, which went on endlessly, was greeted by McLuhan going to the water fountain to bring back two paper cups of water for two people in the audience and then another two until everybody had been served a paper cup of cold water. For some people, the play was a success; for some it was merely a rehearsal; and for others it was definitely an intermission.

Richard Scheckner in his article "Performers and Spectators Transported and Transformed"[4] says that "Theatrical reality is marked . . . non-ordinary—for special use only." He goes on to say, "Performance behavior isn't free and easy. Performance behavior is known and/or practiced behavior—or 'twice behaved behavior'—'restored behavior'—either rehearsed, previously known, learned by osmosis since early childhood, revealed during the performance by masters, guides, gurus or elders, or generated by rules that govern the outcomes as in improvisatory theatre or sports." Scheckner was not talking about McLuhan's seminars but he was talking about the form of encyclic knowledge which was gained as part of a circular or complete education. For "Truth is what acting is all about; once you can fake truth you've got it made."[5] There are many other comments by Scheckner which support McLuhan's policy, such as, "But the Greeks wanted to reduce the possibility that the two competitions—one in writing, the other in acting—although they occurred at the same time and used the same medium, and clearly affected one another, would in practice be reduced to one." McLuhan's references on the effects of alphabetic literacy were instead based on Eric Havelock's writing entitled *Preface to Plato*.[6]

The final exam was to be a thirty-minute test based on any three books out of a reading list of thirty-five. In my mind, the question was, how was McLuhan going to pose the questions in such a way as to find out (a) if we had read three books, (b) which three books, (c) how could he ask one question for each and (d) how would he ever mark them? I was lucky. I had not only read three books, but one-half hour before the exam, using McLuhan's method of probing, I guessed what he would do. He came into the seminar room, took off his coat and hat and said, "Everybody got a pencil and paper? Fine. Take thirty minutes to write down three questions on each of the books you've read." Through this kind of examination, McLuhan was able to (i) explore our ignorance to his advantage, (ii) mark the papers in less time than it took us to write them. Through constant disorientation (a curious word in this context) people began to assume their roles as part of the ongoing study of media and society. Scheckner says, "I call performances where performers are changed 'transformations' and those where performers are returned to their starting places 'transportations.' 'Transportations' because during the perform-ance the performers are 'taken somewhere' but at the end, often assisted by others, they are 'cooled down' and re-enter ordinary life just about where they went in."[7]

McLuhan had been the "transporter" and it wasn't until my initiation at Waterloo Lutheran that I realized how one could take on the role. The students' union had asked McLuhan and Richard Needham to engage in a debate on education as an introduction to the freshman year. McLuhan may have been the "transporter" but he didn't like being transported outside of Toronto so he phoned me at the University of Waterloo and said that I could go on stage for him. When I gracefully declined, he assured me that I could take on the task and that if I merely dissected my opponent's name, I could see what was required of me.

I accepted the challenge in fear and trepidation until I saw the arrangements for Needham, myself and the adjudicator. The three of us were to sit on a stage, behind a table facing the audience with one microphone which was to be passed between us when it was our turn to speak. With good sequential gaps of communication between us created by the time it took to pass around the microphone, there was ample time to conjure up a reply and propose another argument. It turned out rather like a Donald Duck comic strip on education. The microphone was always in search of connections. The effect of the medium was such as to make the debate distant and disconnected.

The question of a change of medium bringing about a transformation of content had struck me earlier when I had gone to the Huron Street School to study "communications" in the kindergarten class. I sat down at the table in the center of the room with my tape recorder and a group of very lively children. All seemed to be going as planned until one little boy asked me what I was doing with the tape recorder. When I replied that I was going to use it to record what the children said, he replied, "Don't you know that people don't talk with their mouths, they talk with their eyes?" This has subsequently led me into the study of creativity and how it survives when people work together on a project. Using television instead of the tape recorder, we have been able to agree with research that says approximately 7 percent of the communications in most meetings is dependent upon an exchange of words, 38 percent upon the tone of the voices communicating, and 55 percent on nonverbal language. It is said of the Japanese, who are highly efficient at lending themselves to a meeting, that "they are always observant of other people. They are intuitive and pay attention. The difference is not in their way of speaking, but in their way of listening. And they watch better. They hear with their eyes and see with their ears.[8] Their awareness of all that surrounds them increases their knowledge so that they can transform a potential conflict into a new resolution rather than merely reacting to it in the form of a debate.

Thus the circular education is not only the making of an encyclopedia; it is also the creation of an attitude. McLuhan encouraged the artist in everyone to come alive. It was not something which could be taught, but rather something which could be caught. In architectural terms, one can teach a student to write a program for a building although it is difficult to draw and build the building to fit that program. If this could be done to perfection, the process should be able to work in reverse, rather like a mystery story which is written backwards. There are few buildings of lasting interest that can be understood in this manner. Just take a building that fascinates you, look at it carefully, and try to play detective by writing the program which might originally have been given to the architect. No two programs will look alike. Only by studying the environmental effect can we uncover the hidden program which makes the building relevant to us. Father Ong, speaking of the Methodist Ramus, has said that, "Ideologically, the world of sound has yielded unwittingly but quite effectively to the world of space."[9] The printed program can arrest space conceptually, while our perception allows it to slip away.

On the eighteenth of January 1984, a CBC news broadcaster announced that the effect of prostitution was such as to make a car a "public space." McLuhan once said that the moon walkers changed the moon from a monument into a junk yard. Would he have added that prostitution had put terrestrial space on the move again? or would he merely refer to the radio news by saying, "The ear turns man over to universal panic."[10]

McLuhan Probes

The higher an executive gets inside any big organization, the sooner he drops out; because he has less and less to do with the operations.

We are as numb in our electric world as the native involved in our literate and mechanical culture.

We have confused reason with literacy and rationalism with a single technology.

Today each of us lives several hundred years in a decade. How can people like us have something in common with their institutions?

Paradox is the technique for seizing the conflicting aspects of any problem. Paradox coalesces or telescopes various facets of a complex process in a single instant.

The ecumenical movement is synonymous with electric technology.

Neither Socrates nor Plato was aware that analytic impulses and the isolated examination of the private self are the effect of phonetic literacy.

Typography cracked the voices of silence.

The effect of extending the central nervous system is not to create a world-wide cry of ever-expanding dimensions but rather a global village of ever-contracting size.

Man's right to his own ignorance might be said to be his principal means of private identity.

"Numbed to death by booze and tranquilizers" is an average strategy for "keeping in touch" with a runaway world.

Tribal man has no awareness of sex in our fragmented sense.

A cliché is an act of consciousness: total consciousness is the sum of all the clichés of all media or technologies we probe with.

The artist is the man in any field, scientific or humanistic, who grasps the implications of his actions and new knowledge in his own time. He is the man of integral awareness.

The unconscious is a direct creation of print technology, the ever-mounting slag-heap of repeated awareness.

Communication, creativity, and growth occur together or they do not occur at all. New technology creating new basic assumptions at all levels for all enterprises is wholly destructive if new objectives are not orchestrated with the new technological motifs.

New art is sensory violence on the frontiers of experience.

There is no storyline in modern art or news—just a date line. There is no past or future, just an inclusive present.

Marshall McLuhan

Inside on the Outside,
or the Spaced-Out American

Probing the hidden element of space
behind such diverse phenomena as privacy,
group speech, television, facial behavior,
and literacy suggests that "simultaneous structures . . .
are eating out the heart of American institutions."

North Americans may well be the only people in the world
who go outside to be alone and inside to be social. This hidden
ground of our corporate awareness surfaced for me when I was to
give a talk to some British advertisers about the North American
attitude to advertising. By way of illustrating the considerable
difference between the two attitudes, I mentioned our resistance
and rejection of ads in movies. For some years I had mentioned
this attitude to graduate students who were quite aware that
Europeans make no objection to advertising in theaters and
movies, until one student volunteered the observation: "We take
our dates to movies to be alone, and don't wish to have our privacy
invaded." At that point I began to make more observations
concerning our attitudes to space in domestic and public buildings, and also our attitudes to space as expressed in literature.

The North American quest for privacy out-of-doors, and our
turning indoors to the home as a friendly group space holds very
firm in Thoreau and Whitman and in Henry James and many
others. Reading Lord Durham's *1839 Report* I was struck by the
following passage:

The provision which in Europe, the State makes for the
protection of its citizens against foreign enemies, is in

America required for what a French writer has beautifully and accurately called the "war with the wilderness." The defense of an important fortress, or the maintenance of a sufficient army or navy in exposed spots, is not more a matter of concern to the European, than is the construction of the great communications to the American settler; and the State, very naturally, takes on itself the making of the works, which are matters of concern to all alike.[1]

What stood out starkly for me was the phrase "war with the wilderness." I suddenly realized that this phrase defined our attitude to the out-of-doors and our typical acceptance of the indoors as a friendly refuge. Since then, Margaret Atwood's remarks in *Survival* have increased my awareness of the hidden *ground* of our attitudes to inner and outer space:

> The war against Nature assumed that Nature was hostile to begin with; man could fight and lose, or he could fight and win. If he won he would be rewarded: he could conquer and enslave Nature, and, in practical terms, exploit her resources. But it is increasingly obvious to some writers that man is now more destructive towards Nature than Nature can be towards man; and, furthermore, that the destruction of Nature is equivalent to self-destruction on the part of man.[2]

Whereas we accept the phone as an invader of our
homes, we are by no means ready to leap outside our homes
for socializing in the way which the videophone demands.

Maybe that is why Bell Telephone had to give up the videophone after spending millions on research and experiments. Picking up the videophone, we are literally "on the air" as much as if we were in a broadcasting studio. North Americans have not developed institutions suited to socializing away from home. It is not only in the movie and in the theater that we seek privacy, but also at restaurants and in nightclubs.

Another problem of the videophone relates to a very deep factor in the North American idea of going outside the home. We are probably the only people in the First World who use only our private voices when we leave our homes. British and Europeans alike put on a group voice, or some variety of "standard" English, French, German, etc. In contrast, we associate group voices in America with unassimilated ethnic groups and Southerners, considering all of these to be socially comic. Group, rather than private, voices are normal in all the rest of the world, forming the principal base of class society. It would seem possible, then, that the reason for the classless character of American society is not so much economic, as the use of private instead of group speech. Whenever group speech surfaces as a form of elitism in America, it at once becomes part of the repertory of humor.

The North American also goes outside to be alone, both for work and for play, so that the coffee break as a form of socializing on company time can be remembered by many as a kind of social revolution. The English Charlie Chaplin was so struck by this strange lack of sociability of North Americans in public places that he based his entire saga on the little man who goes out and finds nobody to talk with. Chaplin's films stress the failure of policemen to chat, and also of waiters and employers, and even of fellow workers. Recently a French visitor was reporting that Europeans take for granted that the Chaplin saga is a documentary of American life. The same Frenchman spoke of the alarm felt in France at the obvious (to them) decline of intellectual life seen in the smaller numbers of diners at cafes. We, on the other hand, try to measure the level of intellectual life by the number of serious books read at home in silence and privacy.

D.H. Lawrence, in his introduction to Edward Dahlberg's *Bottom Dogs*, may well have misread the entire American attitude to the out-of-doors and to social life by imposing his U.K. idea of uniformity on the American. He read the American need for privacy when out-of-doors as a metaphysical revulsion from human contact as such, completely unaware of the *figure-ground* relationship whereby the American finds indoors the warmth and sociability which the European cultivates outside the home. It is true that Lawrence perceived the American as *figure* against the *ground* of a vast and recalcitrant continent. However, Lawrence transferred his U.K. feeling for inner and outer spaces to a new world which long before had radically reversed the older use and meaning of these forms:

This is, roughly, the American position today, as it was the position of the Red Indian when the white man came, and of the Aztec and of the Peruvian. So far as we can make out, neither Redskin nor Aztec nor Inca had any conception of a "good" god. They conceived of implacable, indomitable Powers, which is very different. And that seems to me the essential American position today. Of course the white American believes that man should behave in a kind and benevolent manner. But this is a social belief and a social gesture, rather than an individual flow. The flow from the heart, the warmth of fellow-feeling which has animated Europe and been the best of her humanity, individual, spontaneous, flowing in the thousands of little passionate currents often conflicting, this seems unable to persist on the American soil. Instead you get the social creed of benevolence and uniformity, a mass will, and an inward individual retraction, an isolation, an amorphous sepa-rateness like grains of sand, each grain isolated upon its own will, its own indomitableness, its own implacability, its own unyielding, yet heaped together with all the other grains. This makes the American mass the easiest mass in the world to rouse, to move. And probably, under a long stress, it would make it the most difficult mass in the world to hold together.[3]

If Europeans complain about our lack of friendliness in elevators and restaurants and theaters, visitors to Europe have long com-plained about how seldom they get to visit any European homes.

The entire paradox of the "reversed space" of the North American frustrated Henry James who made it a psychological crux in his novels, regarding it as "the complex fate" of being American. James's delight in presenting his American *personae* to European bewilderment is a very rich subject indeed, but one which depends entirely on understanding the peculiar American quest for solitude in the wilderness, and discovering thereby a privacy and a psychic dimension which Europeans cannot encom-pass or understand. The conflict in the mind of Henry James had occurred earlier in the life and work of Hawthorne. The latter had also confused the North American quest for privacy out-of-doors with a weak concession of autocratic values and thereby a betrayal of democratic values. In going outside to be social, the European seemed more democratic than the North American going outside to be alone.

> To state the case succinctly: Hawthorne's compulsive affirmation of American positives, particularly in the political sense, led to a rejection of the idea of solitude; and solitude as an expression of aristocratic withdrawal sided with Europe rather than America when the two traditions stated their respective claims.[4]

Henry James finally clarified the conflict by a confession about his personal life which he confided to Hamlin Garland:

> He became very much in earnest at last and said something which surprised and gratified me. It was an admission I had not expected him to make. "If I were to live my life over again," he said in a low voice, and fixing upon me a somber glance, "I would be an American. I would steep myself in America, I would know no other land. I would study its beautiful side. The mixture of Europe and America which you see in me has proved disastrous. It has made of me a man who is neither American nor European. I have lost touch with my own people, and I live here alone. My neighbors are friendly, but they are not of my blood, except remotely. As a man grows old he feels these conditions more than when he is young. I shall never return to the United States, but I wish I could."[5]

Perhaps the most obvious and least noticed
feature of going outside to be alone in North America
is seen in the role of the car in our lives.

The North American car is designed and used for privacy. Unlike the European car, it is a big enclosed space, well suited to the business of meditation and decision-making. Almost as much as TV, the car demands peripheral vision which undermines the "tunnel vision" needed for reading. The motor car, then, for us is not only a means of transportation, but a way of achieving a deeply needed privacy when outside.

It goes without saying that there is very little privacy in the North American home because we do not seek it there but, rather, outside in our cars. An unexpected factor in changing our attitudes to the inside and outside is in TV itself. TV brings the outside (with all its dangers and violence) into the peacefulness of our homes. If we began 200 years ago by assuming that to be out-of-doors was to be violent in the course of subduing Nature, then this pattern persists in the programming of TV.

The inside/outside flip provides a key to another very special problem—the North American physiognomy.

It has long been a mystery to students of the human countenance why North Americans should have, as Henry James has suggested, "so much countenance and so little face." On this subject W.H. Auden commented in *The Dyers Hand*:

> Every European visitor to the United States is struck by the comparative rarity of what he would call a face, by the frequency of men and women who look like elderly babies. If he stays in the States for any length of time, he will learn that this cannot be put down to a lack of sensibility—the American feels the joys and sufferings of human life as keenly as anybody else. The only plausible explanation I can find lies in his different attitude to the past. To have a face, in the European sense of the word, it would seem that one must not only enjoy and suffer but also desire to preserve the memory of even the most humiliating and unpleasant experiences of the past.
>
> More than any other people, perhaps, the Americans obey the scriptural injunction: "Let the dead bury their dead."
>
> When I consider others I can easily believe that their bodies express their personalities and that the two are inseparable. But it is impossible for me not to feel that my body is other than I, that I inhabit it like a house, and that my face is a mask which, with or without my consent, conceals my real nature from others.[6]

Auden here seems clearly to indicate that Americans do not go outside to socialize facially, whereas Europeans put on a mask when they go outside, in order to preserve their privacy.

The strategy would seem to apply to speech where the American refuses to put on a group voice which would serve to mask his private self, whereas the European uses the "standard" speech as a corporate mask to preserve privacy.

Sorel Etrog, the international sculptor, has illustrated the inside/outside conundrum. The Etrog world presents the tension between the old organic visual world and the new electronic discarnate man. He enacts the conflict between the images of the old assembly line and the pull towards the holistic new primitive man of electric circuitry. The clash between the old connected world and the new world of postures and intervals is dramatized in the mobile hinge metaphors which present a world that grabs but does not relate to traditional values.

The Etrog drama is a conflict between rigid hardware and completely flexible modules that are forms of instant replay. This is a drama of dialogue and interchange between experience and meaning, between percept and concept, which yields up the secrets of the ancient skeleton. Etrog's art reveals the inescapable attention between the outside and the inside as they exchange roles in a space/time action of visions and re-visions. Etrog's images take up where the machine left off with its approximation of primitive abstract art.

In the electric age the mechanical world automatically becomes an art form, an art language of old clichés being transformed into new archetypes. The contemporary world experiences a transformation of the old machine and its consumer products into transcended images of art and archaeology. The mechanical age had pushed man into the machine mold. The man who had been subdued into a mechanism by time/motion studies in the early twentieth century now rebels and flips into his integral primitive state of space/time once more.

Let me conclude with an observation on literacy and illiteracy which Newsweek *evoked by its allusions to me, and then rejected as "over the heads of our readers."*[7]

I realize this is a tantalizing, teasing sort of footnote to a big subject. My feeling, however, is that it is best to put out these observations as a probe if only in order to get some feedback.

This note points to some other facts of the perception and recognition of space. I refer especially to the *fission* experienced by Western man only, from the phonetic alphabet. The separating of our visual faculties from the rest of the sensorium by the phonetic alphabet is nowadays being reversed by electronic experience, and especially by TV.

In the piece "Why Johnny Can't Write" I am cited as a prophet of the current literacy crisis, saying "Literary culture is through."[8] TV simply shaped totally different situations for readers and writers alike. On the one hand, the TV image, with its simultaneous but discontinuous mosaic of millions of illuminated points, is not so much a visual as an acoustic image. Tony Schwartz puts it very well in *The Responsive Chord* when he says that TV uses the eye as an ear.[9] On the other hand, the social environment has, likewise, become a simultaneous mosaic of electric information. That is to say, both the small and the large aspects of the contemporary world have none of the continuous, connected qualities that go with alphabetic writing, and none of the qualities that go with visual or "rational" space. To say, therefore, that "literary culture is through" is not an opinion but an observation of a dominant and constitutive situation.

Discontinuous matter arrived in 1900 with quantum mechanics (Max Planck). Multilocational art (later called Cubism) arrived at the same time. In 1900 Freud's *Interpretation of Dreams* appeared, bypassing the continuous and rational world of consciousness and restoring the mythic and discontinuous world of dream. Serious artists in all fields began to alert consciousness to the new situation. Arthur Miller's essay "1949: The Year It Came Apart" details a more immediate sense of the situation that came with the TV public. Up until the eve of TV there had been a kind of homogeneous audience from New York to San Francisco.

In many ways it was a good audience, but the important point to remember is that it was the only one, and therefore catholic. Traditionally it could applaud the Ziegfeld Follies one night and O'Neill the next, and if it never made great hits of Odets' plays, it affected to regard him as the white-haired boy. Both O'Neill and Odets would privately decry the audience as Philistine and pampered, but it was the audience they set about to save from its triviality, for they could not really conceive there could be another.[10]

The simultaneous audience has nothing in common with the sequential one stretched from New York to San Francisco, just as the Johnny who sits in the classroom of 1975 has nothing in common with the Johnny who sat there in 1955. The new Johnny has very little private identity and no tunnel vision of any conceivable goals in life. This, again, is not a value judgment, but simply a structural observation, since there cannot be deferred goals in a simultaneous world. Immediate quality of life and complex role-playing takes over from the visual point of view and the pursuit of goals. Mildred Hall and Edward T. Hall make an observation about a flaw in Western consciousness that dearly concerns the future of America. Their point needs to be focused directly upon the future of literacy in the United States.

> The most pervasive and important assumption, a cornerstone in the edifice of Western thought, is one that lies hidden from our consciousness and has to do with man's relationship to his environment. Quite simply the Western view is that human processes, particularly behavior, are independent of environmental controls and influence.[11]

It needs to be noted that the strategies for saving literacy, or the Western way of life, are always pointed to the *content* of specific programs. No heed is given to the effects of the new man-made environments in reshaping the perceptual life of the young. It is obvious that if man-made environments are destroying the institutions of American society, then these environments can also be altered in such ways as to restore and to sustain the desired way of life. This desired effect actually calls for a suspension of the simultaneous structures that are eating out the heart of American institutions. Should this appear to be too great a sacrifice to demand, there would at least have been confrontation. Would not a deliberate decision be preferable to the current mood of absentminded incompetence and drift?

Barrington Nevitt

Via Media with Marshall McLuhan

Or say that the end precedes the beginning,
And the end and the beginning were always there
Before the beginning and after the end.
And all is always now.

T.S. Eliot, *Four Quartets*

In the early morning, on the last day of 1980, Marshall McLuhan left history to enter eternity. He had long recognized every end as a new beginning, while constantly exploring how means become ends that transform not only our intentions but also our psyches and societies. "Etherealized" via electric media, WE are *there* and THEY are *here* instantly as discarnate minds, transferable potentially anywhere or broadcast simultaneously everywhere. We have had the experience but have we missed its meaning?

Exploring cultural biases created by the media ecology

The vast horizons of western Canada, where McLuhan was born in 1911, beckoned him further to explore the vastness of inner space. His interest in medieval and modern English led McLuhan to study at Cambridge during the 1930s. His doctoral thesis on "The Place of Thomas Nashe in the Learning of His Time" revealed how the meanings of "ancient" and "modern" reversed according to the rising and falling influence of the oral and written traditions in the "schools" of western Europe. Their relative power was manifested by the varying importance attached to grammar, logic, and rhetoric in the classical *trivium* of the dominant educational establishment. As a professor of English in North America, McLuhan was also the first to perceive the shift from visual to audile-tactile sensory bias, when radio and televison began to dominate the written word.

We can begin to understand McLuhan and his "contributions," as we come of electric age, by recognizing that he was neither some kind of "structural phenomenologist" in philosophy; nor "Left, Right, or Center" in ideology; nor merely a "media guru" in popular culture. McLuhan was above all an "artist" engaged in sharpening percepts, rather than concepts, beyond the categories of scientists and humanists alike, which his *Understanding Media* suggests rather than defines: "The artist is the man in any field, scientific or humanistic, who grasps the implications of his actions and of new knowledge in his own times. He is the man of integral awareness."[1] McLuhan was much more concerned with expanding human wisdom than increasing scientific knowledge. As an artist, he deliberately juxtaposed ordinary things in extraordinary ways that "displace percepts" to achieve fresh vision. Whereas *percepts* are the raw sensory experience of our direct encounter with existence, *concepts* are extracted from repeated percepts of past experience. Jokes are percepts, not concepts. We cannot reduce percepts to concepts, which are the foundation of science and philosophy, for classification automatically converts present insight into hindsight. But converting concepts into percepts, like exposing "the emperor's clothes," may go beyond a joke!

For pre-Socratic Greeks, every word reverberated across their entire culture like the divine *logos* "with centers everywhere and boundaries nowhere." For Europeans before the Age of Reason, words still "participated" experience: medieval Latin *perceptum* referred simultaneously to both sensory impact and psychic response. Today, there is no word for "percept" in any European language but English. "Perception," on the other hand, has become a "buzz-word" ignoring ancient wisdom that: "*Perception* is a relation among relations apprehended in our sensory lives."

Reviving complementarity and dialogue with human maturity

In Shakespeare's day, Gutenberg had already pushed reason to Othello's "ocular proof" that ultimately led to the Cartesian dichotomies of Madame la Guillotine. Today, the two-bit wit of the computer exceeds the *logical maturity* attainable by any man, just as the *human maturity* of Everyman—the ability not only to recognize the underlying unity, but simultaneously to appreciate the conflicting emotions induced by the paradoxes of existence—is unattainable by any computer.

While those who still worship the Goddess of Reason without Rime or Rhythm were striving to "prove" that maximum security is achievable through their logic of Mutual Assured Destruction, McLuhan and his associates were trying to revive the ancient human wisdom of Yin/Yang to "manifest" in new form what Chinese sage Wang Fu had observed long ago: "Poverty arises from wealth, weakness derives from power. Order engenders disorder, and security, insecurity." Complementarity is the process whereby effects become causes. Today, as causes and effects merge instantaneously via media, the new common ground is neither container nor category but boundless outer and inner space.

McLuhan avoided argument with people engaged in tossing around the weight of their knowledge to put each other down; he did not seek followers but welcomed fellow explorers ready for dialogue to organize shared ignorance in order to discover large patterns rather than small details. McLuhan was more concerned with exploring the unlimited process of exploration itself than in its limited results; and he considered "ideas" and "theories," that others imputed to him, as unperceiving "McLuhanism." He regarded individual claims for priority as not only irrelevant but also as counterproductive for this process of continual *hendiadys* (Greek: one by means of two) that converted breakdowns into breakthroughs.

My own experience of this intensely stimulating dialogue began in 1964 and continued until the end of 1980. I was first attracted by McLuhan's reverberations of pre-Socratic wisdom that had long influenced my own thinking not only in the history and philosophy of science but also in the development of international communication.

Recognizing the human consequences of technological innovation

At that time, McLuhan had already shown in *The Mechanical Bride: Folklore of Industrial Man* how the modern "tyrant rules not by club or fist, but, disguised as a market researcher, he shepherds his flocks in the ways of utility and comfort," and maintains this tyranny by "a popular dream art that works trance-like inside a situation that is never grasped or seen. And this trance seems to be what perpetuates the widely occurring cluster image of sex, technology, and death which constitutes the mystery of the mechanical bride."[2] By making another inventory of current advertisements some twenty years later, McLuhan revealed the flip from "business is our culture" to *Culture Is Our Business*.[3]

By 1960, Edmund Carpenter and McLuhan had jointly edited *Explorations in Communication* with many collaborators who outlined the shape of things to come.[4] In *The Gutenberg Galaxy* McLuhan reported the subliminal effects that print had had in transforming Western psyche and society. In tune with our electric times, McLuhan chose deliberately to present his findings as a *mosaic* that embodied depth perception of many micro-worlds combined to re-present the macro-world of Western man.[5] For having reported the psychic and social consequences of print, not only its services but also its disservices, many book-lovers still accuse book-writer McLuhan of being a book-hater.

In *Understanding Media: The Extensions of Man* by using life itself as his laboratory, McLuhan continued to manifest how the technological extensions of man constantly change his natural environment and thereby his human nature: "The effects of technology do not occur at the level of opinions or concepts, but alter sense rations or patterns of perception steadily and without any resistance."[6] Only by learning to anticipate these effects can we now survive media fallout.

During 1965, through McLuhan and his son Eric, I began to appreciate James Joyce as "the first *human* engineer." Having found no existing language adequate to replay the multisensory experience of mythic giant Finn, successively lulled and aroused by technological innovations—"thunders of the gods"—that had transformed him from paleolithic to civilized man and back again, Joyce invented Finneganese for his parable of *Finnegans Wake*, which gives us "the keys to Given!" (not only the mechanical but the musical keys to both data and Heaven). About to replay the cycle, "Finn, again" had learned how to anticipate rather than merely react to the material, mental and social consequences of his major innovations. The Joycean keys are the common ground for mutual understanding among McLuhan's companions.[7]

Like Francis Bacon, who recognized the complementarity of EAR and EYE by writing "in Aphorism" and "in Method" for *The Advancement of Learning* of his day, McLuhan set out with us to explore the conflicts and the complementarities of oral and visual cultures, from pre-Socratic to postliterate, in order to discover and compare their hidden process patterns. Like Edgar Allan Poe, "father of symbolist poetry and the detective story," we always began by making an inventory of perceived material, psychic, and social effects, rather than any preconceived causes. In contrast to Dr. John Henry Watson, who was constantly trying to fit any available facts into some convenient theory, we approached our problems like Detective Sherlock Holmes, who used science as a probe and never had any theories until "all the facts were in" at the denouement. Like the medieval court jester, we also used jokes as playful probes to expose hidden grounds of grievance *directly*.

In this process, *understanding* is neither a point of view nor a value judgment. Understanding is achieved by making inventories of effects as causes that relate modes of dynamic perception; they are neither definitions of concepts nor expressions of opinion, since all patterns of perception merge and metamorphose in the very act of exploration and discovery. By avoiding value judgments, they serve as guides to insight and to comprehension through *re-cognition* of the *dynamic structures* that occur in every process. In replaying such patterns, we take no sides but many sides, also the inside. For *truth* is neither a label nor something to *match*. Truth is something we *make* with all our senses in a conscious process of remaking the world, as that world remakes us.

Perceiving invisible environments by organizing ignorance

Toward the end of the 1960s, we began to convert the visual *figure/ground* vocabulary of structuralism into a multisensory probe. In *Take Today*, we explored the changing figure/ground relations during the metamorphosis of man as an extension of nature into Nature as an extension of man through major technological innovations. We indicated how new process patterns have superseded old groundrules, as software replaces hardware by "etherealization," in today's new ground of information traveling at the speed of light. And we suggested how to bypass hitherto "inevitable Fate."[8]

In this quest we were aware that nothing has any meaning alone but only as a *figure* to which attention is devoted in relation to its *ground* which tends to remain hidden. The figure/ground relation is constantly changing as grounds become figures and vice versa. A century ago, mathematician Charles Dodgson (Lewis Carroll) demonstrated that the meaning of anything, even meaning itself, is not merely what it says in its definition but what it *does* in its context.

Whereas the normal scientist strips natural language of its cultural heritage to match one word with one meaning by exact definition for his colleagues, the real poet seeks the "exact word" to reverberate across the culture shared with his audience so that each participant may recreate the poet's own experience. By deliberately shifting familiar figures into strange grounds, symbolist artists also create the *surreal*—a shoe alone on a highway rather than on somebody's foot—that imbues the familiar with new meaning.

Communicating with people and between machines

To say that "the medium is the message" is a symbolist statement that deliberately stresses hitherto ignored effects of the *medium* or ground at the expense of the obvious *program* or figure involved in the transformation process of human communication. Whereas *Understanding Media* considers the program as content, *Take Today* reconsiders how users "put on the medium," like a cloak or mask, and become its *content*, as they make sense or *meaning* individually. The *message* is always the totality of effects, material, mental, and social, regardless of the *intent*. The consequences of printing were far greater than any book ever printed, just as the repercussions of electric media speedup are far vaster than any broadcast program. Likewise, to say that TV viewing is an audile-tactile, rather than a visual, experience is to emphasize the shift in sensory responses from literate to nonliterate modes in the process of *synesthesia*—the constantly changing interplay of all the senses—exploited by artists who understand their media. Thus art precedes science precisely because percepts precede concepts.

Paradoxically, the dominant communication metaphor of our electric information age is a *transportation theory* that treats information software like material hardware; it is concerned only with *matching* output to input "signals" transmitted through "noise" in telecommunication "channels." Semantic aspects of communication are irrelevant to this engineering problem of communicating between machines rather than people. Academics, who apply this model and assume that communication media are neutral, still continue vain attempts to correlate violence in society with *violence on the media*.

By contrast, McLuhan and his coworkers constantly study the *violence of the media*, for they recognize that every artifact, whether software or hardware, is a communication medium that *transforms* its users. Human communication is by re-presentation, not replica. While communication media serve to enlarge our scope of action and our patterns of awareness, they also produce environments that numb our powers of attention by sheer pervasiveness. New media constantly give rise to new climates of thought and feeling in a perpetual interplay with older forms. Instead of increasing human understanding, as technologists still hope, we can now observe that our global environment of information traveling at superhuman speed has decreased human tolerance and mutual understanding everywhere. By wiping out all former images we had of ourselves, it is depriving us of both identities and goals. When all barriers of private consciousness are overwhelmed, the resulting form of awareness is a tribal dream; and, as McLuhan was the first to point out, the fragility and insecurity of tribal life lead to violence as a quest for identity in preliterate and postliterate societies alike.

Converting breakdowns into breakthroughs
by process pattern recognition

Electric speedup has also stretched the previously unconscious into a new kind of consciousness that we now call by various names: "intuition," "insight," "breakthrough," or "process pattern recognition" that require using all our wits and senses. The source of our breakdowns has thus also provided the ground for breakthroughs. But, as McLuhan once remarked, "Communicating anything new is always a miracle!" And he also declared, "All my writing is satire intended to wake up readers."

Hitherto, every culture has tried to find its bearings in the experience of earlier times by translating the new and unfamiliar into old familiar forms of being—metaphors (Greek *metapherein*: to carry across). Languages, like cybernetic models and general systems theories, are metaphors that now hinder understanding of our present existence, for that requires anticipating the mental and social effects of our means upon our ends by using all our wits and senses directly. By contrast the dominant Law of Implementation automatically converts the new into the dead by using the old means.

McLuhan was not only among the first to point out that the technological extension of each sense makes its own space, but also to recognize the differing structures of the giant metaphors created by the tribal *ear* and the civilized *eye*. VISUAL SPACE, where *things* are connected *separately*, has separate centers with fixed boundaries, and action is through connections. Visual space is like the mind's EYE characterizing the normal left-hemisphere cerebral activity that dominates the thinking of literate people who think in terms of words and visual models. It is the chosen domain of civilized man and scientists concerned with *matching the old*. ACOUSTIC SPACE, where processes are related *simultaneously*, has centers everywhere and boundaries nowhere, and action is in the gaps. Acoustic space is like the mind's EAR characterizing the normal right-hemisphere cerebral activity that dominates the thinking of nonliterate people who think in terms of multisensory images. It is the natural habitat of natural man and artists concerned with *making the new.*

Visual and acoustic space structures are *incommensurable* like history and eternity, but also *complementary* as exemplified by McLuhan and Harley Parker in *Through the Vanishing Point: Space in Poetry and Painting.*[9] Nevertheless, visual space structures pushed to the speed of light flip into acoustic patterns. The electric world retrieves the tribal village—everybody HERE. And, by time compression, history becomes mythic—all times NOW.

Today's invisible ground of electric information has created a new vortex of power, a giant rim-spin that has changed the meaning of all the old visible figures. An innovation, whether hardware or software, is a figure that intensifies or enhances some related figure or ground by *frontspin*, while it simultaneously replaces or obsolesces still others by *backspin*. Obsolescence does not necessarily lead to destruction but metamorphosis. Although the typewriter obsolesced handwriting, it also transformed writing into an art form while retrieving similar forms that had previously been obsolesced. Today, there is more writing of more kinds than ever. This pattern of retrieval is examined in *From Cliché to Archetype*.[10] Likewise, any process pushed to the extreme of its potential will break down or metamorphose or reverse its original effects by *chiasmus*. Hitherto, these visible and invisible process patterns have been largely ignored by philosophers and scientists whose concepts have blocked their percepts.

Discovering the Laws of the Media, past, present and proposed

Since the early 1970s, we have been exploring the *Laws of the Media*—every artifact—by a "tetrad" of four questions that represent the simultaneous interplay of major patterns perceivable in all processes:[11]

A. What does it intensify or enhance?
B. What does it replace or obsolesce?
C. What does it revive or retrieve of similar nature, previously obsolesced?
D. What does it flip into when pushed to the extremes of its potentials?

We have had the meaning *after* the experience with the *Phonetic Alphabet* that:

A. Enhances private authorship and individual ego;
B. Reduces oral-aural memory;
C. Retrieves and revives secret inner life;
D. Reverses into history, as a corporate record of private life.

We can have the meaning *with* the experience via electric media by *Instant Replay* that:

A. Amplifies cognitive awareness;
B. Obsolesces purely visual images;
C. Retrieves memory through participation (in A);
D. Flips individual experience into process pattern recognition.

The phonetic alphabet gave us a first look at human thinking but prevented us from recognizing the effects of any artifact on anybody. The electric media gave us a second look at human thinking as an artifact and enabled us to anticipate the effects of every human artifact on everybody. We can also bypass the assumptions of self-reference, not conceptually but perceptually, by a tetrad of *The Tetrad*:

A. Intensifies awareness of inclusive structural process and "formal causality";
B. Obsolesces logical analysis and "efficient causality";
C. Retrieves resonance of metaphor in C/B = A/D and C/D and C/A = B/D;
D. Reverses hardware technology into information software.

By thus probing the assumptions underlying our thinking, we can continue to search with the eternal explorer, Marshall McLuhan, for an epistemology of human experience in perceptual rather than conceptional terms throughout history and sub-specie *aeternitatis*. In his end is his beginning.[12]

Marshall McLuhan with Hubert Hoskins

Electric Consciousness
and the Church

Hoskins: In various articles and in your books, *The Gutenberg Galaxy* and *Understanding Media* and *The Medium Is the Massage,* you have probed a new way of envisaging technical media as what you call extensions of our human faculties and our consciousness, and I suppose millions of people by now have heard in the form of a slogan the expression, "The medium is the message." I take it you reject the idea that what is most effective for change is what used to be called the content of a communication: what really counts is not the what but the how.

McLuhan: Yes. It might be illustrated by saying that the English language is an enormous medium that is very much more potent and effective than anything that is ever said in English, but anybody who uses that medium invokes or resonates the totality of it even with the most trivial remark. Our own mother tongues are things in which we participate totally. They change our perception. So that if we spoke Chinese we would have a different sense of hearing, smell and touch. The same is true of printing, radio, movies and TV. They actually alter our organs of perception without our knowing it. We are never aware of these changes. It's like fish in water. Fish know nothing about water, and yet it is the only element they enjoy.

Hoskins: And part of your argument, I take it, is that we have, in the West at any rate, passed through periods of culture—which you have described as literate or sequential or logical—in which men have become capable of abstracting themselves from this environment, of individualizing, segregating and so on, and these have

159

been periods in which religion—for example, Christianity—has evolved in terms of verbalism.

McLuhan: I don't think it was accidental that Christianity began in the Greco-Roman culture. I don't think that Christ would have suffered under Ghengis Khan with the same meaning as under Pontius Pilate. The Greeks had invented a medium, the phonetic alphabet, which, as Eric Havelock explains in his book, *Preface to Plato,* made it possible for men to have for the first time in human history a sense of private identity. A sense of private substantial identity—a self—is utterly unknown to tribal societies to this day. Christianity was introduced into a matrix of culture in which the individual had enormous significance; but this is not characteristic of other world cultures by any means.

Hoskins: Why is it that Christianity, which began in a preliterate and oral society, very quickly became deposited, became embodied, in propositions known as dogmas and so on—became a matter of very high definition, to use your own terminology? Do you regard this as a fundamental aberration?

McLuhan: These issues were all raised at the First Council in the quarrel between Paul and Peter. Paul was a cultivated Greco-Roman who wanted Christianity for the whole world. Peter thought that it had to be filtered through Judaic culture in order to be valid. Today all these ancient issues are alive again. One of the amazing things about electric technology is that it retrieves the most primal, the most ancient, forms of awareness as contemporary. There is no more past under electric culture—every past is now—and there is no future. It is already here. You cannot any longer speak geographically or ideologically in one simple time or place; we are now dealing with very universal forms of experience. So the fact of Christianity having begun in the Greco-Roman culture really is of enormous significance. And I don't think theologians have specially heeded this matter. The effect of TV on the young today is to scrub their private identity. The problem of "private" identity versus "tribal" involvement has become one of the cruxes of our time. This was the big clash between Peter and Paul; and I don't think it was ever more alive as a problem than right now.

Hoskins: Would you agree that the answer that Christianity was for the private individual was the one which predominated from late medieval times onwards and reached its climax perhaps in the Protestant Reformation; and that ever since we have had this highly explicit, highly verbalized, propositional manifestation of what passes at any rate for the Christian revelation?

McLuhan: I am myself quite aware that there is a great contrast between perceptual and conceptual confrontation; and I think that the death of Christianity, or the death of God, occurs the moment they become concept. As long as they remain *percept*, directly involving the perceiver, they are alive.

Hoskins: But concept surely enters into the process at a very early stage. Take the Fourth Gospel: is this where God begins to die?

McLuhan: The revelation is of thing, not theory. And where revelation reveals actual thingness, you are not dealing with concept. The thingness revealed in Christianity has always been a scandal to the conceptualist. It has always been incredible. The credibility gap as far as thought is concerned has always been enormous. This is an issue raised in the Book of Job, where faith and understanding were put at totally opposite poles. Job was not working on a theory but on a direct percept, and all understanding was against him, all concept was against him, he was directly perceiving a reality, revealed to him.

Hoskins: If what you are saying is right, I still don't see how such an activity as theology is possible even in theory.

McLuhan: I should think that it is very much a pastime, and in the sense of a rehearsal of "past times." It is not personal and direct confrontation. Theology is one of the games that people play, in the sense of theorizing; but in the sense of direct percept and direct involvement with the actuality of a revealed thing, there need be no theology in the ordinary sense of the word.

Hoskins: What do you think of the kind of activity carried on by your colleague in Toronto, Professor Leslie Dewart? In *The Future of Belief,* I believe Dewart is arguing that there can be no future for most forms of traditional theism, for the wholly transcendent God? Do you think he's talking nonsense here?

McLuhan: No, I think he's just conceptualizing.

Hoskins: You would regard this as a game?

McLuhan: Pure game.

Hoskins: A useless game?

McLuhan: Not necessarily more useless than any other game. Most games are a tremendous catharsis for pent-up emotions and frustrations. But there has always been the great clash between works and concepts in religion, and I think that theology can perhaps become a work, a part of the *Opus Dei*, part of the prayerful contemplation of God. Insofar as theology is contemplation and prayer, it is part of the contemplation of the thingness and the mysteries.

Hoskins: This is using the term "theology" in a rather unusual way.

McLuhan: It should ideally be the study of the thingness, of the nature of God, since it is a form of contemplation. Insofar as it is theoretic or an intellectual construction, it is a pure game, though perhaps a very attractive one. It's a game that can equally be played with any oriental theology. It has no more relevance to Christian theology than it has to Hindu theology.

Hoskins: I'm not quite clear about your distinction between concept and percept. If I were to say that the traditional Christian doctrine of the Incarnation can be expressed in the phrase "Christ is the medium and the message," is that a percept or a concept?

McLuhan: It's a percept, because as Christ said over and over again in his own life, it is visible to babes, but not to sophisticates. The sophisticated, the conceptualizers, the Scribes and the Pharisees, had too many theories to be able to perceive anything. Concepts are wonderful buffers for preventing people from confronting any form of percept. Most people are quite unable to perceive the effects of the ordinary cultural media around them because of their theories about change which prevent them from perceiving change. It never occurs to people that a satellite environment can alter the perceptions of the entire human race. They have no theory that permits them to obtain such a concept of metamorphosis. The fact is we "perceive" the satellite environment whether we conceive it or not. The percept is what does the work in changing our experience and our organs of perception. The satellite environment has completely altered the organs of human perception and revealed the universal pollution.

Hoskins: Do you think that these modifications of consciousness which you see taking place are going to open up a new world of perception, so that religious experience as the perception of revelation is something which society will be able to realize much more concretely? In future, will there be worship? And what kind of worship? Will it be made concrete in liturgy?

McLuhan: The need for participation in groups and in social forms always requires some code whether verbalized or in the form of costume and vestment, as a means of involvement in a common action. Today, for example, the plain-clothes priest, or the plain-clothes nun, presents a sort of CIA or FBI scandal. It is one of the ludicrous hangups of our time. What the young are obviously telling us is: we want beards, we want massive costumes and vestments for everybody. We do not want any of this simple, plain, individual stuff. We want the big corporate role. The young have abandoned all job-holding and specialism in favor of corporate costuming and role-playing. They are in the exact opposite position of Hamlet, who lived in an age when roles were being thrown away, and Machiavelli and individuals were emerging. Today Machiavelli has been thrown away in favor, once again, of role-playing. The Church, in the sense of being an administrative bureaucracy of ordinary human beings, is never very much aware of what is going on. A bureaucracy by definition has its thing to do regardless of change, and it always perpetuates long after it's irrelevant. The Church today as a bureaucracy is in a way a very comic set of hangups and is no more relevant in its strategies than Don Quixote was when confronted with Gutenberg. He rode madly off into the Middle Ages hoping that it was the future.

Hoskins: Do you see any prospect of it becoming relevant? Or of its adopting a program?

McLuhan: I think one of the factors that is compelling relevance in our time is the speed of change. At electric speeds patterns become so clear that even bureaucrats begin to get the message. This is new, though: things used to change gradually enough to be imperceptible, but today the patterns of change are declaring themselves very vividly because of the speed at which they occur. That is what pollution comes from: pollution is merely the revelation of a changing situation at very high speeds. We now regard all our institutions as polluted, because we can see that they have many patterns that have nothing to do with the function they are supposed to perform. So the young become intolerant; they become aware, through the speed of information, of all the knowledge that only adults were privy to in the past. The young simply then move in as actor rather than as audience. So participation today is a universal pattern in which audience becomes active. There is no more audience in our world: on this planet the entire audience has been active and participant. Naturally religion undergoes tremendous changes under these conditions. And administration undergoes tremendous changes: all forms of authorization and administration and teaching and every sort of political and military establishment are altered by this fact. It is very high speeds and access to universally available information that make this awareness possible. Now its effect on religion is as drastic as its effect on military or other objectives. All forms of sham, all forms of irrelevance, all forms of routinized repetition are swept aside, and going with that clean sweep is this wiping out of the old private identities of centuries of cultural heritage. Now, how much we can survive without any private identity is, I think, a question for religion to consider. "Is there life before death?" somebody once asked. It has become a much more relevant question than the old one about life after death. If there is no longer such a thing as a private individual because of our electric culture of total involvement, then the question about life after death becomes irrelevant. Individualism in the old nineteenth-century sense has been scrubbed right off our culture, and many people find themselves completely bewildered by this change.

Hoskins: Might not Christianity offer us some hope of reconciling the individual with the collective?

McLuhan: Christianity definitely supports the idea of a private, independent metaphysical substance of the self, and when there is no cultural basis for this in the technological culture, then Christianity is in for trouble. When you have a new tribal culture confronting an individualist religion, there is trouble.

Hoskins: You yourself believe in the divine revelation. It cannot be ephemeral? It is indestructible?

McLuhan: It doesn't matter at all what people think about it.

Hoskins: Well, it matters in the sense that it is for people.

McLuhan: It matters to them; it certainly would affect their future, or their future existence. But as far as the society of men is concerned, the private opinion about any of these matters is quite insignificant: the revealed and divinely constituted fact of religion has nothing to do with human opinion or human adherence.

Hoskins: So what you are really saying is that, as you see it, the Church as an institution has no relevant future.

McLuhan: In its merely bureaucratic, administrative and institutional side I think that it is going to undergo the same pattern of change as the rest of our institutions. In terms of, say, a computer technology we are heading for cottage economies, where the most important industrial activities can be carried on in any individual little shack anywhere on the globe. That is, the most important designs and the most important activities can be programmed by individuals in the most remote areas. In that sense, Christianity in a centralized, administrative, bureaucratic form is certainly irrelevant.

Hoskins: Suppose we envisage the Church as a community, founded upon the Christian myth of revelation in Christ: what future for that?

McLuhan: The word "myth" in this connection, of course, is properly used, because it is the Greek word for "word"; the *mythos* is "word," *logos*; myth is anything seen at very high speeds; any process seen at a very high speed is a myth. I see myth as the super-real. The Christian myth is not fiction but something more than ordinarily real.

Hoskins: Exactly. But what I am asking is: do you see any prospect of the Church being transformed from a traditional kind of institution into a mythical community or a community based on this myth?

McLuhan: The Church has in various periods consisted of hermits in very scattered little huts and hovels in all sorts of backward territories. It could easily become this again, and in the age of the helicopter I see no reason why the Church should have any central institutions whatever. So any of the visible forms of the Church could undergo total transformation and dissipation, but this would have no relevance to the central reality and thingness of the revealed and divinely constituted Church. Naturally people who share such awareness of the divine thing enjoy their community: they enjoy being together. And so nothing is ever going to prevent Christians, in that sense, from congregating. But the forms in which they will congregate or organize their activities and help one another—those forms are capable of indefinite transformation. And I don't think they are of very much importance. Not so long as the divine fact—and that includes, as far as I am concerned, the divine sacraments—is available to communities and to the Christian faithful. As long as there is the means of communion, social and divine, there is an indefinite number of forms in which this can be achieved. It just happened that with the coming of very heavy technologies after Gutenberg the Church began to get very heavily centralized, railway style. But in the age of the airplane, the railway centralism which favors very centralized bureaucracies, big nation-states and so on is dissolved. The Church as a massive centralized bureaucracy is certainly passé.

Hoskins: What changes do you envisage coming about through the advent of a "global village" situation, where cultures in various stages of development—cultures with quite diverse histories and quite diverse presents—are flung together. How do you envisage this affecting the immediate future of Christianity?

McLuhan: This has already happened. Because of electric speeds we have had the entire primitive or backward world thrown into our Western life, as a direct responsibility both to feed and to teach; and many of these areas had been Christianized by missionaries, like Biafra or North Vietnam.

Hoskins: I was thinking more of the ancient cultures of the East.

McLuhan: They, too, have had much contact with Christianity at various times. India was one of the first Christianized areas, and so today their presence in the Christian community is as real as any Western one. I don't think there are any more geographic or ideological barriers to a Christian community. An Indian or a Negro or a Korean beside you in the same church is no more strange today than members of your own family.

Hoskins: I was thinking, though, of the great cultures which I think you would hesitate yourself to call religions at all: the anthropologies, as I believe you call them, Hinduism, Buddhism and so on.

McLuhan: I don't think of them as religious except in an anthropological sense. They are not, as far as I am concerned, the thing—revealed divine event—at all. They have all the fascination of any other massive cultural achievement. They were rendered obsolete at the moment of the Incarnation and they remain so. They are games that people play. There's nothing to prevent any one of them from becoming an incidental means of illumination of some aspects of Christian community. We coexist with all these forms as we coexist with all the languages of the world. They are in fact part of the cultural languages of the world. They are part of the technologies of the world—which again are languages.

Hoskins: I'd like just to read you a passage in *Understanding Media*, one of those rare passages in which you appear to predict, or even to prophesy. It reminded me when I read it of the closing part of

The Phenomenon of Man by Teilhard de Chardin, although you refer in this passage to Bergson's critique of language and consciousness:

> Languages as the technology of human extension may have been the Tower of Babel by which man sought to scale the highest heavens; and today, computers hold out the promise of instant change of any code or language into any other code or language. The computer promises, in short, by technology, a Pentecostal condition of universal understanding and unity.

Now are you here predicting, are you prophesying, are you trying to say something historical, or transhistorical, are you trying to say something that lies beyond history?

McLuhan: Well, I think that we live in posthistory in the sense that all pasts that ever were are now present to our consciousness and that all the futures that will be are here now. In that sense we are posthistory and timeless. Instant awareness of all the varieties of human expression constitutes the sort of mythic type of consciousness of "once-upon-a-timeness" which means all time, out of time. It is possible that our new technologies can bypass verbalizing. There is nothing inherently impossible in the computer, or that type of technology, extending consciousness itself—as a universal environment. There is a sense in which the surround of information that we now experience electrically is an extension of consciousness itself. What effect this might have on the individual in society is very speculative. But it has happened—it isn't something that's going to happen. Many people simply resort instantly to the occult, to ESP and every form of hidden awareness, in answer to this new surround of electric consciousness. And so we live, in the vulgar sense, in an extremely religious age; and I think we are moving into an age which, in popular notion at least, is probably the most religious that has ever existed. We are already there.

Louis Forsdale

Marshall McLuhan and the Rules of the Game

I first met Marshall McLuhan in 1955 and we were friends for the rest of his life. We corresponded often, he spoke in my classes dozens of times, he bounced my children on his knee, and, because he preferred dialogue in public presentations, we hit the road, at times, as a team. We were drafting a book together before his death (*Art as Survival in the Electric Age*). I knew him well, then. Here are some thoughts about a friend I miss.

Back to 1955. A naive assistant professor, I was asked to organize one of several two-day seminars to celebrate the inauguration of a new president at Teachers College, Columbia University. Participants in this seminar were to ponder the relationships between mass communication and education. My major task was finding someone to write a brief, provocative opening paper. After scanning the field of possible candidates, my thoughts turned to McLuhan, whose work I had come across in the occasional journal published out of the University of Toronto, *Explorations in Communication*. For some reason I hadn't seen *The Mechanical Bride*, his media book of 1951.

I was scared. Would he come? And, if he did, had I spotted a genius or a nut? After all, I didn't have tenure then.

Marshall agreed to write the paper and attend the seminar. He stayed at my apartment, and, as we walked to the meeting on the first morning, he told me he felt like a man entering the enemy camp.

"Why?" I asked.

"Teachers College has a reputation of following a 'let's-do-anything'–party line. I guess it's true, isn't it?"

"No," I replied, a bit nervous about contradicting my guest

speaker. "The only party line I know of here is doing the best work we can, keeping education at the front of our minds."

"That's good to hear," he replied. "There are a lot of rumors out there."

I report the conversation here only because it was the first time I spotted McLuhan's conservative nature. His writing seemed quite the opposite. I learned through the years, however, that he saw his work in communication, as did I, as a continuation of the great tradition of liberal inquiry in Western culture. He was also radical, but only in the sense of getting at the root of matters. He felt the blustery winds of change all about him, and he tried to steady the boat, not to capsize it.

From that two-day seminar comes a verbal snapshot which, even after twenty-nine years, remains the paradigmatic, McLuhan-intellectual image for me. It's been written about before. Here is my version.

He read his paper before the group of fifteen or so members of the *ad hoc* seminar, representatives invited from both the academic and business communities of New York City. When he had finished, I called for reactions. A distinguished sociologist responded instantly, anger signaled by his scarlet face.

"It's so chaotic I don't know where to begin," he sputtered, "but let's start with the first paragraph."

Before he could shape his distress into question or comment, McLuhan spoke: "You don't like that idea? I've got others."

That anecdote is a major key to McLuhan's style of thinking. He often refused to participate in tight, lineal discussion or debate, preferring to stimulate people with symbolic jabs. Eighteen years later, when introducing him to an audience of five hundred at Teachers College, I characterized his style as one of "academic free-association." Because I've never seen the technique used with such purity in a college setting, I will discuss its merits.

When free association occurs on the couch, and one is taken on a guided tour of those associations by a competent psychiatrist, a pattern of unconscious outlook becomes apparent. Knowing one's psychodynamics can help move one forward. McLuhan's "academic free association" method (my term not his) took us on a guided tour of a bigger world—that of communication at large. He helped us see that world in a new way, releasing us from enshackling dogma. The new vision was both exhilarating and frightening, as any profoundly new vision can be.

Ideas spewed from him, and he seldom self-censored them, thus bending a cardinal academic rule. With an amazing lack of inhibition, he made daring ideational leaps without first preparing a safety net, or, perhaps more accurately, without even indicating which trapeze he was heading for. And, with a few exceptions, that was the style which fit him best. In classes I've heard Marshall try to explain the meaning of a cryptic comment or a metaphor, and it seldom worked, generally ending in confusion. His head was wired in a special way, something for which we should be thankful.

Stravinsky, caught off guard in 1913, couldn't explain "Le Sacré du Printemps" to a belligerent audience had he wanted to. McLuhan caught a generation off guard, and explanations or interpretations were best left to others. Books and articles have already been addressed to such interpretations of McLuhan, but I haven't yet seen the kind of work that would be most useful— something akin to Martin Gardner's *The Annotated Alice*[1]—an "explication de texte," filled with as many roots of McLuhan's ideas as can be discovered, as well as an account in more traditional prose of what his poetic essays were about. That would be a translation, of course, and thus, would involve a risk. But I think the risk is important to take until more of us understand his style.

One of the big problems about Marshall's communicative behavior is that people couldn't pigeon-hole him. Was he a philosopher, a sociologist, an historian, a pop commentator, a prophet, a critic, and, if so, of what? Marshall tried to help define his method with the comment that finally became a rote response for him, "I probe things," and, although he told people quite directly that his style stemmed from the symbolist poets, that meant little to most. In a piece published in *The New York Times* in 1966, he was quoted as saying, perhaps in desperation: "People make a great mistake trying to read me as if I were saying something. . . . I don't want them to believe me. I just want them to think."[2] How direct can a man be? And yet, one can choose from that statement what one wants. One can take the first part, which leads to: "Aha, he admits he isn't saying anything," or one can emphasize the second part of the statement, which leads to "That's what great teachers do; they stimulate thought."

And stimulate thought he did, and does. I conduct a graduate seminar on McLuhan every other year. Whether the students are pro or con, they finally are unable to dismiss him. His intellectual output is volatile. I've never found a class bored with his ideas; angry, defiant, defensive, awestruck, bewildered, inspired—yes; bored, never.

Two things about McLuhan need to be said again and again. The more obvious of the two is that he was an artist, not a scientist. That has been asserted frequently, but somehow it doesn't wash for many McLuhan watchers, particularly wary ones. Yet, without understanding this fact, and accepting it, one can never come to grips with the tensions, the gaps, the leaps found in his writing or speaking.

The less obvious of the two, and a point that has been made only infrequently, is that he was generous in overestimating the readiness and grasp of his audiences. I personally saw that quality repeatedly when he spoke in my classes. He might, for example, quote from memory a lengthy passage from his beloved Shakespeare (or Joyce, or Eliot), always prefacing it with a comment such as, "You all know the passage, of course." Most of us knew bits of it. No one in the room knew it as he did. But he assumed—and it was not a game—that the material was in everybody's memory bank.

Let me illustrate these two points—his role as an artist, and his stance with respect to audiences—by going back again to 1955.

I have found the original copy of the paper Marshall wrote for that 1955 seminar. It's on onion skin, typed on a grouchy machine that skipped spaces in the middle of words. That was pre-secretary, pre-staff (except for his wife, Corinne), pre-agent, pre-fame. And the nine-page, double-spaced document has packed into it many of the themes he played with throughout his life.

I would like to quote the final two paragraphs, not because they will appear new to readers, but because they show glimpses of his style of thinking and writing at a fairly early point in his thinking about the effects of media change. They will also permit me to point specifically to some aspects of that style. The paper was titled "Educational Effects of the Mass Media of Communication," and, prior to these ending paragraphs he had developed his claim that contemporary electronic media were blowing down the walls of museums, businesses, libraries, and schools. . . .

In such an age, with such resources, the walls of the classroom disappear if only because everybody outside the classroom is consciously engaged in national and international educational campaigns. Education today is totalitarian because there is no corner of the globe or of inner experience which we are not eager to subject to scrutiny and processing. So that, if the educator old-style feels that he lives in an ungrateful world, he can also consider that never before was education so much a part of commerce and politics. Perhaps it is not that the educator has been shouldered aside by men of action so much as he has been swamped by high-power imitators. If education has now become the basic investment and activity of the electronic age, then the classroom educator can recover his role only by enlarging it beyond anything it ever was in any previous culture. We cannot hope simply to retain our old prerogatives. Our bridges are gone and the Rubicon is yet to cross? We have either to assume a large new role or to abdicate entirely. It is the age of paratroopers.

Yes, we must substitute an interest in the media for the previous interest in subjects. This is the logical answer to the fact that the media have substituted themselves for the older world. Even if we should wish to recover that older world we can do so only by an intensive study of the ways in which the media have swallowed it. And no matter how many walls have fallen the citadel of individual consciousness has not fallen nor is it likely to fall. For it is not accessible to the mass media.[3]

A book could be devoted to those two paragraphs. The bold ideas, global in scope, staccato in style, unmodified by the usual "ifs," "perhaps," "howevers," are literary pronouncements. A poet who modifies—and I'm now further defining his artistic niche as a poet, broadly defined—is finished after the first line. Those few lines are punctuated with hand grenades. The metaphor "It is the age of paratroopers" is poetically brilliant, given the date of 1955. I would never have used the question mark after "and the Rubicon is yet to cross?" but that detail is the kind that separates the pedestrian from the elegant. It stops the rhythm momentarily, jolting the reader. Few contemporary writers were more aware of linguistic effect than McLuhan.

His solution to the problems of education is devastatingly simple: zap the old subjects—history, the arts, economics—and study the media. Everything else will follow. Notice, too, the way he reaches that conclusion. Without paragraphs of logical maneuvering, he simply vaults from here to there. On reflection, the leap is clear, whether one agrees with it or not. Finally, in this tiny dissection, what do those final two sentences mean? One can guess without external information: there's a core within the individual—an essence, a steady-state internal guidance system—that won't be affected by mere mass media. Introducing external information, one knows that McLuhan was a deeply religious man. He also understood the psychological defense mechanisms that shield our symbolic selves from invasive pressure, but psychologists, for example, would have said it differently.

Yes, the writing is congruent with McLuhan's "poetic" way. He was true to himself. The lack of verbal connective tissue betrays his attitude to his audience. He complimented them by saying, in essence, "You don't need all the details. It's clear, or at least provocative, without unnecessary flab." (Very cool indeed.) Many understood his manner; many didn't. That is true, not only of the readers/hearers of this little piece, it is true of all of his work.

The first time I walked the halls of Saint Michael's College with Marshall, I asked him how his colleagues felt about him.

"Most of them think I'm off the wall; totally bonkers," he said.

"Why?"

"They don't like what I'm trying to do, I suppose."

I have a different theory. I suspect that their attitude stemmed from a feeling of violation because Marshall departed in manner from many of the written and unwritten ground rules of scholarly discourse.

He was also, by designation, a professor of English, but what he addressed was hardly a traditional study of English. Nor did he address his subject in a traditional way. He told me at times of his consternation when colleagues didn't embrace the concept that English was a subset of media studies. "English is a mass medium," he said matter-of-factly, assuming that colleagues would welcome the challenge to expand their domains. He believed more in the power of an idea than in the security of turf.

McLuhan was obsessed by the realization that the media were

blinding and that we were like men who stared at the sun and, left only with afterimages, struggled to regain the original vision through a kind of jigsaw process.

The pieces turned up only through diligent observation in a life-long scavenger hunt. He was "guilty" of selectively picking up ideas that would flesh out the puzzle. If the ideas worked, they went into the puzzle; if they did not work, they were tossed away. Such behavior is tabu in the sciences, although much of the scholarly community does precisely the same thing, consciously or unconsciously nudging facts to support a position, conveniently forgetting the ones that don't. Artists *must* do it.

That incompleted, unfinished, obsessive image puzzle remains one of the major contributions from anyone in any field in the twentieth century. We see its general shape clearly, and perhaps half the pieces. That's what he was all about: see the form, the pattern. His head was an echo chamber filled with the reverberating theme: "See the form, see the form; don't sell your soul for a pot of message."

The pieces to fill out the image consisted of what he frequently called "discoveries." These discoveries, as he learned to say, were percepts, the re-envisioning of the world through—in his case—sophisticated yet childlike senses. He was forever excited about new insights, communicating them in scribbled notes, or, after getting a secretary, in dictated letters. ("Making lots of interesting discoveries. . . .") Sometimes they came in unexpected telephone calls from Toronto, or from an airport almost anywhere, seeking a welcome ear for a "discovery," and always asking for new jokes, which were an indispensable nutrient for him. ("Humor keeps the synapses oiled," he once told me.)

His "discoveries" were shortly translated into cryptic proclamations in print. Those who knew his symbolist shorthand understood. Those who didn't called him careless, or worse.

Calling McLuhan careless is a bit like calling Picasso sloppy. Both McLuhan and Picasso had done their homework, had paid their dues by learning the "proper" rules of the game. Both practiced those rules diligently until they reached a certain plateau from which they saw a different vision. Both rushed then from idea to idea, celebrating new vistas. For both, new images required new forms. And both were "merely" inviting the rest of us to see the view.

Many took McLuhan's communicative behavior as a cop-out by someone who didn't want to engage in tight, logical thinking. It was no cop-out. While much of the scholarly world was massing troops of fact, as in a grade B movie, and marching them straight into the swamps of obviousness, Marshall engaged in a kind of guerilla warfare against obsolete processes, his sensitive radar targeting opportune images. He was nearly alone, and he trusted his instincts. We follow now in his footsteps.

Marshall was at once an intimidating man, and a generous and loving one. He was intimidating, not only because of his wide-ranging knowledge, but also because he was always "on." Obsession, by definition, demands that. The wheels keep whirring. For some of us they whir silently; for others, orally. And McLuhan was an oral man.

It was often difficult, for example, to have him as a house guest. Imagine waking up, still slightly premetabolic, to see, through bleary eyes at the breakfast table, a cheerful face and hear through spongy ears a booming comment, continuing from the night before, sounding something like: "yes, an oral culture is much less interested in the individual than is a visual culture. It's obvious, of course, but it has to be said. And, we're no longer a visual culture. Television isn't visual, it's tactile."

In twenty-five years I seldom held a "small talk" conversation with Marshall. That burning, obsessive insight was his everlasting focal point. I listened, nodded, put in a word here or there, and returned to listening. His behavior, or my acquiescence to it, was often annoying to me, even when I understood that he needed to rehearse his thoughts aloud, to study the responses of a live audience, as might a bard of old, to get the feel of the phrases, to put the set pieces of his brilliant repertoire in place. He often got angry when interrupted in his oral explorations, as many of us do when working through our thoughts silently. His anger would quickly subside, however, for he was a compassionate man.

Still, the point is that he was an oral man. (Yes, he wrote some fourteen books and hundreds of articles, but, again, they are the work of a poet, and poets—except for a minor few—hear the words.) I sent him the draft of a chapter for a book I was writing on him, asking for his observations. He was quick to reply. "It's O.K.," he said, "but you say too little about orality."

Marshall knew his worth, certainly after *Understanding Media* created its tidal wave, he felt that Vanguard Press had a failure of vision when they remaindered *The Mechanical Bride*. He bought as many copies of the book as he could, and stored them temporarily in a friend's basement in Manhattan. I went with him one Saturday to lug away the dozens of copies. He never said, "Some-day this will be valuable," but he gave me half a dozen copies in a silent gesture. Although he was bitter, he chose to share both disappointment and potential with a friend. Loyalty was one of his prime values.

It seems to me that many searchers have approached McLuhan upside down. In honest bewilderment about what to make of him, too many have dismissed his work, saying, in effect, "He didn't meet me halfway in this intellectual process. It's unfair."

The question is this: how does one behave in the presence of a genius? The answer is clear. You learn his/her language, seek to share his/her vision. Then, and only then, is rejection sensible.

To ignore McLuhan is a grave risk. There are signal people for different periods. They capture, in whatever medium, the images and rhythms of the time, or of times to come. Recently J. David Bolter nominated Alan Turing, the great British mathematician and predictor of the digital computer, as a symbol of the age we are entering.[4] I have no problem with that, but there should also be another symbol. Marshall McLuhan should stand as the man who suggested how to see our age. Being in an age does not necessarily tell us how to study our circumstances. McLuhan told us. Others have suggested approaches, too, but none with McLuhan's passion and precision.

Granted, McLuhan violated many of the established ground rules as he helped us see new ways to move through the present no man's land between the Mechanical Age and the Information Age. We must learn his rules for playing the new game of locating ourselves in the maelstrom.

Why, then, has he been dismissed by so many? Some, under-standing him, think he is wrong. Fine. Others, failing to under-stand, want to demolish the structure, or, at least, bring him down to their level.

A close Iranian friend of mine tells a poignant joke which he feels represents a certain kind of Middle Eastern mentality. The mentality is not confined to that area of the world. The story is this.

Parviz and Ali are walking down the street together in Tehran. They see before them an extremely tall ladder, perhaps three meters in height, leaning against the front of a building. Nobody is on the ladder, or even nearby.

Parviz, the more adventurous of the two, goes to the ladder, beckoning Ali to come with him. Parviz checks quickly to see if anyone is around, and then climbs quickly to the top of the ladder. From there he looks out over Tehran, breathtaken.

From below Ali can see that Parviz is deeply moved by what he sees, and calls up, "Parviz, what is it?"

"It's the view, Ali; it's incredible. Come on up. You'll see something unbelievable."

At the bottom, Ali hears the invitation to transcend himself, somehow, and he wants to go up the ladder, too. But there's a problem: Ali is frightened silly of heights. That ladder is terrifying to him, so he silently pouts and sobs.

A passerby sees the distressed Ali, scans as best he can the situation with Parviz, and gently asks Ali, "Excuse me. May I help in some way?"

"Well, thank you, I do have a problem, but I don't think you can help," says Ali, telling the stranger about the awesome view Parviz has seen at the top of the ladder. "He wants me to come up."

"Well, I'll help," says the passerby. "I'll be glad to steady the ladder. Go on up."

"No, although I thank you," says Ali. "You don't see the problem. I don't really want to go up. I'm too frightened. But would you help me bring him down?"

Let me leave my comments there, ending on a story I never had a chance to share with Marshall McLuhan. He would have liked it even if it wasn't a one-liner, his favorite genre.

Marshall McLuhan

The Brain and the Media
The Western Hemisphere

While the Western world remains
dominated by the logic of the left brain hemisphere,
its art and entertainment are moving right—
"a formula for complete chaos."

In writing on "one of the most fascinating and fastest growing areas of the brain research, . . . hemispheric dominance," Robert J. Trotter chooses the Inuit people of Northern Canada as an example of a culture where "the other hemisphere" is dominant. The Inuit language was discovered to reflect "a high degree of spatial, right hemispheric orientation. Linguistic studies rate it as being the most synthetic of languages [American English being at the other end of the same scale]."[1] Inuit sculptures, lithographs and tapestries were "without apparent linear or three-dimensional analytic orientation." Art, then, also afforded "a unique opportunity to observe people carrying out work that demands tremendous spatial skills."

Because the dominant feature of the left hemisphere is linearity and sequentiality, there are good reasons for calling it the "visual" (quantitative) side of the brain; and because the dominant features of the right hemisphere are the simultaneous, holistic and synthetic, there are good reasons for indicating it as the "acoustic" (qualitative) side of the brain.

Visual space, as elucidated in Euclidean geometry, has the basic characters of lineality, connectedness, homogeneity and stasis. These characteristics are not found in any of the other senses. On the other hand, acoustic space has the basic character of a sphere whose focus or center is simultaneously everywhere and whose margin is nowhere. It is the "acoustic" pattern of "simultaneous comprehension" which gives the right hemisphere the power of "facial recognition." The synesthetic interplay among all of the senses too would seem to relate mainly to the right hemisphere. That Trotter selects a nonliterate society for observation and illustration points also to the fact that societies that have not developed the use of the phonetic alphabet tend to exhibit the same right-hemispheric orientation. Nonliterate cultures are mainly oral/aural, even when they cultivate some nonphonetic form of writing such as Sanskrit. On the other hand, literate cultures tend to be visual and dependent on left-hemisphere reasoning. The dominance of either the left or the right hemisphere is largely dependent upon environmental factors. Thus the lineality of the left hemisphere is reinforced by a service environment of roads and transportation, and logical or rational activities in legal administration. The dominance of the right hemisphere, on the other hand, depends upon an environment of a simultaneous resonating character, as is normal in oral societies. Today, when the visual culture of industrial societies has been greatly influenced in an acoustic direction by the simultaneous environment of electronic technologies, the dominance of the left hemisphere can no longer be taken for granted.

The invention of the phonetic alphabet created
a visual environment of services and experiences
which contributed to the ascendancy or
dominance of the left, or lineal hemisphere.

This conjecture is consistent with the findings of the Russian neurophysiologist Luria who found that the area of the brain which controls linear sequencing and, hence, mathematics and scientific thinking, is located in the prefrontal region of the left hemisphere:

> The mental process for writing a word entails still another specialization: putting the letters in the proper sequence to form the word. Lashley discovered many years ago that sequential analysis involved a zone of the brain different from that employed for spatial analysis. In the course of our extensive studies we have located the region respon-

sible for sequential analysis in the anterior regions of the left hemisphere.[2]

Luria's results show that the expression "linear thinking" is not merely a figure of speech, but a mode of activity which is peculiar to the anterior regions of the left hemisphere of the brain. His results also indicate that the use of the alphabet, with its emphasis on linear sequence, stimulates dominance of this area of the brain in cultural patterns. Luria's observations provide an understanding of how the written alphabet, with its lineal structure, was able to create the conditions conducive to the development of Western science, technology, and rationality.

The notion of space is important to clarify. When neurophysiologists assign a vague "spatial" property to the right hemisphere, they are referring to the simultaneous and discontinuous properties of audile-tactile and multiple other spaces of the sensorium. The Euclidean space of analytic geometry is a concept of the left hemisphere of the brain, while the multidimensional spaces of the holistic sensorium are percepts of the right hemisphere of the brain. Where the phonetic alphabet comes into play, the visual faculty tends to separate from the other senses, making possible the perception of abstract Euclidean space. The rise of Euclidean geometry offers a direct parallel with the rise of phonetic literacy; and phonetic literacy, in turn, is coexistent and coextensive with the rise of logic.

The rise of phonetic literacy and logic
and hence of left-hemispheric dominance
can be seen in the history of ancient Greece.

Phonetic literacy in Athens and Greece was an intensely disruptive force, as explained by Phillip E. Slater in *The Glory of Hera* and by Karl Popper in *The Open Society and Its Enemies*. Slater is concerned with the break-up of Greek family life and the rise of the new democratic and competitive individualism as pronounced reactions against all the new qualities of mind and spirit released by the impact of literacy.[3] Popper asks, "How can we explain the fact that outstanding Athenians like Thucydides stood on the side of reaction against these new developments?"[4] What the big tribal leaders of Athens such as Thucydides were trying so hard to resist was what in effect was a violent transition from the holistic institutions of their oral society (right hemisphere) to the fragmented and scientific bias of the visual revolution evoked by the onset of literacy and individualism (left hemisphere).

The same literacy, which destroyed the traditional institutions of Athens, created an abstract rationalism inseparable from the new dominance of the left hemisphere: "But at this time, in the same generation to which Thucydides belonged, there rose a new faith in reason." Literacy played a role in the breakdown of Greek tribalism by separating the individual from the group, and contributed to the so-called democratic individualism climaxing in the Peloponnesian War in the fifth century.[5] The present electronic age, in its inescapable confrontation with simultaneity, may present the first serious threat to the dominance of the left hemisphere since that time.

However, hemispheric dominance does not mean there can be no interplay between the hemispheres.

No matter how extreme the dominance of either hemisphere in a particular culture, there is always some degree of interplay between the hemispheres, thanks to the *corpus collosum*, that part of the nervous system which bridges the hemispheres. The Oriental cultures provide a good example of this interplay. With their extreme cultivation of the right hemisphere, which invests their lives, their language, and their writing with artistic delicacy, still the Chinese exert much left-hemisphere bias and quality in their practicality and their concern with moral wisdom. However, their stress falls heavily on a particular use of space as explained by Chiang Yee:

Indeed the use of space is one of the Chinese painter's most coveted secrets, one of the first thoughts in his head when he begins to plan his composition. Almost every space in our pictures has a significance: the onlooker may fill them up with his own imagined scenery or with feeling merely. There was a Chinese poet of the Sung dynasty, Yeh Ch'ing Ch'en, who wrote the sorrows of a parting and described the scene as follows:

Of the three parts Spring scene, two are sadness,
And the other part is nothing but wind and rain.

Who would venture to paint this scenery, but yet who
would deny the truth of it? This is what we leave to the well-
disposed blank, more eloquent than pictorial expression.[6]

Chiang Yee is explaining that the Chinese use the blank, the
interval between things, as the primary means of getting "in
touch" with situations. Nothing could be more expressive of the
properties of the right hemisphere in contrast to the left, for the
left hemisphere "sees" space as an interval which must be *logically*
connected, filled and bridged. Such is the dictate of lineality and
visual order.

The Japanese attitude to social relationships as "a constant
readjustment to our surroundings" is another illustration of an
Eastern understanding of space. This attitude is the extreme
contrast to the Western or visual "point of view" which assumes a
fixed position from which to examine each situation and seeks to
"connect" situations and relationships rather than "tune." Kakuzo
in *The Book of Tea* expresses the continued adjustment to the
surroundings of the part to the whole:

The Taoists claimed that the comedy of life could be made
more interesting if everyone would preserve the unities.
To keep the proportion of things and give place to others
without losing one's own position was the secret of success
in the mundane drama. We must know the whole play in
order to properly act our parts; the conception of totality
must never be lost in that of the individual. This Laotse
illustrates by his favorite metaphor of the Vacuum. He
claimed that only in vacuum lay the truly essential. The
reality of a room, for instance, was to be found in vacant
space enclosed by the roof and walls, not in the roof and
walls themselves. The usefulness of a water pitcher dwelt
in the emptiness where water might be put, not in the form
of the pitcher or the material of which it was made.
Vacuum is all potent because all containing. In vacuum
alone motion becomes possible.[7]

Today, the paradox is that the most recent
Western technologies are electronic and simultaneous,
and are thus structurally right hemisphere and
"Oriental" in their nature and effects.

This situation, of course, is not new, having begun with the telegraph one hundred years ago. But the overwhelming foundation or *ground* of the Western world remains lineal, sequential and connected, in its legal institutions, and also in its education and commerce, while its entertainment and its art are representative of right-hemispheric structures. A formula for complete chaos. The *ground* of the Oriental right hemisphere, meantime, is rapidly acquiring some of the hardware connectedness of the left-hemisphere Western world. Yet, as we have seen, the right-hemisphere culture is at least always intensely aware of *ground*, and in fact prefers the experience of participation in *ground*, while members of Western culture are able to detach themselves from participation in the *ground* through individualism and the advent of phonetic alphabets.

Nowhere is this more evident
than in the Western approach to
the study of media and its effects.

The left-hemispheric Westerner approaches the study of media in terms of linear motion or sequential transportation of images as detached *figures* (content), while the right-hemisphere approach examines the *ground* of media effects instead. For example, the Shannon-Weaver model of communication is an extreme example of the lineal bias in communication: it is a kind of pipeline model of hardware container for software content. It stresses the idea of "inside" and "outside" and assumes that communication is a kind of literal *matching* rather than making. Claude Shannon notes:

> The fundamental problem of communication is that of reproducing at one point either exactly or approximately a message selected at another point. Frequently the messages have *meaning*.[8]

In point of fact, the side effects of any communication system tend to be an entire environment of interfacings, a kind of subculture which accompanies the central "service" or channel of communication. For example, the side effects of the Alaska oil pipeline might mean that the entire native population would be deprived of its environmental livelihood with its construction. Or equally, the system of roads and services that accompany the motor car alter the entire face (and odor) of any society. In the same way, the side effects of telephone or radio assume a complex system of electric technology which transforms the entire society.

There is a paradox that the "hardware" channels of radio and telephonic communication contribute to an extraordinary "software" effect. When people are on the telephone or on the air, they have no physical bodies, but are only abstract images. The result is a discarnate man, an effect which the Shannon-Weaver theory would simply designate as *noise*. Minus his body, the user of a telephone or radio is also minus his private identity.

Wilson Bryan Key

Watch the Background,
Not the Figure

I first met Marshall McLuhan in San Juan, Puerto Rico, during 1966. He appeared as keynote speaker at a conference of *The Young President's Association*—a group of several hundred U.S. corporate executives who had headed their own organizations with over a million dollar annual gross before the age of forty. The program described the Canadian professor as "A Prophet of Corporate Communication." One of my major concerns, as president of a business research corporation at the time, was study and research on communication. I attended McLuhan's session.

For two solid hours he spoke in a stream-of-consciousness assault upon his audience. The presentation was a virtuoso recital of intellectuality—eloquent references to an army of authors, philosophers, artists, theologians, and other prestigious names I recalled from my student years. He eloquently flayed the corporation heads for their misdeeds, superficialities, greed, shortsightedness, and amorality. At the end of the lecture, during which the audience listened with intense concentration, there was an enthusiastic response.

The question and answer period was extraordinary. The titans of U.S. commerce and industry interrogated their speaker as though he had gained access to the fabled philosopher's stone. I had only one small problem with my first adventure with the McLuhan intellect—I was uncertain that I had understood clearly even one thing he had said during the lecture. I was not certain anyone else in the audience had understood. Nevertheless, I had a strong, specific feeling that whatever it was he had lectured about was extremely important. Many others, I discovered, shared these impressions. Over the remaining days of the conference, the executives talked incessantly about McLuhan's lecture. There appeared to be a general feeling that McLuhan had gained access to the future, had discovered a predictive technique which might unveil the world into which they and their corporations were heading. These affluent, well-educated men and women were some of the toughest, most hard-nosed, no-nonsense business leaders in the world. They were clearly impressed by the Canadian professor.

I was impressed, at the time, perhaps more with the executives' reaction to Marshall McLuhan than to the content with which he appeared to deal. I had a lot of trouble pinning McLuhan's content down to specifics. Shortly after the conference, I began to read his books. They were inspired metaphorically, but as with the lecture, for some reason, I simply could not put my finger precisely on what he was getting at. For several months, however, I persevered in my attack upon *The Mechanical Bride, Understanding Media, The Medium Is the Message,* and *The Gutenberg Galaxy.* Many months later, at a conference in Berkeley, I still struggled with *Galaxy,* carried it in my car for spare moments of reading.

One afternoon, during lunch with several graduate students, one alluded to the problems of studying the effects of the unconscious mentation system upon modern life and society. Though McLuhan's name was never mentioned, I suddenly perceived the connection. This, finally, appeared to be McLuhan's subject matter—though in none of his books had he directly alluded to the unconscious, subconscious, subliminal, etc. The sudden revelation was upsetting—it appeared, now, so obvious, as do most revelations after they are revealed. At the time, I could not understand why this had been so difficult for me to comprehend. I had yet to evolve an appreciation of the power of perceptual defense or of repression. From that moment on, McLuhan's work became lucid, intellectually provocative, exciting, even humorous, and deeply relevant to survival in the chaotic world North Americans had built for themselves or in which they had inadvertently entrapped themselves.

The following year, I found myself in London, on the faculty of the University of Western Ontario. My first Toronto visit included a meeting with Marshall McLuhan. The man's personality and discourse were every bit as provocative and exciting as his books. It appeared that McLuhan had, somehow, tapped into his own unconscious system, perhaps through some technique of autohypnosis into which he had stumbled. Over the following years, we met every few weeks—often for lunch or dinner. Those conversations were important events in my life. We would go on intensely for several hours, finally say goodbye, and I would return to London—turned on for a week or more, over the new ground which had bubbled to the surface. Several weeks later, we would meet again. He invariably began precisely where he had left off during the earlier visit, as though he had pushed the forward button on a tape recorder installed somewhere in his brain. When we were finished, he would switch off until our next meeting. We shared a mutual respect for human individuality, creativity and intellectual entrepreneurship. This collaboration endured until shortly before his death, when I left Canada and returned to the United States.

I have often tried to pin down and reflect upon just what it was I gained from the McLuhan involvement. I recall, with pleasure, our exciting bull sessions which left me clawing away at most of my treasured assumptions for days afterward. I shall always be grateful for the "Introduction: Media Ad-Vice" he wrote for my book *Subliminal Seduction*. Three weeks after I had dropped off the first rough draft manuscript with a note requesting an introduction, he phoned. "I should have known all this was going in," he said apologetically. "You've embarrassed me!"

I replied, "I always thought you knew. At some level of knowing, I was certain you knew. The use of subliminal stimuli," I tried to explain, "is only a logical extension of many ideas you wrote or talked about. If what you have said was valid, then we should find certain techniques in media. I looked! There they were!"

I have periodically reread this introduction over the years, and am convinced it is a masterpiece. I have, though, heard numerous critics rant and rage over this evaluation of advertising, almost ignoring my own attacks upon our media systems of misinformation in the body of the book. One German reviewer referred to McLuhan as a "dangerous fool," virtually ignoring the rest of my book in his review.

I shall never forget McLuhan's kindness and thoughtfulness during a two-year intense combat with UWO over my research and writing which administrators in the University attempted to ridicule, censor, and destroy, with the encouragement of Canada's media industry. Finally, under threat of judicial intervention of my solicitor, UWO awarded me $64,000 in return for my resignation. At the height of the battle, McLuhan often called or wrote a note urging that I not let the Philistines win, but, he counseled, one day the problem would end; life would go on, to focus upon the future—not the present. This concern, from a dear and caring friend, came at critically important points during the polemic. McLuhan once wrote a note telling me to remember that Louis Pasteur was expelled from virtually all the scientific and medical organizations of his time, for his discovery of germs. He added angrily, "The idiots still attempt to suppress ideas!"

There were many kindnesses from McLuhan, both large and small, but invariably expressed at moments when the world appeared its most threatening. I doubt there were many people, throughout his long life, who experienced McLuhan without being affected in their understanding of their world(s)—even those who most heatedly disagreed with him. I have often found it difficult to tolerate fools. I consider this intolerance my major personality defect. I usually will attempt to be polite, but, when pressed for time or patience, I sometimes shoot from the hip and behave quite rudely. I am ashamed of this. McLuhan, by contrast, displayed the patience of Job. Like many public figures, McLuhan was a magnet for the disturbed, the maladjusted, the disenfranchised, and the idiosyncratic. They literally swarmed about him, as though he could resolve their dilemmas with a wave of his vocabulary. They intruded cruelly into his time, into his privacy, and into both his personal and professional life. McLuhan's kindness and sympathy for the distraught was legion. I never saw or heard him turn away anyone who needed kindness, understanding, human sensitivity or simply an ear into which they could pour their perplexities. Even when exhausted or working intensely on a project, he always found the time to deal with troubled individuals, though it cost him dearly, in lost time and energy. I still envy McLuhan his humanity; perhaps, in retrospect, this was even more important than his philosophical insight, though both were inextricably interconnected.

A principal knee-jerk reaction to McLuhan from students and many of his colleagues was, "I cannot understand what he is talking about!" As our relationship continued over the years, I realized the comment was profound. Indeed, they did not understand, but not for their assumed reasons, for which they, unfairly, blamed McLuhan. Actually, these people did not want to understand—perhaps as some basic characteristic of WASP repression. English Canada, much like the U.S., is a highly repressed society. The Anglo-Canadian culture hides from itself a large portion of the interesting, exciting and sometimes frightening things it is doing to itself. R.D. Laing, the British psychiatrist, might describe this repression as "The Secrets of the Family." McLuhan chuckled gleefully once when I told him he was one of the most dangerous writers of this century—dangerous to all the treasured mythologies which precariously hold together what we fantasize as Western Civilization.

Much to his credit, McLuhan infuriated the mediocrities, the uncreative, conventional-wisdom types who proliferate on Canadian (and U.S.) faculties. They often made him the object of their petty jealously and intolerance as they searched for someone to criticize who had deviated from their popular concept of "normal." Several of these actually fashioned temporary, parasitic careers, as they merchandized crude attempts to embarrass, criticize and expose as ridiculous, McLuhan's work. I was often fascinated by the intolerant, vicious and elaborate attacks upon McLuhan I would overhear in faculty clubs throughout Canada. These were usually expressed by individuals who had not read his books, never heard him speak nor had the slightest notion of his subject.

If anyone allowed himself to understand McLuhan and the object of his probes, or the strategies behind his richly humorous prose, his put-on became comparable to Nero's fiddling while Rome burned to the ground, or, in a more contemporary context, while the ICBMs sizzle as they warm up in their silos. In spite of the most serious undertones in his work, McLuhan was fun—great fun, if you enjoyed this kind of gentle, though deeply penetrating, intellectual gymnast. It was enormous fun, if you were equipped to handle it, emotionally and intellectually, but McLuhan was rarely consistent, predictable or, most importantly, conventional in his wisdom. His insights stirred and stimulated the creative imaginations of liberal humanists throughout the world.

In private life, however, McLuhan often appeared the arch-conservative in his political and social views—somewhere, I sometimes thought, to the right of Torquemada. His Catholicism, to which he had converted while a graduate student at Cambridge, was omnipresent in everything he wrote or spoke. He was, indeed, a Christian who fervently believed in his faith, but not with the easy, hypocritical phrases of the Fundamentalist Biblepushers, but by the example he tried to set in his daily life. It was frequently difficult to reconcile the astute, critical scholar of history, the brilliant, worldly (catholic, in its nonreligious sense) student of human foible and frailty, with the simple faith he appeared to exhibit toward his God. I once questioned him about the conflict and inconsistency I perceived, between blind faith and intellectual integrity. He replied simply, "I am a Catholic! That resolves most of my dilemmas. I can get on with my work. Period!"

I recall a delightful, leisurely dinner at his home. We were well into a second bottle of superb Beaujolais when Corinne, the lovely Texan who ran the McLuhan establishment, and I drifted off into a pleasant repartee over the question of reincarnation. I was determined, I told her, to return as an alley cat in Beverly Hills. Corinne, not to be outdone, preferred the life of a butterfly in a cherry orchard. Suddenly, McLuhan's face turned grim. He appeared quite upset. "Please," he cautioned Corinne, "let's change the subject!" Everyone at the table became very concerned at his apparent discomfort. McLuhan proceeded, slowly at first, but with increasing eloquence, to cite page and paragraph of several Papal Encyclicals on the subject of reincarnation. Even a light, conversational discussion of the subject, he explained, was grounds for excommunication. About the only reliable aspect of McLuhan was his thorough unpredictability.

Perhaps my greatest debt to McLuhan was the change he induced, gradually, in my own view of the world. I began adult life at eighteen with four and a half years in the military, where life was often reduced to its simplest common denominator—survival. My later life, both professional and personal, had, likewise, been continually involved in some topical combat or polemic of the moment. Sometimes I won, sometimes I lost, but intense involvement was sustained in whatever was going on at any particular time. In well over three hundred research studies I had written for governments and corporations, my chief concern was, usually, to assess the day's wins and losses. In media research, my preoccupation had usually been with comparative content and other narrowly defined questions, such as which soap opera or news program reached the largest audience and sold the heaviest quantity of merchandise. I had always believed, from my occupational perspective, that this is what the world was all about—today's battle plan, bodycount and the one for tomorrow, and the day after and the day after, etc.

McLuhan's long-term effect upon my life and my work, as viewed some half a dozen years after our last encounter, was to move me back away from the firing line. He, somehow, manipulated me, via our long sessions, into looking at the war, instead of individual battles. I had been quite good at battles, even though I often lost major wars. As he put it, "Concentrate upon ground (background), not merely upon figure. Figure will usually mislead, distract and confuse."

I now perceive what those corporation presidents found useful in McLuhan's work, quite possibly without a clear, conscious realization of what he had given them. A corporation president is almost solely preoccupied with the future of his institution, and whatever it may produce. Corporate bodies have suites full of executives whose preoccupation is with the present—today's issues, counter issues, wins and losses, day-to-day survival. Presidents, of virtually all large institutions, are the only employees paid for their orientation toward the future.

One CEO of a multinational corporation said, at the 1966 conference after McLuhan's lecture, "My primary concern is what we will be doing ten years from now. I have a staff of able people who worry about what we do from day to day. I try to keep out of their way and let them do their jobs. I do not have the slightest idea of what we will produce ten years from now, but the success of my job depends upon finding out. You cannot find out anything if you become emotionally mired in day-to-day combats. I spend my life with ideas most of our executives would consider trite, boring, even irrelevant to the corporate survival, if they consciously thought about them at all—which is most unlikely. I must seek out structures, trends, evolutions, new perceptions of old ideas, what goes on beneath the surface of conscious preoccupation."

Subliminal or unconscious perception, and its effects upon cultural value systems and behavior, was the central focus for much of McLuhan's writing. He once described the most meaningful dimension of any environment (media or otherwise) as whatever is taken for granted, unquestioned or unchallenged, ignored as irrelevant to daily life, common, apparently unthreatening, invisible because of its banality and ordinariness, lacking in distinction—those portions of reality in every cultural system which few individuals take seriously. He admonished that, whenever your logic tells you something is irrelevant nonsense, unworthy of serious consideration, go back and take another look. Our minds trick us, usually, into overlooking or ignoring what is really going on. All humans, he believed, are extremely vulnerable—especially those who believe they are not. The most dangerous threats to survival and adjustment for individuals, corporations, societies, and nations are these consciously unattended aspects of daily life. These are the hidden time bombs most likely to do us in. Usually, we will never know, understand, or even suspect what it was that actually struck us down.

McLuhan appeared horrified at North America's blind acceptance of banality and topical events in its media—pseudo-information, if you will. He viewed this as the perceptual anesthesia which could ultimately bring us all to the end—the final cataclysm. A principal survival concern, in media, was how one segregated the informational wheat from the chaff, the banal from the profound, the actual from the pseudo; in short, the ability to discriminate between fantasy and reality.

McLuhan appeared enormously amused over the incongruous notion that, the more formal education consumed, the less well-informed people became. He once considered the phenomenon as a possible law of the media. He was appalled at the trivialization of North American university education—the steady erosion of language studies (especially in the language departments), classical history, art, cultural investigations, and philosophical insights. He commented that, every year, in the university classroom, students generally became less and less literate, less articulate, and less able to cope with the world's greatest ideas. I suspect this obvious deterioration in intellectual ability bothered him very much. He deeply cared about his students.

Media content defined as *news, advertising* or by the equally meaningless label *entertainment* (these are totally integrated concepts in North American commercial media) absorbs most individuals each day via print or broadcast. Little, if any, of their content is ever consciously remembered. Media content which initially appeared so vital, significant, powerfully threatening or supportive and fundamental to continued existence, imperative to a comprehension of the world—all of this "hype" usually reduces, after a good night's sleep, into little more than a vaguely recalled impenetrable maze of generalized emotional impressions and obscure facts. Many of us save the likes of *Time* magazine, literally to save time, to preserve the facts, perspectives and personalities for future use. (We seldom get around to looking at these archives however.) One of McLuhan's favorite puns was about a man who entered an antique store, asking, "What's new?"

Repetitive topical events accumulate, of course, in the psyche and contribute to residual value systems—such as increasing the tolerance level for violence or sexual promiscuity. Nevertheless, the detailed minute grist from the mills of media have almost no effect on the value systems through which individuals and cultures survive or perish. Topicality serves only the short-term goals of media's economic viability through the management of audience size and its demographic and psychographic characteristics. For these audiences, the media both consume and save time—quite unproductively, as a rule.

Another of McLuhan's useful insights was *perceptual overload*— the anesthetizing produced by the overwhelming bombardment of the individual by media, coming in from all sides at all hours. It becomes extremely difficult to "know" consciously at any given moment just what is happening in the world around us. In fact, he concluded, the more immersed and involved in the media the more unlikely that a person would achieve true awareness. To achieve my survival-oriented insight into reality, it is necessary to step outside the system and question every assumption prevalent within the system. Once again, background, not foreground or figure, contains the significant information about who we are, where we are going, and what we are likely to do when we arrive.

McLuhan argued that one must subtract the merely topical to reveal the residual ground—the reality of any sociocultural system. Listen, he would say, to what individuals, groups, or societies *mean*, not what they *say*, about how they perceive themselves. Their assumptions, most often, are the opposites of the reality.

I am not certain the metaphor "man for all seasons" would be entirely appropriate for Marshall McLuhan. He was, perhaps, not a thorough, well-organized, methodical scholar—and, quite possibly, he laughed too much at the ironies which surrounded him. In his dialogues, he would often begin in one direction, find he was on a dead-end street, abruptly reverse the whole argument he had developed, and plunge full-speed in the opposite direction. Nevertheless, McLuhan was an unforgettable trip, an experience few of his students will ever forget.

It would be absurd to say blithely that Marshall McLuhan will never be forgotten. As the world staggers on toward its ultimate destiny, much will and has been forgotten—perhaps especially those individuals who crossed streets with their cultural systems, and compelled their contemporaries to endure unflattering, self-critical re-evaluations. McLuhan will not, however, ever be forgotten by us—those whom he inspired, stimulated, encouraged and challenged. He was a great teacher—one of the very greatest.

Marshall McLuhan

A Last Look at the Tube

With TV, Shakespeare's "All the world's a stage" flips into "all the stage is a world," in which there is no audience and everybody has become an actor, or participant. When one says that "the medium is the message," it is to point out that every medium whatsoever creates an environment of services and disservices which constitutes the special effect and character of that medium. Tony Schwartz points out that one of the major aspects of the TV image is that it uses the eye as an ear, since it is a resonating audile-tactile form of innumerable gaps that have to be filled in by the viewer:

> In watching television, our eyes function like our ears. They never see a picture, just as our ears never hear a word. The eye receives a few dots of light during each successive millisecond, and sends these impulses to the brain.[1]

It is this open-mesh image that is so entirely involving, even to the point of inducing semihypnotic trance; and this raises a matter that confuses many people not familiar with the structural character of our sensory experience. It was the symbolists who had stressed the character of the discontinuous as the key to tactility and involvement: their structures were never continuous or connected statements so much as suggestive juxtapositions. As Mallarmé put it: "To define is to kill. To suggest is to create." The simultaneous world of electric information is always lacking in visual connectedness and always structured by resonant intervals. The resonant interval, as Heisenberg explains, is the world of touch, so that acoustic space is simultaneously tactile.

Any medium presents a figure whose ground is always hidden, or subliminal. In the case of TV, as of the telephone and radio, the subliminal *ground* could be called the discarnate or disembodied user. This is to say that when you are "on the telephone," or "on the air," you do not have a physical body. In these media, the sender is sent, and is instantaneously present everywhere. The disembodied user extends to all those who are recipients of electric information. It is these people who constitute the *mass* audience, because mass is a factor of speed rather than quantity, although popular speech permits the term mass to be used with large publics.

Discarnate man, deprived of his physical body, is also deprived of his relationship to Natural Law and physical laws. As a discarnate intelligence, he is as weightless as an astronaut, but able to move very much faster. Minus the physical mesh of Natural Laws, the user of electronic services is largely deprived of his private identity. The TV experience is an inner trip, and is as addictive as any known drug. The discarnate TV user lives in a world between fantasy and dream, and is in a typically hypnotic state which is the ultimate form and level of participation.

The world of fantasy is an inner world whereas the world of dreams tends toward outer orientation and aspiration and deferred gratification. On the other hand, fantasies are instant and are their own satisfaction. The discarnate TV user, with a strong bias toward fantasy, dispenses with the real world, even in the newscasts. The news automatically becomes the real world for the TV user and is not a substitute for reality, but is itself an immediate reality. Death on TV is a form of fantasy.

> On television, violence is virtually the sole cause of death; it is only on soap operas, and then very rarely, that anyone dies of age or disease. But violence performs its death-dealing service quickly, and then the victim is whisked off camera. The connection of death to real people and real feelings is anonymous, clinical and forgotten in the time it takes to spray on a new and longer-lasting deodorant.[2]

The fantasy violence on TV is a reminder that the violence of the real world is much motivated by people questing for lost identity. Rollo May and others have pointed out that violence in the real world is the mark of those questing for identity. On the frontier everybody is a nobody, and therefore the frontier manifests the patterns of toughness and vigorous action on the part of those trying to find out who they are.

A more characteristic form of identity quest under electric conditions is the universal theme of nostalgia. When our world exists only in fantasy and memory, the natural strategy for identity is nostalgia, so that today revivals occur so frequently that they are now called "recurrences" (in the recording industry). In his book *Do It*, Jerry Rubin wrote after the trial:

> Television creates myths bigger than reality. Whereas a demo drags on for hours and hours, TV packs all the action into two minutes—a commercial for the revolution. On the television screen, news is not so much reported as created. An event happens when it goes on TV and becomes myth. . . . Television is a nonverbal instrument, so turn off the sound, since no one ever remembers any words that they hear, the mind being a technicolor movie of images, not words. There's no such thing as bad coverage for a demo. It makes no difference what's said: the pictures are the stories.[3]

The social myth is a kind of mask of one's time, a "put on" which is also a form of body language. It is this body language which relates the TV form to the right hemisphere of the brain and brings us directly into relation to TV politics. Whereas the left hemisphere is sequential and logical, verbally connected and syntactic, the right hemisphere is simultaneous and acoustic, emotional and intuitive. The electric environment tends to give a lot of stress and power to the right hemisphere, just as the old industrial and literate environment had given corresponding dominance to the left hemisphere. The left hemisphere had been favored by the worlds of literacy, and of market organization with its quantitative goals and specialist structure. These worlds have been increasingly obsolesced by the instant environment and instant replays that enhance the simultaneous character of the right hemisphere.

Electronic or discarnate man is automatically committed to the primacy of the right hemisphere. In political terms the instant mask, a mythic structure, gives sudden prominence to the charismatic image of the political leader. He must evoke nostalgic memories of many figures that have been admired in the past. Policies and parties yield to the magic of the leader's image. The arguments in the Ford–Carter debates were as insignificant as the fact of their party affiliation.

If discarnate man has a very weak awareness of private identity and has been relieved of all commitments to law and morals, he has also moved steadily toward involvement in the occult, on one hand, and loyalty to the superstate as a substitute for the supernatural on the other hand. For discarnate man the only political regime that is reasonable or in touch with him is totalitarian—the state becomes religion. When loyalty to Natural Law declines, the supernatural remains as an anchorage for discarnate man; and the supernatural can even take the form of the sort of megamachines of the state that Mumford talks about as existing in Mesopotamia and Egypt some five thousand years ago. The megamachines of North America, for example, can take the form of the fifty-three–billion–dollar ad industry for manipulating our corporate psyches, or they can be the equally vast security systems constituted by what Peter Drucker calls our "pension fund socialism."

> Through their pension funds, employees of American business today own at least 25 percent of its equity capital, which is more than enough for control. The pension funds of the self-employed, of the public employees and of school and college teachers own at least another 10 percent, giving the workers of America ownership of more than one-third of the equity capital of American business.[4]

Meantime, our own megamachine for daily living presents us with the world as "a sum of lifeless artifacts," as Erich Fromm explains:

> The world becomes a sum of lifeless artifacts; from synthetic food to synthetic organs, the whole man becomes part of the total machinery that he controls and is simultaneously controlled by. He has no plan, no goal for life, except doing what the logic of technique determines him to do. He aspires to make robots as one of the greatest

achievements of his technical mind, and some specialists assure us that the robot will hardly be distinguished from living men. This achievement will not seem so astonishing when man himself is hardly distinguishable from a robot.[5]

When the viewer himself becomes a kind of discarnate information pattern, the saturation of that pattern by an electric environment of similar patterns gives us the world of the contemporary TV user. This is a parallel to the computer—the only technology that lives on, and produces, the same material.

Eric McLuhan

The Genesis of *Laws of the Media*

The "Laws of the Media" project began in the mid-seventies when the publisher of *Understanding Media* asked my father to revise it for a second edition.

Whenever my father started work on a book, he began by setting up a dozen or so file folders and popping notes into them as fast as observations or discoveries occurred to him. Often the notes would be on the backs of envelopes or on scraps of paper, in his own special shorthand. Sometimes he would write or dictate a paragraph or two. He included press clippings, advertisements and photocopies of passages from books with his notes in the margins. He would also include copies of letters he had written, for he frequently used letters as an opportunity to "talk out" an idea in the hope that his correspondent would fire back other ideas or criticisms.

Beginning with about thirty folders, one for each chapter of *Understanding Media*, we added folders for technologies such as personal computers, video recorders and cable TV that had appeared or developed in the decade since *Understanding Media* was published. We reviewed all the criticisms of *Understanding Media*. We found two kinds—those that dealt with matters of fact (e.g., "it was 1830 and not 1842") and those that might be called "matters of frustration." The latter was by far the largest area. Though voiced in dozens of ways by serious readers who claimed the book was "difficult" or "impossible to read" or who objected to the style or organization, they seemed to form a chorus of "that's all very well for you, but it's not scientific."

The abrasive, discontinuous style of *Understanding Media* was forged after many redraftings. It was designed to provoke the reader, to jar his or her sensibility into a form of awareness more open to the subject matter—a traditional poetic technique. Faced with the question of how to make it "scientific," my father began a prolonged consultation by questioning everyone he encountered: "What constitutes a scientific statement?" Finally he found the essential clue in Sir Karl Popper's *Objective Knowledge* (1972): "something stated in such a manner that it can be disproven."

The next questions were: "What statements can we make about media that people can test—prove or disprove—for themselves? What do all media have in common? What do they *do*?"

We expected to find at least a dozen factors. By the first afternoon we had discovered three—and each one had been discussed in *Understanding Media*. The first is the notion of *extension*. As an extension of man (the subtitle of the book), every technology extends or amplifies some organ or faculty of the user. The next characteristic is that of *closure*. Our senses strive for equilibrium and when one area of experience is heightened or intensified, another is diminished or numbed. So too one technology displaces another, which is the concept of obsolescence. Our search became more feverish. Do these laws hold in every case? Can anyone, anywhere, verify them by direct observation? Yes, to both questions.

The third factor, discussed in a separate chapter of *Understanding Media,* "Reversal of the Overheated Medium," is *reversal.* Any form pushed to its limit reverses its characteristics. And there matters rested for about three weeks, when the fourth law appeared—*retrieval.* At first we thought that retrieval (the subject of *From Cliché to Archetype* by Marshall McLuhan and Wilfred Watson [New York: Viking Press, 1970]) entailed only the dredging up or recasting of old junk forms as the content of the new form. But retrieval actually involves considerably more.

We found these four laws—and no others. My father spent the rest of his life searching not only for a fifth law, but also for a single case in which one of the first four laws did not apply.

These became the first *Media Laws.* Much was yet to come. The study of the senses and of the ways in which media extend and modify sensibility needed systematic attention. Accordingly we embarked on a full-scale study of visual space and acoustic space and their development by alphabetic and electric technologies. The study is still far from complete. There remains too the study of the other senses and the ways in which they interpenetrate and affect each other.

As we searched for a fifth law, we made further discoveries, the most important of which was the realization of an inner harmony among the four laws. It surfaced when we noticed there were special ratios, and pairs of ratios, among the laws. Furthermore this harmony showed that the laws taken together should exhibit the same structure as metaphor. And they did.

My father continued to exhort colleagues, visitors and students (especially those who attended the Monday night meetings at the Centre) to use the four laws to explore media and to assist him in testing the laws. Gradually, we realized that the laws apply to all the products of human endeavor and to the endeavor itself. One colleague at the university tried them on cancer treatment methods and found they worked. With another associate my father discovered that they applied to the world of business; with another, to Newton's laws of motion. The floodgates burst. Parts of the *Laws of the Media* manuscript underwent successive drafts and were circulated among friends and colleagues for comment. Finding the link to metaphor led to one of the farthest-reaching implications, which tied directly back to the subtitle of *Understanding Media: The Extensions of Man*. Insofar as media are utterings or outerings (extensions), they are not *as* words, they *are* words. We had stumbled upon the key to their verbal structure.

With the help of a grant from the Social Sciences and Humanities Research Council, I was able to assist my father full time during the crucial year 1979 when we extended the application of the laws to the arts and the sciences. We found that everything that man makes and does—every procedure, style, artifact, poem, song, painting, gimmick, gadget, theory—every product of human effort manifested the same four dimensions.

I do not consider it an exaggeration to say that the confirming and detailing of this tie between speech and artifacts has yielded the single biggest intellectual discovery of our time. Yet the four laws are simple. They have the most profound significance for all of the arts and sciences, and not only for erasing the distinction between them. They also provide both the arts and sciences with a common set of tools for forging ahead as well as backward (much the same thing in any case), for constantly mining and revitalizing their traditions, and for using each other as resources.

As people can test for themselves, the laws apply only to human ideas and artifacts: they tell us nothing about animal products such as webs or dams or nests. Does that not confirm the ancient observation that it is chiefly speech that makes us human and distinct from the rest of creation?

Many times over the years as we worked on this book, my father would refer to the works of Bacon or Vico as one would consult colleagues. He realized that he and they, along with other grammarians, had been steering parallel courses, bringing the tools of literary training to bear on the world and our part in it. Several times a year he would return to Francis Bacon's *Novum Organum* or *New Science* and to Bacon's four idols as holding a key to the bias of communication, the forms of blindness imposed by media. It was much the same with Vico's *Scienza Nuova* or *New Science,* that is, while plowing away at etymology and interpretation, Vico was quite conscious of the bias of sensibility stored in language. (Vico had his "fours" as well; grammarians—interpreters and etymologists—are intensely sensitive to patterns and resonances.)

When the "four" pattern of media laws appeared, we quickly reviewed the idols again to see if they showed the same pattern, hoping for quick confirmation, as it were, from another quarter. But this four pattern seemed to be new, and only loosely related even to the classic "big fours," the levels of exegesis and the four causes. Independent confirmation is always reassuring. For many years, whenever my father made some large discovery about media or about sensibility, he would open *Finnegans Wake* and within a few pages (seldom more than three or four) find that Joyce had been there before him and had gone both further and faster. Invariably, this was because Joyce navigated by the lines of force in the language; that is, Joyce usually flew in style whereas Vico and the rest of us could do no more than walk or jog. Still, this time there was no independent confirmation other than from Joyce (but that's another book). My father died before we could work out in great detail how his new discoveries related to the labors of Vico and Bacon. He knew the relations were there and his intuitions had never played him false. *Laws of the Media* carries the subtitle, *The New Science.*

Marshall McLuhan

Laws of the Media

I have been experimenting with developing a series of "Laws of the Media," which I submit herewith for comment and discussion. My purpose is to invite criticism, directed not at me or at my rhetoric, but rather at the substance and contents of my thoughts. It seems to me that historians of technology—and kindred students of the sociology and philosophy of technology, economists, practicing engineers, and the like—might enjoy and profit from attempting to disprove my "laws."

Cognizant of the seeming paradox that a "scientific hypothesis is one that can be disproved," I have put my "Laws of the Media" in a "disprovable" form, hoping that in the course of disproving each of them, many new discoveries might occur.

How did I arrive at these "Laws of the Media"? By a structural approach. The structuralists, beginning with Ferdinand de Saussure and now Lévi-Strauss, divide the approaches to the problem of form into two categories: *diachrony* and *synchrony*. Diachrony is simply the developmental, chronological study of any cultural matter; but synchrony works on the assumption that all aspects of any form are simultaneously present in any part of it. Although I have used the simultaneous approach in arriving at these "Laws of the Media," any one of them is susceptible to the diachronic approach for filling in the historical background and details.

Since electric speeds of information constitute a sort of simultaneous structuring of experience, synchrony, representing all directions at once, is, as it were, acoustic; whereas the diachronic, representing one stage at a time, is visual in its analytical pattern. Few people seem to be aware that visual space and order are continuous, connected, homogeneous, and static. In these regards, visual space is quite different from any other kind of space, be it tactile, kinetic, audile, or osmic (smell). Visual space alone can be divided.

You will note that, although these are called "Laws of the Media," only a few of them deal with communications media narrowly conceived. Instead, I am talking about "media" in terms of a larger entity of information and perception which forms our thoughts, structures our experience, and determines our views of the world about us. It is this kind of information flow—media— which is responsible for my postulation of a series of insights regarding the impact of certain technological developments. I call them "laws" because they represent, as do scientific "laws," an ordering of thought and experience which has not yet been disproved; I call them "Laws of the Media" because the channels and impact of today's electronic communication systems provide the informational foundation upon which we order, or structure, these experiential perceptions.

In formulating these laws, I have utilized what is sometimes called the "scientific method." That is, I have proceeded by induction, even though in the process of induction one discovers many things that could not be merely inducted. The "Laws of the Media" have been shaped by studying the effects of media, so there is always a hidden *ground* upon which these effects stand, and against which they bounce. That is, the law of a medium is a *figure* interplaying with a *ground*. As with a wheel and an axle, there must be an interval between the two in order for the play to exist.

Even if readers might not agree with my underlying structure, approach and methodology, I hope they will examine these sample apothegms for their validity on a historical basis. I am not primarily a historian, so my reference base is not historical. However, I like to test the validity of my laws in terms of history. In other words, do my "Laws of the Media"—derived from my inductive approach to synchronous form—correspond to historical data as viewed from the vantage point of historians of technology? Does the history of technology "prove" or "disprove" my postulates?

A sample of my proposed "Laws of the Media" follows (the four steps of the process are named in the first "law" and assumed for the rest):

I. *Cable TV*
   A. *Amplifies* quality and diversity of signal pickup.
   B. *Obsolesces* diffusion broadcasting.
   C. *Retrieves* early transmission broadcast pattern of point-to-point (ship to shore).
   D. *Reversal* is flip to home broadcasting.

II. *Housing*
   A. Private enclosed visual space (three little pigs).
   B. Cave, tent, wigwam, dome.
   C. Wagon trains, covered wagon (pioneers), mobile home clusters.
   D. High-rise corporate.

III. *Elevator*
   A. For mines, enhanced depth—real low-down.
   B. Steps, ladders—gravity, that is, is levity.
   C. Retrieves hidden treasures—retrieves hierarchy!
   D. Flips into high-rise—new egalitarianism of the elevator.

IV. *Clothing*
   A. Private energy—clothing as weaponry.
   B. Climate—clothing as thermal control.
   C. Mask, trophy, corporate energy.
   D. Conventional attire.

V. *Number*
   A. Plurality—quantity, for example, possessions.
   B. Notches, symbols, tallies.
   C. Math, algebra, zero, blank.
   D. Profile of crowd—pattern recognition.

VI. *Steamboat*
   A. Opens sea for hardware.
   B. The wood sail—uncertainty, exploration.
   C. Creates tourism—programmed pilgrims.
   D. Centralism via sea power (vs. old decentralization of sea power).

VII. *Railway*
   A. Tonnage hardware—horizontal speed.
   B. Country life.
   C. Frontier.
   D. Vertical organization chart; hierarchy—robber barons.

VIII. *Copernican revolution*
   A. Enhances role of the sun (central).
   B. Pushes aside the crystalline spheres.
   C. Retrieves Aristarchus.
   D. Flips into relativity—centers everywhere (decentral) and margins nowhere.

IX. *Xerox*
   A. Speedup of printing process.
   B. Obsolesces assembly-line book.
   C. Retrieves the oral tradition, the committee (the happening).
   D. Reversal is "everybody a publisher."

X. *Microphone—P.A. system*
   A. Amplifies individual speech and rhythm.
   B. Obsolesces the big band, the Latin Mass, grand opera.
   C. Retrieves group participation.
   D. Flips from private to corporate sound-bubble.

XI. *Money*
   A. Transactions.
   B. Barter.
   C. Potlatch (conspicuous consumption).
   D. Credit.

XII. *The wheel*
   A. Locomotion.
   B. Sled, roller, etc.
   C. Roads as river—moving sidewalk—skis, snowmobiles, dune buggy, Skidoo, tank.
   D. Airplane via bicycle.

XIII. *Printing*
  A. Amplification of private, individual handicraft via mechanization.
  B. Oral tradition, also handicrafts and guilds.
  C. Retrieves antiquity, for example, the first Copernican revolution via Pythagoras.
  D. Flips from private writing to corporate consumption, into the big mechanized environment (reading public and worker) of the second Copernican revolution, and the interiorization of the external world via Kantian revolt against Hume, and flips into Romanticism and subjectivism.

XIV. *Instant replay*
  A. Instant replay of experience = cliché. Amplifies cognitive awareness.
  B. Obsolesces the representational and chronological.
  C. Retrieves "meaning."
  D. Flips from individual experience to pattern recognition—archetype.

XV. *Satellite*
  A. Enlarges the planet.
  B. Obsolesces nature.
  C. Retrieves ecology.
  D. Reversal—nature is art form. Retrieves globe as theater. Population goes from spectator to actor.

XVI. *Electric media*
  A. Amplification of scope of simultaneity and service environment as information.
  B. Obsolesces the visual, connected, logical.
  C. Retrieves the subliminal–audile-tactile dialogue.
  D. Etherealization—the sender is sent.

George Sanderson

The Man in the Coach House

McLuhan was original, brilliant, humorous, talkative, authoritative, kindly. An amazing performer, a master juggler capable of tossing up a dazzling arc of ideas, percepts, puns and pontifications. His aphorisms such as, "the medium is the message," terms such as "global village" have become commonplace. Men wept at his funeral. Although he had charisma, he did not seek disciples. He was the stuff from which myths are made. But he is strangely ignored. How can this be explained?

Some think that McLuhan had the bad luck to become famous in the mid-sixties, the decade of bullets and short nights— a period now perceived by the reigning stodgers as a False Age. In those times hippies appeared moo-eyed with psychedelic bliss and visions of love in the grass. Dissidents and conscientious objectors abounded. Later, many felt personally betrayed by the unkept promises that gushed into the political and cultural scene and, for a while (say two summers), pulled us by our secret hopes and our childhood ambitions into the belief that the Age of Aquarius was truly at hand.

No one likes to be duped. And McLuhan not only seemed to be part and parcel of this weird imbroglio, he appeared, to many, as the instigator of the cresting wave that seemed about to smash down on Western civilization. His own grave concerns about the drug culture, the decline of literacy, the movement toward a retribalizing world were not noted. And other stars shone over the Pacific Waters—Marcuse, Laing, Leary, Buckminster Fuller, Norman O. Brown. *The Whole Earth Catalogue* plugged Husserl and hemp. But McLuhan's voice, because of its reverberatory peal, its authority, was heard and identified and remembered after the other toners dropped into semi-obscurity. Thus for many, McLuhan's name became indissolubly linked with that strange decade that arose above the waves with John F. Kennedy's election and subsided with the assassinations of Martin Luther King and Bobby Kennedy.

This is one answer, but it is not entirely satisfying. Here is another.

McLuhan is an individual without an institution. McLuhan's cause, his set of perceptions has not been taken up by any group, establishment or institution in the way that the scientists adopted Einstein or Darwin, the philosophers Wittgenstein or Heidegger. No organized group of supporters promotes his thought, or attempts to show its importance. One would expect the universities to have become McLuhan's natural champions. But McLuhan and the Academics never got along. The reasons for this are complex.

McLuhan's comprehensiveness, his inclusiveness, is foreign to the academic scene, where success is usually achieved through specialization. Today's scholar or scientist selects a tiny, neat, well-defined topic, something microscopic, overlooked, or even invisible. Once chosen, this molecule of mystery is grasped with the pincers supplied by the current methodology, analyzed, dissected and categorized. The results end up in a learned journal where they are safe from prying eyes. Today's scholars have become micro-professors, lords of quarkdom puffing towards grants, tenure, promotion, prestige. McLuhan's vision, rich with insights drawn from every field, from every age, and united in an integral tapestry, is too gigantic for those with Lilliputian ambitions.

And McLuhan's originality is even more unacceptable. If McLuhan is right, many fundamental assumptions concerning the origin and development of our Western culture have to be radically revised. The intellectual establishment becomes terribly anxious when its implicit and explicit ambitions are challenged. Timid professors often become paladins and hurl themselves at the offending doctrines. But usually they need only use a kind of patient dismissal or kindly neglect. The most effective technique is to construct a kind of master grid in which the original thinker is given his little square. Now the challenger is in his proper place, surrounded by his kin. The living (i.e., dangerous) thinker has now become tame, manageable, innocuous.

Since Plato and Aristotle, the Western world has exploited the domesticating power of classification. Walker Percy, in his wonderful essay "The Loss of the Creature," calls this process "devaluation by theory." The uniqueness, the specialness of a thing is sacrificed by our need to place everything in categories. By means of the process of classification and analysis we tame and exploit the world. Furthermore, McLuhan, in showing how theory is the child of technē, deromanticizes the history of ideas. And he grievously offends the sensibilities of the Academy by *pointing* at things. It is rude to point in the halls of Academe.

When American intellectuals get bored, they often send out for European ideas. Uncrated, these lovelies are seductively complex and loaded with exotic terminology. McLuhan did not offer the academics the sanctuary of a slick methodology and the fearsome jargon such as we find in the discussions which utilize terms from semiotics or structuralism or postmodernist ideologies and techniques. These jazzy French and German imports offer the intellectual a sophisticated labyrinth in which one may wander indefinitely, skirting the edges of gauzy Nietezschean abysses, converting history into a game of Dungeons and Dragons and uncovering undreamed-of tensions and deceits in Western society.

Compared to these European "nouveautés," McLuhan is all nuts and bolts. He deals in perceptions, i.e., things one can point at, touch, smell and hear. Live things that assault us, ruin lawns, speed down highways, move through the air. Trying to grasp the world, "à la McLuhan," draws one perilously close to the unclassifiable world-pool that we do not want to confront—the world of individual, unique things, each never quite itself in its movement and unknown purpose. Each, even in its resemblance to other things, strange. And we ourselves stranger than anything else.

McLuhan's own institution became a possible model for creative learning in the electronic age. While he was away at Fordham in 1968, his friend and colleague, Arthur Porter, obtained a small coach house for him behind Saint Michael's University library. Porter's efforts were to have important consequences. When McLuhan returned, he put on his coach house the way a man puts on his favorite jacket. This small building became a true world center, a space where the great northern owl could really hoot. Visitors from every continent came to talk and question. Prime ministers, rock stars, academics, artists, students, writers, met and mixed and laughed, and listened to the great owl. In the midst of this coming and going, McLuhan sent out an amazing number of intensely argued, insight-filled letters to painters, scholars, scientists, businessmen. At the same time he was producing articles, coauthoring books and giving talks around the world. He had also begun the *Laws of the Media*, and his work alone will undoubtedly contribute immensely to the process of understanding technologies. McLuhan's energy was astonishing; where did it come from?

Some of the contributors have emphasized the importance of McLuhan's strong religious belief. There is no doubt that his faith gave him the confidence to run like a colt through the fields of *dasein*, and to laugh at the gorgon of flux. But those who knew McLuhan also testify to the importance of his wife Corinne, who stood calmly and impressively in the center of his life, an essential part of McLuhan's hidden ground. Marg Stewart, his amazing secretary, was another part of the ground as was his executive assistant George Thompson and his agent Matie Molinaro. Here we have some of the basic conditions (but not the causes) for the success of McLuhan's Coach House years. With this basic support, McLuhan constructed an extensive network which he animated and from which he drew strength. When he died, the network disappeared, the members cut off abruptly from each other by the disappearance of the mother node.

McLuhan's center had much in common with a form of education that developed in Ionia and the Aegean after the phonetic alphabet fell fizzing into the Hellenic culture like an alpha seltzer. Thinkers like Pythagoras began to explore the intellectual potentialities of the emerging Hellenic culture. Plato and Aristotle themselves became nuclei for the literate traditions which perpetuated their thoughts, and carried their basic intuitions into the history of our civilization. The phonetic script and its first important creation, Greek Culture—related to each other as form to matter—were set for their encounter with the Judeo-Christian tradition.

McLuhan showed that the approaching Electronic age would have certain similarities to the acoustic, tribal period of Homeric Greece. Both ages required a multisensory response to surrounding environments. Nonliterate cultures rely on oral means for the transmission of culture. In our age we can see the role that music, especially rock, plays in the lives of the young, and TV gives us our archetypal micro-epics, our nightly Odysseys. But whereas the culture of the prephonetic Greeks was continuous with an immemorial oral tradition, our electronic age is discontinuous with the preceding print culture, and this induces a kind of cultural amnesia.

When Pascal pointed out that memory is necessary for all the operations of reason, he was affirming a traditional philosophical axiom. The individual, deprived suddenly of all his memories, would be unable to think or speak or even run for office.

Our humanity depends on a continuous act of recollection. Can we retain the basic values of our civilization if we cannot look into our past, personal and racial, as a person looks down into a deep lake on a calm day and discerns regions, layers, minnows, larger fish, depths and deeper depths? Can we keep the bubble of self-consciousness inflated, when it is pierced by quotidian arrows? Without practicing this kind of memory, recollective, quasimeditative, orienting, the house of self tumbles and is replaced by the nomad's tent. Without a sense of self we become victims of the immediate response, prisoners of now, unable to place ourselves within the temporal context. Unable finally, even to think the self, we float on a glittering sea of simultaneity, our responses merely trophic. Or, spread out like marmalade on the plain of the present, we remain pressed flat against the surface of events. As institutions shiver under the strain of adapting to life at the speed of light they no longer serve to aid us in the remembrance of things past.

The reaction to *Letters of Marshall McLuhan,* edited by Corinne McLuhan et al. (Oxford, 1987), was interesting within the context of our discussion. Many reviewers displayed a high degree of hostility. Some of these reviewers were distinguished writers and poets. Their anger seemed inexplicable and they gave no evidence of having actually read the book except to pick out substantiating examples of the intellectual vices they attributed to McLuhan. Amazingly, no attention was paid to McLuhan's basic ideas, repeated in letter after letter. The cause of this irrational response was anticipated and explained by McLuhan when he remarked that "the mere moralistic expression of approval or disapproval, preference or detestation, is currently being used in our world as a substitute for study."

We can perceive the truth of this remark if we look at the continuous moralizing commentary found in editorials, serious magazines, journals and on TV. When the critics turn their attention to education, the media, politics or practically any evolving institution or social process, we seldom experience anything other than a series of traditional denunciations, often delivered with great energy and earnestness. Since few critics are creative, we seldom learn anything. But we are urged towards indignation and anger. As a concrete example of what would have annoyed McLuhan, a major U.S. magazine recently had a seminar on the crisis in high-school education. Only one panelist made a passing reference to the possible effects of TV and radio on the young, despite the fact that it is common knowledge that the average North American viewer now spends four or five hours a day watching TV. There was much talk about excellence, discipline and the communication of the love of learning, etc. . . . but no recognition of the electronic *ground* which has fundamentally altered the sensibilities and feelings of youth. The same lack of awareness is evident when political and social institutions are discussed. Editorialists lay bare every injustice. The attacks are unremitting and humorless. Vigorous editorializing will change the world.

It is a truism that when humans are deprived of their ability to speak, the human personality is in danger. We are talking animals, and much everyday talk has its share of criticism and gossip. But the talk of the intellectual is of another kind, since most intellectuals do nothing but talk or write. They don't fix shoes, repair cars, go fishing, bowl, or even do the shopping. They *have* to speak, and their discourse is almost entirely corrective, moralistic, reproving, self-righteous. And their tone is usually one of unquestioned superiority. The fundamentalist haranguers, who recently found themselves engulfed in scandal, constitute the lower end of the spectrum of self-righteous critics whose more sophisticated cousins march triumphantly through the pages of reputable newspapers and serious periodicals and who glare at us from TV screens. When someone like McLuhan comes along and says that people who merely spend their time announcing their own preferences for old values when the world is collapsing and everything is changing at a furious pitch are not acting like serious persons, we can anticipate the results. If we take McLuhan seriously and start trying to perceive and understand the effects of media, we must forgo the pleasures and rewards of being mini-Jeremiahs.

Thus we have two more reasons why McLuhan is ignored. If taken seriously, he threatens many who have achieved eminence through attacks on the morality of the day. Their egos are at stake and their personal stability is threatened by the dread of speechlessness. This silence is more dreadful than the silence of the immensities which terrified Pascal. Unlike Pascal, the modern critic can pray to no God outside or inside the Cosmos. He is sustained by his membership in the tribe, hurling his voice into the hollow chorus of denunciation, or synchronizing his word processor with the multitudes who make criticism their living. McLuhan's reproach that such activity obscures the real problem is, because of its practicality, reminiscent of a remark by Chesterton. When asked which book he would select if abandoned on a desert island, he did not ask for a Bible, but rather a manual on ship building.

McLuhan's thought, the thought of any pioneer who forces us to deepen our self-knowledge, makes demands, not so much on our intellect as on our will. A man's character is his fate according to Heraclitus. Understanding issues that deal with human nature, its problems, its depressing potentialities and exalted hopes requires a human intelligence. Human intelligence remains undeveloped unless we grasp our own suffering and learn the lessons it teaches. Self-knowledge is the product of this process and self-knowledge is seldom pursued because it involves a lifelong friendship with a jerk.

When we are young we believe that the unifying vision, the insight that will make sense of it all, the world mess, and ourselves, comes from some act of the intellect. And we study logic, or philosophy or biology or meditative techniques in hopes that the pieces will suddenly assemble and reveal a coherent pattern. When we get older, we realize that intelligence is never enough. We realize the importance of will and the helplessness of intelligence. The latter cannot understand anything important, anything that has not been gained by effort, by determination, by striving, by patience. It does not know how to profit from loss. In trying to understand McLuhan's vision we have to remember that vision is really an act of the will.

McLuhan asked us to consider the *effects* of technological change rather than concentrate on the obvious contents of media. Our everyday perception is imprisoned in traditional habits of thinking and perceiving. Excluding some serendipitous restructuring of our normal perception, only the will can lead us to reconfigure our lives and habits so that we have a chance to experience things afresh.

Although McLuhan was puzzled and sometimes distracted by the resistance which his perceptions aroused, we must not think he was daunted by this opposition and neglect. He remained an explorer to the end, and George Thompson, his executive assistant, insists that the real McLuhan has to be envisoned in a typical setting, at his large table in the Coach House early in the morning. The table is covered with books, papers, letters, clippings, articles, magazines. Mrs. Stewart is typing upstairs. McLuhan is roaring through the days' newspapers, tearing out items of interest, asking George to Xerox something and send it somewhere. McLuhan is like a boy at the beginning of summer holidays. Everything dull is over and everything important is waiting to be discovered and he is saying, "It's a new day, George; every day's a new day, George. What are we going to find today?"

The man who ate the morning news was beginning another day.

McLuhan Probes

The Russians find it unbearable to have "eyes" around their environment. Just as we hate the idea of having "ears" in our own—e.g., the microphone in the embassy eagle. The Russians live much more by ear than we do. Realism—perspective art—is avant-garde for them. When you have the means of realistic representation, you also have the means of mechanical production. Mechanical production comes out of visual realism in the Western world. What we think of as realism is to the Russian absolute phantasy.

For the specialist is one who never makes small mistakes while moving toward the grand fallacy.

Art is a cliché probe that scraps older environments in order to retrieve other clichés that have been tossed aside earlier.

The story of modern America begins with the discovery of the white man by the Indians.

To say that any technology or extension of man creates a new environment is a much better way of saying that the medium is the message. This environment is always "invisible" and its content is always the old technology. The old technology is altered considerably by the developing action of the new technology.

An actor puts on his audience as a poet puts on his language. A stripper puts on her audience as she takes off her clothes.

The invention of a typography confirmed and extended the new visual stress of applied knowledge providing the first uniformly repeatable commodity, the first assembly line and the first mass production.

The new electric environment of simultaneous and diversified information creates acoustic man. He is surrounded by sound— from behind, from the side, from above. His environment is made up of information in all kinds of simultaneous forms, and he puts on this electrical environment as we put on our clothes, or as the fish puts on water.

The new organization man is an oral man with a heart of type.

New styles are really responses to new environments, and fashion is always looking into a rear-view mirror to find something nostalgic to revive. The need to remove is merely the need to feel secure with something that was once familiar.

Nobody yet knows the languages inherent in the new technological culture.

At seventy-three, Groucho Marx pities the poor parent of the permissive era: "What you should do with kids is slug hell out of them when they're small. Explain to them what life is about, and if they don't obey, give them the cat-o'-nine-tails." Groucho is merely anticipating what the TV kids will do to theirs. When identity disappears with technological innovation, violence is the natural recourse.

The pornograph came in the nineteenth century with the visual specialism of photograph.

There is absolutely no inevitability as long as there is a willingness to contemplate what is happening.

Notes

Marshall McLuhan

The Role of New Media in Social Change

1. Lynn White, *Medieval Technology and Social Change* (Oxford: Oxford University Press, 1962).
2. Siegfried Giedion, *The Beginnings of Architecture* (Princeton, N.J.: Bollingen Foundation, Princeton University Press, 1964).
3. Milic Capek, *The Philosophical Impact of Contemporary Physics* (New York: Van Nostrand, 1961).
4. J.J. Gibson, "Observations on Active Touch," *Psychological Review* 69, no. 6 (November 1962): 477–491.
5. E.H. Gombrich, *Art and Illusion* (New York: Pantheon Books, 1960), 18.
6. Gibson, "Observations on Active Touch," 487–488.
7. Leo Bogart, "Comic Strips and Their Adult Readers," in *Mass Culture* (Glencoe: The Free Press of Glencoe, 1957): 189–199.

T.W. Cooper

The Unknown McLuhan

1. Barbara Rowes, "If the Medium Didn't Get McLuhan's Message in the 1960s, Another One Is on the Way," *People*, September 20, 1976, 82–91.
2. Personal interview with W.T. Easterbrook, October 28, 1973.
3. H. Marshall McLuhan, "G.K. Chesterton, a Practical Mystic," *Dalhousie Review* 15 (1936): 464.
4. McLuhan, "Chesterton," 462.
5. H. Marshall McLuhan, "Francis Bacon: Ancient or Modern," *Renaissance and Reformation* 10, no. 2 (1974): 98.
6. H. Marshall McLuhan, "George Meredith as a Poet and Dramatic Novelist" (M.S. diss., University of Manitoba, April 1934), i.
7. McLuhan, "Chesterton," 462.

8 H. Marshall McLuhan and Barrington Nevitt, *Take Today: The Executive as Dropout* (Don Mills: Longman, 1972), 54.

9 Abraham Rotstein, "Innis: The Alchemy of Fur and Wheat," *Journal of Canadian Studies* 12, no. 5 (1977): 6.

10 H. Marshall McLuhan, Foreword to *Empire and Communication*, by Harold Innis (Toronto: University of Toronto Press, 1950, 1972), vii.

11 Personal interview with H. Marshall McLuhan, Toronto, August 1978.

12 Personal interview with George Steiner, Toronto, October 1974.

13 H. Marshall McLuhan, Seminar, University of Toronto Centre for Culture and Technology, October 1974.

14 Personal interview with H. Marshall McLuhan, April 1, 1976.

15 Interview with McLuhan, April 1, 1976.

16 H. Marshall McLuhan, Seminar, University of Toronto Centre for Culture and Technology, December 1973.

17 Personal interview with H. Marshall McLuhan, August 17, 1978.

18 Interview with McLuhan, August 17, 1978.

19 Interview with McLuhan, August 17, 1978.

20 Personal interview with W.T. Easterbrook, November 1973.

21 H. Marshall McLuhan, interview by G.E. Stearn, in G.E. Stearn, *McLuhan, Hot and Cool* (New York: Signet, 1967), 292.

22 Rowes, *People*, 84.

23 Personal interview with Bede Sullivan, Victoria, August 1976.

24 Tom Wolfe, in Stearn, *McLuhan*, 31.

25 During the 1976 Christmas season the hospitable McLuhan invited me to join his family for dinner. One of his twin daughters, Mary, had flown in with her daughter from California. After Corinne McLuhan had served us a tasty turkey and McLuhan's four-year-old granddaughter had entertained us with well-memorized lyrics, a McLuhan trademark, we adjourned upstairs to screen Norman McLaren's animated film, *Fiddle De Dee*. The sound track consisted of a virtuoso fiddler's rendition of "Listen to the Mocking Bird." No sooner had we heard four bars of the song than "Grandfather" McLuhan began to sing along. After Grandpa had been singing for a few measures, Corinne began to sing along also. The innocent boyish joy exhibited by Marshall when he recognized a favorite tune was just as genuine as his love for bouncing probes off sounding boards. McLaren's film suggested neither soliloquies nor questions to McLuhan; this was not an occasion to consider the meaning of media. Another simple, down-to-earth facet of the man had leapt out of his kangaroo pouch.

26 Personal interview with W.T. Easterbrook, April 1974.

27 Interview with Easterbrook, April 1974.

28 Claude Bissell, "The Humanities and Technology," Ghana Humanities Lectures. Lecture IV, 14.

29 H. Marshall McLuhan with Wilfred Watson, *From Cliché to Archetype* (New York: Pocket Books, 1970, 1971), 166.

Marshall McLuhan

Media and the Inflation CROWD

[1] Brooks Adams, *The Law of Civilization and Decay (n.p.,* 1896; repr., Salem, N.H.: Essay Index Reprint Service, Ayer Co., 1943).

[2] General Creighton Abrams, *Toronto Star,* August 9, 1973.

[3] H. Marshall McLuhan and Barrington Nevitt, *Take Today: The Executive as Dropout* (New York: Harcourt, Brace, Jovanovich, 1972), 84.

[4] McLuhan and Nevitt, *Take Today,* 223.

[5] McLuhan and Nevitt, *Take Today,* 104.

[6] Elias Canetti, *Crowds and Power* (London: Victor Gollancz, Ltd., 1962), 187.

Marshall McLuhan

At the moment of Sputnik the planet becomes a global theater in which there are no spectators but only actors

[1] Elizabeth Longford, *Victoria R.I.* (London: Weidenfeld & Nicolson, 1964), 562.

[2] Alphonse-Marie-Louis de Lamartine, quoted in H. Marshall McLuhan, "Joyce, Mallarmé, and the Press," in *Interior Landscape: The Literary Criticism of Marshall McLuhan,* ed. Eugene McNamara (New York: McGraw-Hill, 1969), 5.

[3] Louis L. Snyder and Richard B. Morris, eds., *A Treasury of Great Reporting* (New York: Simon & Schuster, 1962).

[4] Norman Mailer, *Miami and the Siege of Chicago* (New York: New American Library, 1968).

[5] H. Marshall McLuhan and Barrington Nevitt, *Take Today: The Executive as Dropout* (New York: Harcourt, Brace, Jovanovich, 1972).

[6] Michel de Montaigne, quoted in Donald M. Frame, *Biography of Montaigne* (New York: Harcourt, Brace & World, 1965), 83.

[7] Montaigne, quoted in Frame, *Biography.*

Marshall McLuhan

Violence of the Media

[1] "No Victim, No Pornography," *The Listener* (December 1975/January 1976): 858.

[2] Mildred Hall and Edward T. Hall, *The Fourth Dimension in Architecture: The Impact of Building on Man's Behavior* (Santa Fe, N.M.: Sunstone Press, 1975).

[3] Erik H. Erikson, *Identity, Youth and Crisis* (New York: Norton, 1968), 59.

[4] F.R. Miale and Michael Selzer, *The Nuremberg Mind* (New York: Quadrangle, 1975).

[5] Stanley Milgram, as quoted in Miale and Selzer, 7.
[6] Milgram, as quoted in Miale and Selzer, 8.
[7] Milgram as quoted in Miale and Selzer, 9.
[8] James Reston, "Pre-election Blues," *Globe and Mail,* March 16, 1976.
[9] Reston, "Pre-election."
[10] David Halberstam, *Atlantic* (February 1976), 64.
[11] Halberstam, *Atlantic,* 65.
[12] Halberstam, *Atlantic,* 70.

John Culkin

Marshall's New York Adventure

[1] H. Marshall McLuhan, "Report on Project in Understanding New Media," U.S. Office of Education, 1960.

Fred Thompson

Monday Night Sessions

[1] James R. Brandon, *Kubuki, Five Classical Plays* (Cambridge: Harvard University Press, 1975), 43.
[2] Johan Huizinga, *Homo Ludens* (Boston: Beacon Press, 1950).
[3] Barrington Nevitt, "Cultural Biases," *The Communication Ecology* (Toronto: Butterworths, 1982), 58–75.
[4] Richard Scheckner, "Performers and Spectators Transported and Transformed," *Kenyon Review* 3, no. 4 (1981): 83.
[5] Scheckner, "Performances," *Kenyon Review,* 86–87.
[6] Eric A. Havelock, *Preface to Plato* (Cambridge: Harvard University Press, 1965).
[7] Scheckner, "Performances," *Kenyon Review,* 91.
[8] Liane Sebastian, *Peaks and Mountains, Japan in Aspen* (Chicago: Sebastian Graphics, 1980), 25.
[9] Walter J. Ong, *Ramus, Method and the Decay of Dialogue* (Cambridge: Harvard University Press, 1958), 290.
[10] Dennis Duffy, *Marshall McLuhan,* Canadian Writers Number 1, New Canadian Library (Toronto: McClelland and Stewart Ltd., 1969), 26.

Marshall McLuhan

Inside on the Outside, or the Spaced-Out American

[1] John George Lambton Durham, *1839 Report on the Affairs of British North America,* volume 2 (Oxford: Clarendon Press, 1912), 91.
[2] Margaret Atwood, *Survival* (Toronto: Anansi Press, 1972), 60.

3 D.H. Lawrence, Introduction to *Bottom Dogs,* by Edward Dahlberg (New York: Simon & Schuster, 1930), ix–x.

4 Marius Bewley, *The Complex Fate* (London: Chatto and Windus, 1952), 57.

5 Hamlin Garland, *Roadside Meetings* (New York: Macmillan, 1930), 461.

6 W.H. Auden, *The Dyers Hand* (New York: Random House, 1948), 193–194.

7 "Why Johnny Can't Write," *Newsweek,* September 8, 1975, 58.

8 "Why Johnny," *Newsweek.*

9 Tony Schwartz, *The Responsive Chord* (New York: Anchor Press/Doubleday, 1973).

10 Arthur Miller, "1949: The Year It Came Apart," *New York,* December 30, 1974.

11 Mildred Hall and Edward T. Hall, *The Fourth Dimension in Architecture: The Impact of Building on Man's Behavior* (Santa Fe, N.M.: Sunstone Press, 1975), 7.

Barrington Nevitt

Via Media with Marshall McLuhan

1 H. Marshall McLuhan, *Understanding Media: The Extensions of Man* (New York: McGraw-Hill, 1964), 65.

2 H. Marshall McLuhan, *The Mechanical Bride: Folklore of Industrial Man* (New York: Vanguard Press, 1951), vi, 101.

3 H. Marshall McLuhan, *Culture Is Our Business* (New York: McGraw-Hill, 1970).

4 Edmund Carpenter and H. Marshall McLuhan, eds., *Explorations in Communication* (Boston: Beacon Press, 1960).

5 H. Marshall McLuhan, *The Gutenberg Galaxy: The Making of Typographic Man* (Toronto: University of Toronto Press, 1962).

6 McLuhan, *Understanding Media,* 18.

7 Eugene McNamara, ed., *The Interior Landscape: The Literary Criticism of Marshall McLuhan 1943–1962* (New York: McGraw-Hill, 1969).

8 H. Marshall McLuhan and Barrington Nevitt, *Take Today: The Executive as Dropout* (New York: Harcourt, Brace, Jovanovich, 1972).

9 H. Marshall McLuhan and Harley Parker, *Through the Vanishing Point: Space in Poetry and Painting* (New York: Harper & Row, 1968).

10 H. Marshall McLuhan and Wilfred Watson, *From Cliché to Archetype* (New York: Viking Press, 1970).

11 Marshall McLuhan, *Laws of the Media* (Toronto: University of Toronto Press, 1988).

12 Kathryn Hutchon and Eric McLuhan, *City as Classroom* (Agincourt, Ont.: Book Society of Canada, 1977); Barrington Nevitt, *The Communication Ecology: Representation versus Replica* (Toronto: Butterworths, in preparation).

Louis Forsdale
Marshall McLuhan and the Rules of the Game

1   Martin Gardner, ed., *The Annotated Alice* (New York: Clarkson N. Potter, 1960).
2   Wallace Turner, "Understand McLuhan [sic], by Him," *The New York Times,* November 22, 1966.
3   H. Marshall McLuhan, "Educational Effects of the Mass Media of Communication" (Paper delivered at seminar to celebrate inauguration of a new president, Teachers College, Columbia University, New York, 1955), 9.
4   J. David Bolter, *Turing's Man: Western Culture in the Computer Age* (Chapel Hill: The University of North Carolina Press, 1984).

Marshall McLuhan
The Brain and the Media:
The "Western" Hemisphere

1   Robert J. Trotter, "The Other Hemisphere," *Science News* 109 (April 3, 1976): 218.
2   A.R. Luria, "The Functional Organization of the Brain," *Scientific American* (March 1970): 71–72.
3   Phillip E. Slater, *The Glory of Hera: Greek Mythology and the Greek Family* (Boston: Beacon Press, 1968).
4   Karl Popper, *The Open Society and Its Enemies* (Princeton, N.J.: Princeton University Press, 1950), 178.
5   Popper, *The Open Society and Its Enemies,* 178, 180.
6   Chiang Yee, *The Chinese Eye: An Interpretation of Chinese Painting* (Bloomington, Ind.: Indiana University Press, 1964), 189–190.
7   Okakura Kakuzo, *The Book of Tea* (Rutland, Vt. and Tokyo, Japan: Charles E. Tuttle, 1906), 44–45.
8   Claude E. Shannon and W. Weaver, *The Mathematical Theory of Communication* (Urbana, Ill.: University of Illinois Press, 1964), 31.

Marshall McLuhan

A Last Look at the Tube

[1] Tony Schwartz, *The Responsive Chord* (New York: Anchor Press/Doubleday, 1973), 14.

[2] Frank Mankiewicz and Joel L. Swerdlow, *Remote Control: Television and the Manipulation of American Life* (New York: Quadrangle/The New York Times Book Company, 1978), from unrevised galley proofs.

[3] Jerry Rubin, *Do It,* as quoted in Malcolm Muggeridge, *Christ and the Media: London Lectures in Contemporary Christianity* (Toronto: Ecclesia Books, Hodder & Stoughton, 1977), 67.

[4] Peter Drucker, *The Unseen Revolution* (New York: Harper & Row, 1976), 1.

[5] Erich Fromm, *The Anatomy of Human Destructiveness* (Greenwich: Fawcett, 1975), 389.

Contributors

Articles

Claude Bissell is the former president of the University of Toronto. His book, *The Young Vincent Massey*, was published by the University of Toronto Press in 1981.

John Culkin is currently Executive Director of the Center for Understanding Media in New York City, and has recently published several articles on literacy and alphabet reform.

Thomas W. Cooper is the author of *The Television and Ethics Bibliography* (Emerson College 1986). He is currently teaching at Emerson College in Boston.

G.M. Feigen, M.D., is a San Francisco surgeon, writer, TV host. In 1965, with the late Howard Gossage, Feigen founded the consultation firm Generalists, Inc.

Louis Forsdale was professor of communication and education, Teachers College, Columbia University, New York.

Jane Jacobs is the author of *Cities and the Wealth of Nations: Principles of Economic Life* (Random House 1984). She lives in Toronto.

Wilson Bryan Key is the author of *Subliminal Seduction* (New American Library 1976) and more recently, *The Clam-Plate Orgy* (New American Library 1980). Dr. Key is president of Mediaprobe: The Center for the Study of Media, Inc.

Eric McLuhan teaches communications at York University in Toronto. He is a partner in McLuhan and Davis, Communications, in Toronto. *Laws of the Media* was published by the University of Toronto Press in 1988.

Matie Armstrong Molinaro was Marshall McLuhan's friend and agent. She is president of Canadian Speakers' & Writers' Service Ltd., Toronto and is, with Corinne McLuhan and William Toye, one of the editors of *Letters of Marshall McLuhan* (Oxford 1987).

Barrington Nevitt is a former colleague of Marshall McLuhan and coauthored *The Executive as Drop-Out* (Longmans 1972). He is the author of *Prospects for Peace,* published by Gamma Institute Press, Montreal, in 1985.

Walter J. Ong, S.J., is University Professor of Humanities and professor of humanities in psychiatry at Saint Louis University, Missouri, and the author of many books, including *Orality and Literacy: The Technologizing of the Word* (Methuen 1982).

Fred Thompson is a professor with the faculty of environmental studies in the School of Architecture, University of Waterloo.

Symposium

John Cage produced *John Cage Etchings, 1978-1982,* which was published by Point Publications, 1982.

Barry Day is vice-chairman of McCann-Erickson Worldwide.

Pierre Emmanuel was a leading French poet and member of the French Academy.

Martin Esslin is Professor of Drama at Stanford University. His latest book is *The Field of Drama* (Methuen 1987).

Gerald O'Grady is the director, Center for Media Study, State University of New York at Buffalo.

Edward T. Hall is the author of *The Hidden Dimension* (Doubleday 1966) and *The Dance of Life: The Other Dimension of Time* (Doubleday 1984).

Robert Hittel was a friend of Marshall McLuhan and lives in Fort Lauderdale, Florida.

Hugh Kenner's latest book is *A Sinking Island: The Modern British Writers* (Knopf 1988).

William Kuhns is the author of *The Post-Industrial Prophets: Interpretations of Technology* (Harper & Row 1970).

Norman Mailer's latest book is *Tough Guys Don't Dance* (Random House 1984).

Corinne McLuhan was wife to Marshall McLuhan. She is editor, with Matie Molinaro and Bill Toye, of *Letters of Marshall McLuhan* (Oxford 1987).

Harold Rosenberg's publications (University of Chicago Press) include *Art and Other Serious Matters* (1985), *Discovering the Present* (1985) and *The Case of the Baffled Radical* (1986).

Arthur M. Schlesinger, Jr., is the author of many books, including *The Cycles of American History* (Houghton Mifflin 1986).

Margaret Stewart was Marshall McLuhan's secretary. She now lives in Washago, Ontario.

George Steiner's latest book is *Antigones* (Oxford University Press 1986).

George Thompson was a long-time executive assistant to Marshall McLuhan. He lives in Toronto.

Pierre Eliot Trudeau was prime minister of Canada from 1968 to 1984.

Walker Percy's latest book is *The Thanatos Syndrome* (Farrar, Straus & Giroux 1987).

Bruce W. Powe is the author of *A Climate Charged* (Mosaic Press 1984) and *The Solitary Outlaw* (Lester and Orpen Dennys 1987).

Bruce Powers teaches at Niagara University. He is coauthor with Marshall McLuhan of *The Global Village: Transformations in the World, Life and Media in the Twenty-first Century* (Oxford 1989).

John Wain's latest book is *The Free Zone Starts Here* (Delacorte Press 1984).

Charles Weingartner is the author, with Neil Postman, of *How to Recognize a Good School* (Phi Delta Kappa 1973).

Patrick Watson, a well-known TV producer and journalist, has just completed the TV documentary *The Struggle for Democracy.*

Tom Wolfe's recent book is *The Bonfire of the Vanities* (Farrar, Straus & Giroux 1988).